ALBERT AND DAVID MAYSLES

INTERVIEWS

CONVERSATIONS WITH FILMMAKERS SERIES
PETER BRUNETTE, GENERAL EDITOR

ALBERT AND DAVID MAYSLES
INTERVIEWS

EDITED BY KEITH BEATTIE

UNIVERSITY PRESS OF MISSISSIPPI / JACKSON

www.upress.state.ms.us

The University Press of Mississippi is a member of the Association of American University Presses.

Manufactured in the United States of America

First printing 2010
∞

Library of Congress Cataloging-in-Publication Data

Albert and David Maysles : interviews / edited by Keith Beattie.
p. cm. — (Conversations with filmmakers series)
Includes filmography and index.
ISBN 978-1-60473-364-8 (cloth : alk. paper) — ISBN 978-1-60473-365-5 (pbk. : alk. paper) 1. Maysles, Albert—Interviews. 2. Maysles, David—Interviews. 3. Motion picture producers and directors—United States—Interviews. I. Beattie, Keith, 1954–
PN1998.3.M39752A43 2010
791.4302'330922—dc22

2009019924

British Library Cataloging-in-Publication Data available

CONTENTS

INTRODUCTION

"INTERVIEWS ARE superfluous . . . The film is our statement," insists David Maysles in an interview reprinted here. David Maysles and his brother Albert exemplified the statement by making a number of the best known and most highly respected documentary films of the late twentieth century. Their films *Salesman*, *Gimme Shelter*, and *Grey Gardens*, among other works, are landmarks in documentary film history. While the aesthetics of what became known in the United States as direct cinema (which, confusingly, is often loosely referred to by the name of its French counterpart, *cinéma vérité*) are important to their films, a strict adherence to an observational direct cinema is not the sole or exclusive characteristic of the films. In a number of interviews included in this volume Albert Maysles tends to summarize the brothers' approach to filmmaking in terms of what he sees as the need for a documentary filmmaker to respond to specific situations and exigencies. Within this approach the brothers were willing to restyle and re-inflect—and even abandon—extant principles and understandings of direct cinema in their approach to filmmaking (thereby casting doubt on assumptions concerning direct cinema as a proscribed set of practices).

Attendant on the brothers' films are the interviews collected here. Any sense of the superfluousness of interviews is overcome even within those interviews and discussions which inevitably tend to duplicate the focus of questions which have been posed in other such conversations. A sense of duplication and overlap highlights issues and concerns which are especially pertinent or which, as the interviewers recognize, require further explication or elaboration. What is particularly interesting in this relation is the way in which David or Albert Maysles seeks to "open up" a question, using a question as a way of not merely presenting information on the specific topic at hand, but of reflecting on a range of issues, themes, concepts, and concerns relevant to their filmmaking. In this way many of the interviews reprinted here offer especially valuable insights into the field of documentary filmmaking in general, and the form of observational direct cinema practiced by the Maysles brothers in particular.

Film history has tended to approach the innovations in documentary filmmaking wrought by direct cinema in terms of the development of new technology, in particular portable cameras and synchronised lightweight sound recording equipment. Such a technological determinism overlooks the fact that beyond various technologies direct cinema constituted a reworked relationship between filmmakers and subjects. The ethics of the Maysles' documentary filmmaking are grounded in humanist practices summarized by the brothers in a number of the interviews in this volume in the words trust, respect, compassion, engagement, and empathy. The words bespeak a special bond between filmmaker and subject.

This bond or contract informs the discussion of many of the films addressed here, among them *Salesman*, which is referred to at length in the interviews with Bob Sitton, Robert Phillip Kolker, and Alan Rosenthal. The allusion by certain contemporary critics to a breaking of the bond between filmmaker, subject, and audience in *Gimme Shelter*, a foundational "rockumentary" produced by the Maysles brothers in 1970, is addressed in the conversations with Calvin Pryluck and Robert Phillip Kolker. The close bond in the filming process between filmmaker and subject is elaborated in the brothers' comments on *Grey Gardens* (see Calvin Pryluck, Jackson Pellow, and Anne S. Lewis). The focus on the family in *Grey Gardens*, in the form of the interactions between mother and daughter, Edith Bouvier Beale and Edith Bouvier Beale II—"Big" Edie and "Little" Edie (aunt and cousin of Jacqueline Kennedy Onassis)—is extended in *The Burks of Georgia* (a film discussed in the interview conducted by Judith Trojan). Comparisons and contrasts between the Beales and the Burks implicate family dynamics and the role of class in social organization, a topic often obscured or ignored in other representations of family life. Beyond the bond between filmmaker and subject is the relationship of filmmaker and audience, a connection which is especially pronounced in the case of *Grey Gardens*, a film which enjoys an almost cult following and has spawned a Broadway musical, a feature film adaptation, and the 2006 work *The Beales of Grey Gardens*, edited from outtakes of footage shot for the original film.

One way in which the relationship between filmmaker and subject can be understood is in terms of collaboration, defined as mutual respect within terms of a working partnership. Collaboration was the functional basis of the brothers' filmmaking practice, and collaborative relationships with various colleagues informed that practice. The Maysles' collaboration with the environmental artist Christo has resulted in the films *Christo's Valley Curtain, Running Fence, Islands, Christo in Paris, The Umbrellas,* and *The Gates,* which are variously discussed in a number of the conversations gathered here. Elsewhere in the interviews the brothers acknowledge Charlotte Zwerin's contributions to the editing of films such as *Salesman.* Albert Maysles mentions his brief collaboration with Jean-Luc Godard, and in a discussion of work commissioned for television he refers to his ongoing association with the producer and filmmaker Henry Corra. Albert Maysles' collaborative relationship with Susan Froemke and other members of Maysles Films is a feature of his comments on the commissioned film *Concert of Wills,* discussed in the interview with Ann Hassett.

In recent interviews, such as the ones by Geoffrey Macnab, Williams Cole, and Lance Avery Morgan, Albert Maysles talks of his latest projects, including the works-in-progress *In Transit* and *Hand-Held from the Heart,* both of which are shot on high-definition video. Reflecting the long and significant careers of the filmmakers, the interviews collected here range from 1963 to 2007. Beyond an emphasis on issues associated with collaboration, the relationship with subjects and audiences, and the ethics of this relationship, the conversations address and analyse a variety of topics, including among other concerns, the motivations behind the making of the early films, contributions to the work of Drew Associates and the foundations of "direct cinema," the relationship of objectivity and subjectivity in documentary filmmaking, technical aspects of documentary camerawork and sound recording, the status and funding of independent documentary filmmaking, critical reactions to their films (notably *Gimme Shelter* and *Grey Gardens*), and contemporary attitudes to documentary (nonfiction) filmmaking. The range of topics addressed in the interviews is matched by the diversity of sources collected here. Sources from the United States, Britain, and Australia are included, in the form of journals of film criticism and cultural issues, newspapers, book chapters, and internet sites. The interviews remain largely unchanged from their original publication. What emerges from the range of topics addressed in the conversations reprinted in *Albert and David Maysles: Interviews* is an understanding of the Maysles' filmmaking as a complex and rich multidimensional practice.

In this way Jonas Mekas praises the Maysles' style as a complement to the "new journalism," calling their film *Showman* a "nonfictional film novel" (the allusion to novelistic techniques is particularly apt given the brothers' references in interviews to the works of writers such as Hemingway, Thomas Wolfe, and Tolstoy). James Blue and Alan Rosenthal both approvingly quote Jean-Luc Godard's impression that "Al Maysles is the greatest cameraman in America." The "trilogy" of films which Albert Maysles counts as his favorite works—*Salesman*, *Gimme Shelter*, and *Grey Gardens*—are variously assessed here. *Salesman* is referred to as a "marvelous accomplishment—a milestone in film making and in recording the passing American scene" (Bob Sitton); "an intensely moving portrait of an ordinary human being" (Alan Rosenthal); and "one of the richest portraits of the heart of America" (Liz Stubbs). Robert Phillip Kolker summarizes *Gimme Shelter* as a "virtuoso piece," and *Grey Gardens* is called an uncompromising study (Judith Trojan) of a fascinating topic (Brooke Comer). In an essay printed elsewhere, Martin Scorsese (who once had a job as Albert Maysles' lighting assistant) declares that Albert Maysles "truly does have the eye of a poet. . . . When Al is behind the camera, there's a sensitivity to mood, to space and light, to the energy between the people in the room. The camera is an inquisitive presence, but also a *loving* presence, an *emphatic* presence."[1]

The scope of the Maysles' rich film practice is exemplified in their extensive filmography, included here. The filmography lists the films jointly made by Albert and David Maysles, and those made by Albert Maysles since David's death in 1987. In keeping with the particularities of documentary filmmaking the term "filmmaker" replaces "director" and is used to refer variously to a collaborative contribution to and combination of photography, sound recording, and editing. The filmography also includes films made by various filmmakers on which Albert Maysles has served as cinematographer. The accompanying chronology includes major moments in the lives and careers of Albert and David Maysles.

In preparing this volume for the Conversations with Filmmakers series I was assisted by the interlibrary loan units of various institutions. The staff of such facilities demonstrated an admirable persistence in tracking down otherwise difficult to obtain sources. Much of the work on this project was undertaken while I was a Visiting Research Fellow within the School of Humanities, College of Arts and Social Sciences, the Australian National University, Canberra. I am pleased to be able to acknowledge and to thank the School for its assistance. I would also like to thank the interviewers and rights holders who granted me permission to reprint the published interviews which appear here. I requested permission to reprint more articles than I was able to include in this volume. My thanks to all those people who answered my requests. This book is for Dr. Julie Ann Smith whose constant support bespeaks her immense generosity and unparalleled kindness.

KB

Notes

1. Foreword by Martin Scorsese to Albert Maysles, *A Maysles Scrapbook: Photographs, Cinemagraphs, Documents*, copublished by Steven Kasher Gallery, New York, and Steidl Publishers, Gottingen, Germany, 2007. The filmography included in *Albert and David Maysles: Interviews* incorporates details derived from this book.

CHRONOLOGY

1929 Albert Maysles born November 26 in Boston, Massachusetts to first-generation Russian Jewish immigrant parents.

1932 David Maysles born January 10 in Boston.

1944 Albert Maysles graduates from Brookline High School, Brookline, Massachusetts, and serves with Army Tank Corps during World War II.

1949 David Maysles graduates from Brookline High School, Brookline, Massachusetts. Albert Maysles receives a BA in psychology, Syracuse University, Syracuse, New York, and commences teaching psychology at Boston University.

1953 David Maysles receives a BA in psychology from Boston University and serves in Army Military Intelligence School, Oberammergau, Germany. Albert Maysles awarded an MA in psychology, Boston University. Albert Maysles teaches psychology at Boston University.

1955 Albert Maysles leaves his position teaching psychology at Boston University and visits the Soviet Union for the first time to make the film *Psychiatry in Russia*.

1956 David Maysles works as assistant film producer on *Bus Stop* (Twentieth Century Fox).

1957 David Maysles works as assistant film producer on *The Prince and the Showgirl* (Warner Brothers). Albert and David Maysles tour Poland and Russia on a motorcycle, and make their first film together, *Youth in Poland* (unfinished).

1960 Albert Maysles serves as cinematographer on *Primary* and *Yanki, No!*, among other productions for Robert Drew and Drew Associates.

1961 Albert Maysles works as a cinematographer and David Maysles as a reporter and sound recordist on *Adventures on the New Frontier* produced by Robert Drew.

1962 Albert and David Maysles form Maysles Films. The brothers make *Showman* for their new company.

1964 *What's Happening! The Beatles in the U.S.A.* produced by Maysles Films. Albert Maysles serves as cinematographer for Jean-Luc Godard's segment ('Montparnasse et Lavallois") of the omnibus feature, *Paris vu par . . .*

1966 *A Visit with Truman Capote* (also known as *With Love from Truman*) produced by Maysles Films.

1968 Albert and David Maysles make *Salesman*, a direct cinema portrait of a door-to-door Bible salesman. The film is widely and favorably reviewed in the press.

1970 Albert and David Maysles, with Charlotte Zwerin, make *Gimme Shelter*, a record of the Rolling Stones' 1969 concert tour of the U.S., which ended with a disastrous concert at the Altamont Speedway outside of San Francisco. The film is criticized by Vincent Canby and Pauline Kael, while other reviewers defend the film against charges of sensationalism.

1973 The brothers begin a longstanding relationship with the environmental artist Christo Javacheff. Together they make *Christo's Valley Curtain.*

1974 Albert and David Maysles, with Ellen Hovde and Muffie Meyer, make *The Burks of Georgia.* The film *Christo's Valley Curtain* is nominated for an Academy Award.

1976 Albert and David Maysles, together with Ellen Hovde, Muffie Meyer, and Susan Froemke, make *Grey Gardens*, a portrait of a mother and her daughter (aunt and cousin to Jackie Onassis) living in seclusion in a rundown mansion in East Hampton. The film provokes wide critical discussion and a cult-like following.

1987 David Maysles dies of a stroke on January 3 in New York. *Vladimir Horowitz: The Last Romantic* receives an Emmy Award.

1990 Last feature collaboration between Albert and David Maysles, *Christo in Paris*, released three years after David's death.

1991 Albert Maysles receives Cinematography Award at the Sundance Film Festival for *Christo in Paris*. *Soldiers of Music* receives an Emmy Award.

1992 *Salesman* is included on the Library of Congress list of the most historically, culturally, and aesthetically significant films. The film *Brother's Keeper* by Joe Berlinger and Bruce Sinofsky is dedicated to the memory of David Maysles.

1994 Albert Maysles receives a Career Achievement award from the International Documentary Association.

1996 Albert Maysles films *Letting Go: A Hospice Journey.*

1997 Albert Maysles, with Susan Froemke and Bob Eisenhardt, produces *Concert of Wills: Making the Getty Center* for the Getty Trust.

1998 Albert Maysles receives the President's Award of the American Society of Cinematographers, the first time the award is given to a documentary filmmaker. The citation calls him the "father of direct cinema."

1999 The Eastman Kodak Company lists Albert Maysles as one of the world's finest 100 cinematographers.

2000 Albert Maysles films *LaLee's Kin: The Legacy of Cotton.*

2001 Maysles Shorts established as a branch of Maysles Films, to produce commercials and corporate films. *LaLee's Kin* receives the Cinematography Award at the Sundance Film Festival and is nominated for an Academy Award.

2005 Albert Maysles founds the nonprofit Maysles Institute in Harlem as a venue for screening films and training underprivileged children in the techniques of filmmaking.

2008 *Shine a Light,* Martin Scorsese's documentary on the Rolling Stones is released. Almost forty years after he filmed the Rolling Stones in *Gimme Shelter* Albert Maysles serves as a cinematographer on the film.

FILMOGRAPHY

As Filmmakers

1955
PSYCHIATRY IN RUSSIA
Producer: NBC-TV
Filmmaker: **Albert Maysles**
Photography: **Albert Maysles**
Length: 12 minutes

1957
RUSSIAN CLOSE-UP
Producer: **Albert Maysles**
Filmmaker: **Albert Maysles**
Photography: **Albert Maysles**
Sound: **Albert Maysles**
Editing: **Albert Maysles**
Length: 33 minutes

YOUTH IN POLAND (unfinished)
Producers: **Albert Maysles, David Maysles**
Filmmakers: **Albert Maysles, David Maysles**
Photography: **Albert Maysles**
Sound: **David Maysles**

1961
SAFARI YA GARI
Producer: **Albert Maysles**
Filmmaker: **Albert Maysles**
Photography: **Albert Maysles**

Sound: Jerry Feil
Editing: Nell Cox
Length: 8 minutes

1962
ANASTASIA
Producers: NBC-TV, Bo Goldman
Filmmakers: **Albert Maysles**, **David Maysles**
Photography: **Albert Maysles**
Sound: **David Maysles**
Length: 12 minutes

SHOWMAN
Production Company: Maysles Films
Producers: **Albert Maysles**, **David Maysles**.
Filmmakers: **Albert Maysles**, **David Maysles**
Photography: **Albert Maysles**
Sound: **David Maysles**
Editors: Daniel Williams, Tom Bywaters, Betsy Powell
Length: 53 minutes

CURTIS JONES: AN AMERICAN IN PARIS (unfinished)
Producers: **Albert Maysles**, **David Maysles**
Filmmakers: **Albert Maysles**, **David Maysles**
Photography: **Albert Maysles**
Sound: **David Maysles**

1963
CARL SANDBURG READS FROM "HONEY AND SALT"
Filmmakers: **Albert Maysles**, **David Maysles**
Photography: **Albert Maysles**
Sound: **David Maysles**
3 minutes

AT HOME WITH LIFE
Producer: Life Magazine
Filmmakers: **Albert Maysles**, **David Maysles**
Photography: **Albert Maysles**
Sound: **David Maysles**
14 minutes

1964
WHAT'S HAPPENING! THE BEATLES IN THE U.S.A.
Producer: Neil Aspinall for Granada TV

Filmmakers: **Albert Maysles**, **David Maysles**
Photography: **Albert Maysles**
Sound: **David Maysles**
Editor: Danny Williams
Length: 74 minutes

IBM: A SELF PORTRAIT
Producer: Irving Gitlin
Filmmakers: **Albert Maysles**, **David Maysles**
Photography: **Albert Maysles**
Sound: **David Maysles**
Editors: Danny Williams, Kate Glidden
Length: 30 minutes

EMPLOYEE BARRIERS TO SERVICE
Producers: Bell Telephone, Stanley Hirson
Filmmakers: **Albert Maysles**, **David Maysles**
Photography: **Albert Maysles**
Sound: **David Maysles**
Editor: Kate Glidden
Length: 12 minutes

1965
MEET MARLON BRANDO
Production Company: Maysles Films
Producers: **Albert Maysles**, **David Maysles**
Filmmakers: **Albert Maysles**, **David Maysles**
Photography: **Albert Maysles**
Sound: **David Maysles**
Editor: Charlotte Zwerin
Length: 29 minutes

CUT PIECE
Producer: Yoko Ono
Filmmakers: **Albert Maysles**, **David Maysles**
Photography: **Albert Maysles**
Sound: **David Maysles**
Editor: **David Maysles**
Length: 9 minutes

SEAN O'CASEY: THE SPIRIT OF IRELAND
Producer: Twentieth Century Fox
Narrator: Herschel Bernardi
Filmmakers: **Albert Maysles**, **David Maysles**

Photography: **Albert Maysles**
Sound: **David Maysles**
Editor: Elliot Geisinger
Length: 8 minutes

BILL BLASS
Producer: Benton and Bowles
Filmmakers: **Albert Maysles, David Maysles**
Photography: **Albert Maysles**
Sound: **David Maysles**
Length: 8 minutes

1966
A VISIT WITH TRUMAN CAPOTE (also known as WITH LOVE FROM TRUMAN)
Producers: WNWT-TV, **Albert Maysles, David Maysles**, Charlotte Zwerin
Filmmakers: **Albert Maysles, David Maysles**, Charlotte Zwerin
Photography: **Albert Maysles**
Sound: **David Maysles**
Editors: **David Maysles**, Charlotte Zwerin
Length: 29 minutes

DALI'S FANTASTIC DREAM
Producer: Twentieth Century Fox
Filmmakers: **Albert Maysles, David Maysles**
Photography: **Albert Maysles**
Sound: **David Maysles**
Length: 8 minutes

MGM PRESS JUNKET
Producer: MGM
Filmmakers: **Albert Maysles, David Maysles**
Photography: **Albert Maysles**
Sound: **David Maysles**
Length: 20 minutes

ORSON WELLES IN SPAIN (unfinished)
Production Company: Maysles Films
Producers: **Albert Maysles, David Maysles**
Filmmakers: **Albert Maysles, David Maysles**
Photography: **Albert Maysles**
Sound: **David Maysles**

Editor: Charlotte Zwerin
Length: 10 minutes (rough cut)

1967
TONY ROME (featurette)
Producer: Twentieth Century Fox
Filmmakers: **Albert Maysles**, **David Maysles**
Photography: **Albert Maysles**
Sound: **David Maysles**
Length: 8 minutes

PROBLEMS ON OUR HANDS
Producers: Johnson and Johnson, Stanley Hirson
Filmmakers: **Albert Maysles**, **David Maysles**
Photography: **Albert Maysles**
Sound: **David Maysles**
Editor: Edward Packer
Length: 20 minutes

1968
SALESMAN
Production Company: Maysles Films
Producers: **Albert Maysles**, **David Maysles**
Filmmakers: **Albert Maysles**, **David Maysles**, Charlotte Zwerin
Photography: **Albert Maysles**
Sound: **David Maysles**
Sound Mixer: Dick Vorisek
Editor: Charlotte Zwerin
Contributing Editor: Ellen Giffard
Assistant Editor: Barbara Jarvis
Screenplay Scene Settings: Paul Zimmerman
Length: 91 minutes

MOTHER (unfinished)
Producers: **Albert Maysles**, **David Maysles**
Filmmakers: **Albert Maysles**, **David Maysles**
Photography: **Albert Maysles**
Sound: **David Maysles**

1970
GIMME SHELTER
Production Company: Maysles Films

Producers: **Albert Maysles**, **David Maysles**
Associate Producer: Porter Bibb
Filmmakers: **Albert Maysles**, **David Maysles**, Charlotte Zwerin
Photography: **Albert Maysles**, and others
Sound: **David Maysles**, and others
Supervising Editor: **David Maysles**
Editor: Charlotte Zwerin
Contributing Editors: Ellen Giffard, Robert Farren, Joanne Burke, Kent McKinney
Length: 91 minutes

1971
GRAND FUNK RAILROAD: LIVE AT SHEA STADIUM
Producer: Terry Knight
Filmmakers: **Albert Maysles**, **David Maysles**
Photography: **Albert Maysles**, Richard Leacock, Robert Van Dyke Sound: **David Maysles**, Robert Van Dyke
Editor: Muffie Meyer
Length: 50 minutes

1973
CHRISTO'S VALLEY CURTAIN (also known as VALLEY CURTAIN)
Production Company: Maysles Films
Producers: **Albert Maysles**, **David Maysles**
Filmmakers: **Albert Maysles**, **David Maysles**, Ellen Hovde
Photography: **Albert Maysles**
Sound: **David Maysles**, Chalres Groesbeek
Editors: Ellen Giffard, Susan Froemke
Length: 28 minutes

SISTERS (unfinished)
Producers: Peter Beard, Lee Radziwill
Filmmakers: **Albert Maysles**, **David Maysles**
Photography: **Albert Maysles**
Sound: **David Maysles**

1974
THE BURKS OF GEORGIA (also known as THE BURK FAMILY OF GEORGIA)
Producer: PBS-TV (for the *Six American Families* series)
Executive Producer: George Moynihan
Associate Producers: Lisa Director, Paul Wilkes
Filmmakers: **Albert Maysles**, **David Maysles**, Ellen Hovde, Muffie Meyer
Photography: **Albert Maysles**
Sound: **David Maysles**

Editors: Ellen Hovde, Muffie Meyer
Length: 53 minutes

CONRACK (featurette)
Producer: Twentieth Century Fox
Filmmakers: **Albert Maysles**, **David Maysles**
Photography: **Albert Maysles**
Sound: **David Maysles**
Length: 9 minutes

1975
GREY GARDENS
Production Company: Maysles Films
Producers: **Albert Maysles**, **David Maysles**
Filmmakers: **Albert Maysles**, **David Maysles**, Ellen Hovde, Muffie Meyer, Susan Froemke
Photography: **Albert Maysles**
Sound: **David Maysles**
Editors: Ellen Hovde, Muffie Meyer, Susan Froemke
Length: 94 minutes

1978
RUNNING FENCE
Production Company: Maysles Films
Producers: **Albert Maysles**, **David Maysles**
Filmmakers: **Albert Maysles**, **David Maysles**, Charlotte Zwerin
Photography: **Albert Maysles**
Sound: **David Maysles**
Editor: Charlotte Zwerin
Length: 58 minutes

DIANE VON FURSTENBERG: A DESIGNER'S TOUCH
Producer: Sears and Roebuck
Filmmakers: **Albert Maysles**, **David Maysles**
Photography: **Albert Maysles**
Sound: **David Maysles**
Length: 12 minutes

1979
SMIRNOFF STYLE
Producer: Smirnoff
Filmmakers: **Albert Maysles**, **David Maysles**
Photography: **Albert Maysles**

Sound: **David Maysles**
Length: 22 minutes

1980
MUHAMMAD AND LARRY
Production Company: Maysles Films; co-produced with The Deerlake Company
Producers: Marvin Towns, Clifford Towns, Keith Vyse
Filmmakers: **Albert Maysles**, **David Maysles**
Photography: **Albert Maysles**
Sound: **David Maysles**
Editors: Kate Hirson, Janet Swanson
Length: 26 minutes

1981
GOOD LIVING WITH MARTHA STEWART
Producer: Dan Cooper
Filmmakers: **Albert Maysles**, **David Maysles**
Photography: **Albert Maysles**
Sound: **David Maysles**
Length: 25 minutes

1985
VLADIMIR HOROWITZ: THE LAST ROMANTIC
Producers: CBS/Sony, Peter Gelb, Susan Froemke
Filmmakers: **Albert Maysles**, **David Maysles**, Susan Froemke, Deborah Dickson, Pat Jaffe
Photography: **Albert Maysles**, **David Maysles**, Don Lenzer
Sound: Lee Dichter, Lawrence Loewinger
Editors: Deborah Dickson, Pat Jaffe
Length: 88 minutes

OZAWA
Producers: CBS/Sony Classical, Peter Gelb, Susan Froemke
Filmmakers: **Albert Maysles**, **David Maysles**, Susan Froemke, Deborah Dickson
Photography: **Albert Maysles**, **David Maysles**, Robert Leacock, Robert Richman
Sound Engineer: Lawrence Loewinger
Editor: Deborah Dickson
Length: 57 minutes

CHASE MANHATTAN BANK: THE BEGINNING
Producer: Chase Manhattan Bank
Filmmakers: **Albert Maysles**, **David Maysles**

Photography: **Albert Maysles**
Sound: **David Maysles**
Length: 11 minutes

1986
ISLANDS
Production Company: Maysles Films
Producers: Susan Froemke, Joel Hinman
Filmmakers: **Albert Maysles**, **David Maysles**, Charlotte Zwerin
Photography: **Albert Maysles**, **David Maysles**, Robert Richman, Erich Roland, Jeff Simon, Jeff Peterson
Sound: Lee Dichter, Roger Phenix
Music: Scott Cossu
Editor: Kate Hirson
Length: 57 minutes

1987
HOROWITZ PLAYS MOZART
Producers: CBS/Sony Classical, Susan Froemke, Peter Gelb Filmmakers: **Albert Maysles**, Susan Froemke, Charlotte Zwerin
Photography: **Albert Maysles**, Don Lenzer, Vic Losick, George Bottos
Sound: Peter Miller, Gianfranco Cabiddo, Judy Benjamin
Editor: Pam Wise
Length: 50 minutes

1989
JESSYE NORMAN SINGS CARMEN
Producers: CBS/Sony, Susan Froemke, Peter Gelb
Associate Producers: Nell Archer, Ann Cauvin
Filmmakers: **Albert Maysles**, Susan Froemke, Peter Gelb, Charlotte Zwerin
Photography: **Albert Maysles**, Martin Schaer
Sound: Martin Muller
Editors: Charlotte Zwerin, Bernadine Colish
Length: 57 minutes

THE MET IN JAPAN
Producers: CBS/Sony Classical, Peter Gelb, Susan Froemke
Associate Producers: Nell Archer, Valery Gaillard
Filmmakers: **Albert Maysles**, Susan Froemke
Photography: **Albert Maysles**
Editor: Deborah Dickson
Original Music: Wendy Blackston
Length: 21 minutes

SPORTS ILLUSTRATED: THE MAKING OF THE SWIMSUIT ISSUE
Producer: Susan Froemke
Associate Producers: Nell Archer, Douglas Graves
Filmmakers: Susan Froemke, **Albert Maysles**
Photography: **Albert Maysles**, Dyanna Taylor, Alexander Gruszynski
Editors: Geof Batz, Bob Eisenhardt, Pam Wise
Length: 55 minutes

1990
CHRISTO IN PARIS
Production Company: Maysles Films
Producers: **Albert Maysles**, **David Maysles**, Susan Froemke,
Associate Producers: Nell Archer, Valery Gaillard
Filmmakers: **Albert Maysles**, **David Maysles**, Deborah Dickson, Susan Froemke
Photography: **Albert Maysles**, Don Lenzer, Bruce Perlman
Sound: **David Maysles**
Editor: Deborah Dickson
Original Music: Wendy Blackston
Length: 58 minutes

1991
SOLDIERS OF MUSIC: ROSTROPOVICH RETURNS TO RUSSIA
Producers: CBS/Sony Classical, Susan Froemke, Peter Gelb
Associate Producer: Nell Archer
Filmmakers: **Albert Maysles**, Susan Froemke, Peter Gelb, Bob Eisenhardt
Photography: **Albert Maysles**, Wolfgang Becker, Edward Lachman, Martin Schaer
Sound: Martin Muller
Editor: Bob Eisenhardt
Length: 88 minutes

DOWN TO EARTH: FARMERS ON FARMING
Producer: Du Pont Classic
Filmmakers: **Albert Maysles**, Henry Corra
Photography: **Albert Maysles**
Length: 10 minutes

1992
ABORTION: DESPERATE CHOICES
Producers: HBO Films, Susan Froemke
Co-Producer: Nell Archer
Filmmakers: **Albert Maysles**, Susan Froemke, Deborah Dickson

Photography: **Albert Maysles**, Susan Froemke
Editor: Deborah Dickson
Sound Editor: Janet Swanson
Length: 67 minutes

BAROQUE DUET (also known as KATHLEEN BATTLE AND WYNTON MARSALIS: BAROQUE DUET)
Producers: CBS/Sony Classical, Maysles Films, Susan Froemke, Peter Gelb
Filmmakers: **Albert Maysles**, Susan Froemke, Peter Gelb, Pat Jaffe
Photography: **Albert Maysles**
Additional Photography: Greg Andracke, Don Lenzer, Jean de Segonzac
Sound: Roger Phenix, Larry Loewinger, Kenneth Love
Editor: Pat Jaffe
Length: 78 minutes

SPORTS ILLUSTRATED: SWIMSUIT '92
Producer: Susan Froemke
Filmmakers: **Albert Maysles**, Susan Froemke
Photography: **Albert Maysles**, Dyanna Taylor, Christian Blackwood, Christophe Lanzenberg
Editors: Jay Freund, Kathy Doughtery, Juliet Weber
Length: 57 minutes

1993
SPORTS ILLUSTRATED: SWIMSUIT '93
Producer: Susan Froemke
Filmmakers: **Albert Maysles**, Kathy Dougherty, Susan Froemke
Photography: **Albert Maysles**, Dyanna Taylor, Doug Cooper, Christophe Lanzenberg, Gary Steele
Editors: Kathy Dougherty, Bob Eisenhardt
Length: 43 minutes

1994
ACCENT ON THE OFFBEAT
Producers: CBS/Sony Classical, Susan Froemke, Peter Gelb
Filmmakers: **Albert Maysles**, Susan Froemke, Deborah Dickson, Peter Gelb
Photography: **Albert Maysles**
Editor: Deborah Dickson
Length: 56 minutes

THE UMBRELLAS (also known as CHRISTO: THE UMBRELLAS, and THE UMBRELLAS: JOINT PROJECT FOR JAPAN AND USA)
Production Company: Maysles Films

Producers: Henry Corra, Grahame Weinbren, **Albert Maysles**
Associate Producer: Douglas Graves
Filmmakers: **Albert Maysles**, Henry Corra, Grahame Weinbren
Photography: **Albert Maysles**, Robert Richman, Gary Steele, Robert Leacock, Don Lenzer, Richard Pearce, Martin Schaer
Sound: Merce Williams, Ronald Yoshida, Peter Miller, Bruce Perlman, Roger Phenix
Editors: Grahame Weinbren, Sakae Ishikawa
Length: 81 minutes

CONVERSATIONS WITH THE ROLLING STONES
Production Company: Maysles Films
Producer: Susan Froemke
Co-Producer: Douglas Graves
Filmmakers: **Albert Maysles**, Susan Froemke, Kathy Dougherty
Photography: **Albert Maysles**, Adam Kimmel
Sound: Ross Redfern
Editor: Kathy Dougherty
Length: 23 minutes

THE BEATLES: THE FIRST U.S. VISIT
Producers: Neil Aspinall, Susan Froemke
Filmmakers: Kathy Dougherty, Susan Froemke, **Albert Maysles**
Video Production: William Dever
Coodinating Producer: Ron Furmanek
Length: 132 minutes

1996
LETTING GO: A HOSPICE JOURNEY
Producers: HBO Films, Susan Froemke, Douglas Graves
Associate Producer: Susan Brignoli
Filmmakers: **Albert Maysles**, Susan Froemke, Deborah Dickson
Photography: **Albert Maysles**
Sound: L. Mark Sorre
Editor: Deborah Dickson
Length: 90 minutes

1997
CONCERT OF WILLS: MAKING THE GETTY CENTER
Producers: Susan Froemke, Gloria Gerace, Douglas Graves
Filmmakers: **Albert Maysles**, Susan Froemke, Bob Eisenhardt
Screenplay: **Albert Maysles**
Photography: **Albert Maysles**, Christophe Lanzenberg, Christian Blackwood, Robert Richman, Giorgio Urbinelli

Sound: Bruce Perlman, Micheal Reily
Editor: Bob Eisenhardt
Length: 100 minutes

1998
JAMES BALDWIN: THE PRICE OF A TICKET
Producers: **Albert Maysles**, Karen Thorsen
Director: Karen Thorsen
Length: 87 minutes

2000
LALEE'S KIN: THE LEGACY OF COTTON
Producers: HBO Films, Susan Froemke, Douglas Graves
Co-Producer: Douglas Graves
Associate Producers: Charles Loxton, Xan Parker, Susan Sloan
Filmmakers: **Albert Maysles**, Susan Froemke, Deborah Dickson
Photography: **Albert Maysles**, with additional photography by Jim Dollarhide
Sound: Peter Miller, Donald Thomas, Margaret Crimmins, Greg Smith
Editor: Deborah Dickson
Length: 88 minutes

2001
WITH THE FILMMAKER: PORTRAITS BY ALBERT MAYSLES
Producers: IFC Channel, Antonio Ferrera, Larry Kamerman, Rebecca Losick
Filmmakers: **Albert Maysles**, Antonio Ferrera, Larry Kamerman
Photography: **Albert Maysles**
Sound: Antonio Ferrera
Sound Editor: Tony Pipitone
Editor: Matthew Prinzing
Length: 120 minutes (four 30-minute episodes)

2004
NATIONAL ANTHEM: INSIDE THE "VOTE FOR CHANGE" CONCERT TOUR
Production Companies: Maysles Films, Pennebaker-Hegedus Films
Producers: Bill Curren, Frazer Pennebaker, Maureen A. Ryan
Associate Producers: Rebecca Losick, Rebecca Marshall
Filmmakers: **Albert Maysles**, D. A. Pennebaker
Photography: **Albert Maysles**, D. A. Pennebaker
Length: 300 minutes

2005
THIS IS AN ADVENTURE
Producer: Antonio Ferrera
Associate Producer: Rebecca Losick

Filmmakers: Antonio Ferrera, Matthew Prinzing, **Albert Maysles**
Length: 52 minutes

2006
THE BEALES OF GREY GARDENS
Production Company: Maysles Films
Producer: Tanja Meding
Filmmakers: **Albert Maysles**, **David Maysles**, Ian Markiewicz
Photography: **Albert Maysles**
Sound: **David Maysles**
Editor: Michael Hession
Length: 90 minutes

IDA, ELLA, AND WILLA (segment of the omnibus film TIME PIECE)
Producers: Neda Armian, Margaret Bodde, Sadie Tillery
Filmmaker: **Albert Maysles**
Photography: **Albert Maysles**
Length: 10 minutes

2007
THE GATES
Producers: Antonio Ferrera, Maureen Ryan, Vladimir Yavachev
Filmmakers: **Albert Maysles**, **David Maysles**, Antonio Ferrera, Matthew Prinzing
Photography: **Albert Maysles**, Antonio Ferrera, Peter Hutton
Sound: **David Maysles**, Antonio Ferrera
Editors: Matthew Prinzing, Antonio Ferrera
Length: 90 minutes

SALLY GROSS: THE PLEASURE OF STILLNESS
Production Company: Maysles Films
Producer: Tanja Meding
Filmmakers: **Albert Maysles**, Kristen Nutile
Photography: **Albert Maysles**, Kristen Nutile, Sean Williams, Greg Vanderveer, Peter Goldman, Michael Hosenfeld, Anne Alvergue
Sound: Andres Arredondo
Editor: Kristen Nutile
Audio Edit and Mix: Timothy J. Anderson
Music: Robert Poss
Length: 56 minutes

ADDICTION (segment, A MOTHER'S DESPERATION)
Producers: HBO, Susan Froemke
Associate Producer: Rob Meyer

Filmmakers: **Albert Maysles**, Susan Froemke
Photography: **Albert Maysles**
Editor: Paula Heredia
Length: 48 minutes

GREY GARDENS: FROM EAST HAMPTON TO BROADWAY
Producer: East of Doheny (Kelly Gonda, Lou Gonda)
Filmmaker: **Albert Maysles**
Photography: **Albert Maysles**
Length: 50 minutes

Albert Maysles as Cinematographer

1957
POLAND "OUTLOOK"
Producers: NBC-TV, Frank Reuven
Directors: Frank Reuven, Chet Huntley
Photography: **Albert Maysles**
Length: 30 minutes

1959
OPENING IN MOSCOW
Director: D. A. Pennebaker
Photography: **Albert Maysles**
Sound: **Albert Maysles**
Length: 52 minutes

1960
PRIMARY
Producers: Robert Drew, Time-Life, Inc.
Executive Producer: Robert Drew
Photography: **Albert Maysles**, Richard Leacock, D. A. Pennebaker, Terrence McCartney-Filgate
Sound: Robert Drew
Editors: Robert Drew, Richard Leacock, D. A. Pennebaker, Terrence McCartney-Filgate, Robert Farren
Length: 53 minutes

ON THE POLE
Producers: Robert Drew, Time-Life, Inc.
Executive Producer: Robert Drew
Photography: **Albert Maysles**, D. A. Pennebaker, William Ray, Abbott Mills
Sound: Robert Drew

Editor: Robert Drew
Length: 52 minutes

1961
YANKI, NO!
Producers: Drew Associates, ABC-TV
Executive Producer: Robert Drew
Photography: **Albert Maysles**, Richard Leacock, D. A. Pennebaker
Sound: Robert Drew
Editor: Robert Drew
Length: 60 minutes

KENYA: PART I: LAND OF THE WHITE GHOST; PART II: LAND OF THE BLACK GHOST
Producers: Robert Drew, ABC-TV, Time-Life, Inc.
Executive Producer: Richard Leacock
Photography: **Albert Maysles**, Richard Leacock
Sound: Gregory Shuker
Editor: Robert Drew
Length: 60 minutes

X-PILOT
Producers: Drew Associates, ABC-TV, Time-Life, Inc.
Executive Producer: Robert Drew
Photography: **Albert Maysles**, Terrence McCartney-Filgate
Sound: Howard Sochurek, Gregory Shuker
Editing: Robert Drew
Length: 25 minutes

ADVENTURES ON THE NEW FRONTIER
Producers: Drew Associates, Time-Life, Inc.
Executive Producer: Robert Drew
Photography: **Albert Maysles**, D. A. Pennebaker, Richard Leacock, Kenneth Snelson
Sound: Robert Drew, Lee Hall, Gregory Shuker, **David Maysles**
Editing: Robert Drew
Length: 52 minutes

1963
THE THEATER OF TOMORROW
Producers: ABC-TV, Robert Saudek, Mary Ahern
Director: Michael Ritchie
Photography: **Albert Maysles**
Length: 60 minutes

1964
MONTPARNASSE ET LAVALLOIS (segment of the omnibus feature, *Paris vu par . . .* , also known as *Six in Paris*)
Producers: Barbet Schroeder, Films du Losange
Director: Jean-Luc Godard
Photography: **Albert Maysles**, Nestor Almendros
Sound: René Levert
Editor: Jacqueline Raynal
Length: 12 minutes

1966
WHO IS JEAN SHRIMPTON?
Producer: Granada TV
Director: Dick Fontaine
Photography: **Albert Maysles**, David Samuelson
Sound: **David Maysles**
Length: 30 minutes

1968
MONTEREY POP
Producers: Richard Leacock, D. A. Pennebaker
Director: D. A. Pennebaker
Photography: **Albert Maysles**, D. A. Pennebaker, Nick Doob, Barry Feinstein, Richard Leacock, Roger Murphy, Nick Proferes, Jim Desmond
Sound: Wally Heider, Robert Van Dyke, John Cooke
Editors: Nina Schulman, Mary Lampson
Length: 78 minutes

JOURNEY TO JERUSALEM
Producer: Michael Mindlin, Jr.
Director: Michael Mindlin, Jr.
Photography: **Albert Maysles**, Richard Leacock, Stan Hirson, Bruce Martin, Sid Reichman, Joe Ryan
Sound: **David Maysles**
Editors: Robert Farren, Dorothy Tod, Isaac Cohen
Length: 86 minutes

EMERGENCY: THE LIVING THEATRE
Producers: Gwen Brown, Julian Beck, Judith Malina
Director: Gwen Brown
Photography: **Albert Maysles**, Alan Raymond, Frank Simon
Editor: Dan Halas
Length: 29 minutes

1970
REFLECTIONS
Producer: Japan Airlines
Director: Nell Cox
Photography: **Albert Maysles**
Sound: Vic Losick
Editor: Nell Cox
Length: 26 minutes

1977
THE GRATEFUL DEAD MOVIE
Producers: Ron Rakow, Eddie Washington
Directors: Jerry Garcia, Leon Gast
Photography: **Albert Maysles**, **David Maysles**, Stephen Lighthill, Robert Primes
Sound: Pat Jackson
Editors: Jerry Garcia, Susan Crutcher, John Nutt, Lisa Fruchtman
Length: 131 minutes

1983
BOB DYLAN: "DON'T FALL APART ON ME TONIGHT" AND "LICENSE TO KILL" (unfinished music shorts)
Producer: Sony Music
Photography: **Albert Maysles**
Length: 10 minutes (total)

1992
JAMMIN': JELLY ROLL MORTON ON BROADWAY
Producers: Margo Lion, Jac Venza, Nell Cox, Tom Bywaters
Director: George Wolfe
Photography: **Albert Maysles**
Length: 60 minutes

1993
LET THE GOOD TIMES ROLL
Producers: Chris Blackwell, Liz Heller, Stephanie Bennett
Directors: Paul Justman, Gary Legon, Jim Gabour
Photography: **Albert Maysles**
Length: 90 minutes

SEARCHING FOR BOBBY FISCHER
Producer: William Horberg
Director: Steven Zaillian

Photography: **Albert Maysles** (certain scenes; uncredited)
Length: 110 minutes

1996
WHEN WE WERE KINGS
Producers: David Sonenberg, Leon Gast
Director: Leon Gast
Photography: **Albert Maysles**, Maryse Alberti, Paul Goldsmith, Kevin Keating, Roderick Young
Sound: Gary Kelgren, Robert Cardelli, Chris Stone
Editors: Lean Gast, Taylor Hackford, Jeffrey Levy-Hinte, Keith Robinson
Length: 89 minutes

DEM DEUTSCHEN VOLK (also known as *Christo and Jeanne-Claude: Wrapped Reichstag, Berlin—1971–1995; Verhüllter Reichstag*)
Producers: Arte, ZDF, Ex-Nihilo
Directors: Jörg Daniel Hissen, Wolfram Hissen
Photography: **Albert Maysles**, Michael Hammon, Eric Turpin, Jörg Widmer
Editors: Dirk Grau, Götz Filenius
Length: 98 minutes

1999
100 YEARS OF WOMEN
Executive Producer: **Albert Maysles**
Producers: Susan Froemke, Douglas Graves
Director: Susan Froemke
Photography: **Albert Maysles**, Joan Churchill, Trish Govoni, Ferne Pearlstein, Bob Richman, Nancy Schreiber, Dyanna Taylor
Length: 60 minutes

2001
THE PARIS REVIEW: EARLY CHAPTERS
Producer: Edgar Howard
Director: Paula Heredia
Photography: **Albert Maysles**
Length: 53 minutes

ON COMMON GROUND: AN AMERICAN-GERMAN WORLD WAR II REUNION
Producers: David Eilenberg, Jessica Glass
Directors: David Eilenberg, Jessica Glass
Photography: Ethan Vogt, **Albert Maysles**
Length: 88 minutes

2002
STAGES: THREE DAYS IN MEXICO: BRITNEY SPEARS
Producer: Jim Forni
Director: Judy Hoffman
Photography: **Albert Maysles**, Antonio Ferrera, Judy Hoffinan, Jim Morrissette
Length: 60 minutes

2004
MASADA: LIVE AT TONIC, 1999
Producer: Antonio Ferrera
Director: Antonio Ferrra
Photography: **Albert Maysles**
Length: 68 minutes

IN GOOD CONSCIENCE: SISTER JEANNINE GRAMICK'S JOURNEY OF FAITH
Producer: Barbara Rick
Director: Barbara Rick
Photography: **Albert Maysles**
Length: 82 minutes

A DOG'S LIFE: A DOGAMENTARY
Producer: Gayle Kirschenbum
Director: Gayle Kirschenbaum
Photography: **Albert Maysles**
Length: 110 minutes

THE JEFF KOONS SHOW
Producers: Alison Chernick, Marni Deutsch
Director: Alison Chernick
Photography: **Albert Maysles**
Length: 49 minutes

ILLONA, UPSTAIRS
Producer: Melissa Hammel
Director: Melissa Hammel
Photography: **Albert Maysles**
Length: 25 minutes

2005
PRETTY THINGS
Producer: Josh Cramer
Director: Liz Goldwin
Photography: **Albert Maysles**, Josh Cramer, Peter Goldwyn, Keira Stephens,

Liz Goldwyn, Ron Egozi, Maggie Zackheim, Alex Rotaru, Peter Stanglmayr, Jennifer Van Goethem, Philip Maysles, Antonio Ferrera, Vincent Toto
Length: 120 minutes

SEAN O'CASEY: UNDER A COLOURED CAP
Producer: Mary Beth Yarrow
Director: Shivaun O'Casey
Photography: **Albert Maysles**
Length: 81 minutes

COFFEE BEANS FOR A LIFE: MEIN UBERLEBEN IN KOLBUSZOWA
Producer: Andrew Goldstein
Director: Helga Hirsch
Photography: **Albert Maysles**
Length: 90 minutes

STOLEN
Producers: Jen Kaczor, Sally Jo Fifer
Director: Rebecca Dreyfus
Photography: **Albert Maysles**, Rebecca Dreyfus
Editors: Liz Ludden, Markus Peters, Kate Taverna
Length: 90 minutes

2006
NOT A PHOTOGRAPH: THE MISSION OF BURMA STORY
Producer: Eran Lobel
Directors: Jeffrey Iwanicki, David Kleiler, Jr.
Photography: **Albert Maysles**, W. Mott Hupfel III, Leif Husted-Jensen
Editors: Tyler Hubby, Jeff Iwanicki, Anne Renehan, Chris Santo, John Suvannavejh
Length: 72 minutes

WHEN THE ROAD BENDS: TALES OF A GYPSY CARAVAN
Producers: Jasmine Dellal, Wouter Barendrecht
Director: Jasmine Dellal
Photography: **Albert Maysles**, Alain de Halleux
Sound: Mariusz Glabinski
Editors: Margarita Jimeno, Paulo Padilha
Length: 111 minutes

2007
SELF-PORTRAIT WITH COWS GOING HOME AND OTHER WORKS: A PORTRAIT OF SILVIA PLACHY
Producer: Susannah Ludwig

Director: Rebecca Dreyfus
Photography: **Albert Maysles**
Length: 10 minutes

MONTEREY 40
Producer: Erik Himmelsbach
Director: Erik Himmelsbach, D. A. Pennebaker
Photography: **Albert Maysles**
Length: 90 minutes

A PRESIDENT TO REMEMBER: IN THE COMPANY OF JOHN F. KENNEDY
Producer: Robert Drew
Director: Robert Drew
Photography: **Albert Maysles** as cinematographer of footage from *Primary*
Length: 85 minutes

SOUL POWER
Producers: Leon Gast, David Sonenberg, Jeffrey Levy-Hinte
Director: Jeffrey Levy-Hinte
Photography: **Albert Maysles**, Paul Goldsmith, Kevin Keating, Roderick Young
Length: 93 minutes

SHINE A LIGHT
Producers: Steve Bing, Michael Cohl, Zane Weiner, Victoria Pearman
Director: Martin Scorsese
Photography: Robert Richardson; "Camera in hand": **Albert Maysles**
Length: 122 minutes

FOUR SEASONS LODGE
Producers: Andrew Jacobs, Matt Lavine
Director: Andrew Jacobs
Photography: **Albert Maysles**, Justin Schein
Length: 100 minutes

A CASE OF MISTAKEN IDENTITY
Producer: Joseph Jacoby
Director: Joseph Jacoby
Photography: **Albert Maysles**
Length: 60 minutes

Albert Maysles as Interviewee In

1999
Cinema Verite: Defining the Moment; Director: Peter Wintonick
The Wild Ride of Outlaw Bikers; Producer: Peter Jones

2000
The Beatles Revolution; Director: Rudy Bednar

2001
Mick Jagger: The Ultimate Performer; Director: Robin Bextor

2002
Hollywood Rocks the Movies: The 1970s; Director: Patty Irins Specht (**Albert Maysles** uncredited)
Independent View, episode 208; KQED TV
Indie Truth: An Inquiry into the Documentary; Director: Carl Bessai

2004
Michael Moore Hates America; Director: Mike Wilson

2005
Ghosts of Grey Gardens; Director: Liliana Greenfield-Sanders
Tell Them Who You Are; Director: Mark Wexler

2007
How Is It with Phooie; Director: Mike Steinberg
Grey Gardens: From East Hampton to Broadway; Director: **Albert Maysles**
Manufacturing Dissent: Uncovering Michael Moore; Directors: Rick Caine, Debbie Melnyk
My Nose; Director: Gayle Kirschenbaum
A Walk into the Sea: Danny Williams and the Warhol Factory; Director: Esther Robinson
Wild Blue Yonder; Director: Celia Maysles

ALBERT AND DAVID MAYSLES

INTERVIEWS

Albert and David Maysles

MARK SHIVAS/1963

ALBERT AND DAVID MAYSLES showed their first major film *Showman*, about Joseph E. Levine the movie tycoon. Levine is best known for his promotion of *Hercules*, which he bought for £50,000, spending £400,000 on promotion; as a result one out of every eight Americans went to see the film and Levine cleaned up.

Showman was filmed during the period when Levine handled the Loren/De Sica picture *Two Women*. The Maysles followed Levine from New York to Boston, Cannes, and Rome, filming some of his activities. They also followed some of Levine's staff, in particular an aide called Mort who seemed to them to be the most anti-Levine, in the hope of getting another side to the tycoon's character. They had hoped to record the working out of a business deal to its completion: this would have given the film structure. But they were unable to do this and had instead to content themselves with Levine's day to day activities. Luckily, during the three weeks the Maysles spent with him, Levine attended a reunion which told them something about the poverty of his childhood—"He was a rich kid. He had shoes"—and the Oscar Awards presentation took place.

Albert Maysles worked on some of the Drew-Leacock movies, including *Primary*. He takes responsibility for the direction of *Showman*, and his brother David for the editing. When shooting, Albert carries the camera and David the recorder. They, like Drew and Leacock, refuse to "direct" the action in any way, even rejecting the interview as a device, and act as observers only. In the following interview we have, for the sake of simplicity, not distinguished between the two brothers.

M.S.

From *Movie*, no. 8, April 1963. Reprinted by permission of the author.

Q: *What did you tell Mr. Levine that you wanted to do?*

A: That we wanted to spend a lot of time with him, filming him. In the States they are used to this sort of thing from the techniques that are used by magazines, like *Life*. And one of the writers at *Life* had spent a great deal of time, day and night, with him, doing a story on him. Our time spent with him was much less of an imposition because we made no real demands on him. All we asked was to let us be with him when something interesting—we thought—was happening.

Q: *How much film did you shoot for* Showman?

A: Around 30,000 feet, which is not much for this sort of film. Fifteen feet to every one used.

Q: *Were there any guiding principles in what you chose to shoot?*

A: Almost every opportunity we had we shot. We didn't *always* get co-operation from Levine or his people so we had to take advantage of every opportunity when something was happening. We'd ask what was happening each day, and where they were going. One day we rang up and they said nothing was going to happen, and I'm sure that to them it seemed so. But we went to his office and some of his old buddies came in quite unexpectedly. We never had any idea that that was going to happen, but it was marvellous. And that's the way most of it went.

We didn't get a logical and dramatic structure. There was no point you can call a real climax, but I'm not sure that's always necessary. There are other things that compensate for that, like a real revelation of a personality.

Q: *Did you put the camera down if you found anybody acting, or what?*

A: I don't understand the nervousness on the part of the film-makers about what's going to happen when people see the camera. Nothing's going to happen if you don't think too much about it. If you're concerned about the presence of the camera, others are going to be concerned about it. The camera stays on my shoulder all the time so sometimes I am shooting and sometimes I am not. It's in the same position all day long and they can't tell. If they were to think about it, they'd get awful tired of thinking about it. It's like it's part of the room, part of the furniture. How many times have I told people not to look in the camera? Maybe once. But as a general rule I don't have to. Someone looks at the camera, and you just look at them and they look away. You must remember that we're filming people who are very much involved in what they're doing. If you say "Don't look into the camera," as many people do, that's the best signal to be worried about it.

Q: *Do you use the fastest film available, or do you find a balance between the grain and quality and the speed you would like?*
A: We work at the highest speeds but we use normal film. We can work at 1000 ASA and we don't have any problem with grain. We took Plus X film and pushed it to 1000. It's rated normally about 125.

Q: *Would you ever break off during a sequence and show someone doing what he is talking about, while his voice continues on the soundtrack?*
A: Use wild sound, you mean? An interior monologue? We feel that's rather a compromise. We'd rather have the immediate situation and the reactions of people to it. The drama's right in front of you. This kind of inner monologue is almost like narration. Using one or the other you can have almost any picture and justify it by the lines, whereas in an actual situation, the thing is happening before you. The dialogue is pertinent. You're more subjective when you're directing, or using inner monologue or narration, than when you're just observing. Even then you're still subjective in everything you shoot, in the fact that you shoot that thing rather than anything else. In *Showman* it was Levine in action, and if you had cut different material that we had shot, I don't think you would have a different impression of him. We had a hunch ahead of time that there was a sympathetic quality in the man, and we knew because of *Hercules* that he was also probably a pretty rough businessman.

Q: *Would you think you had failed if everyone had the same reaction to* Showman*?*
A: It's interesting to know that people have different reactions to Levine. Some people like him a great deal and are very sympathetic towards him. It works out that way split fifty-fifty—in films with this "objective" approach. *Primary* was that way too. Some people say, "You really did a job on Humphrey," and other people think that Humphrey came out so much better. It has a lot to do with the conceptions that people bring with them to the film which they see.

Q: *Would you ever think of attempting any transference of your techniques to a controlled film?*
A: I think a lot of productions, like *The Connection* and other low budget features could be done much better with a spontaneous camera. But it's very difficult to go half way in something like this, because the

moment that the people accept you in the slightest way as a director of their lives and activities and what they have to say, you've intervened with another kind of relationship, and they're waiting for you to direct them, to control them. Under those circumstances they can't be entirely themselves, which is what we're after.

We have plans for a major film to be made specifically for the motion picture theatre. This film is going to cost about 175,000 dollars, which isn't very much for an American feature production. We'll shoot less than 100,000 feet of film, but it'll take about four or five months to shoot and double that time to edit. It's like the Family of Man exhibition in motion pictures.

The Maysles Brothers and "Direct Cinema"

MAXINE HALEFF/1964

THE STATELY *TIMES* of London is not known for its enthusiasm in giving rave notices, but here's what Maurice Wiggin said in the issue of February 16, regarding *New York Meets the Beatles*, by the Maysles brothers:

> . . . Some of the roughest, crudest, maddest, most vivacious and vervy sound-and-vision I've seen and heard. The admirable intention is to get rid as far as possible of all the intermediaries, the filtering and editorializing elements; to use the recording tools sparely, simply and directly, confronting the viewer with something like the unadulterated truth. It is the self-effacing technique which masquerades as nonexistent.

And, continues Patricia Rowan in the same issue of the *Times*, the Maysles' techniques

> . . . will outdate not only the old-pattern programmes, with their commentators and experts and reporters, but also the old divisions of the creative team, and the concept of the cameraman simply as technician.

A daring and unique style marks the work of the Maysles brothers, Albert and David, whose independent production, *Showman*, was much acclaimed by European critics. What sets it apart is the ability of the Maysles to capture on film actual events that are deeply revealing, maintaining at the same time an excellence of photography and sound.

When filming, Dave does the sound and Al the photography. Joseph Levine is the subject of *Showman*, and he was chosen because the Maysles felt that he had the warmth of personality to make an interesting film. Other occupations and personalities had been considered earlier.

The locale of the fifty-three-minute film ranges from Cannes to Boston to Hollywood to Rome. Many of the events concern Sophia Loren's winning of the Academy Award for her performance in *Two Women*, which Levine distributes.

The Maysles shot Levine informally in many private and public situations. They did not ask for a release until after they had shown Levine the unedited footage. At first, Levine refused to give his approval, but after the Maysles edited the film, Levine consented to a television release only. The Maysles say they never want to work without a release again. Because television stations and networks prefer documentaries produced under their own supervision by staff personnel, the Maysles have encountered great difficulty in placing *Showman* on television. Despite the uncertain financial returns on *Showman*, the two brothers have recently produced a second film, concerning the hectic American tour of the popular British singing group, The Beatles.

Ideally, Al and Dave would like to produce their films for motion picture theatres. "Some people say that the audience won't sit through a long documentary, because it is not emotionally involving," says Dave. "But we think that, properly done, this kind of film can be the most emotionally involving. We wish to show people living their own lives and speaking their own thoughts with a minimum of structuring of events by the film maker." The next film that the Maysles plan to do on their own is to be about the problems of a pregnant single girl. Conceding that such a project entails invasion of privacy, Dave states that many people are sympathetic to working in such a film through a desire to explain their lives. "If society is going to understand itself," believes Dave, "then it is not going to keep these people from telling their story. We use the camera in such a way that its presence is not detrimental to the people in the film who go about their business. I don't think anybody knows enough about a subject to impose his own ideas. We are trying to find out what people are saying. You would think that our method is impersonal, that it doesn't have feeling, but it is exactly the opposite. Through the whole thing runs a kind of emotion that is involving. We try to develop techniques and equipment that won't interfere with the subject and won't interfere with our story telling."

The Maysles' equipment has been specially designed by them and is being continually changed and improved. The camera is basically an Auricon movement with an Angenieux zoom lens. Because it weighs twenty pounds and is balanced, it can be carried for long periods on the cameraman's shoulder without strain. Because of the balance, the cameraman can put his hands into his pockets or can hold the lens with both hands to operate the zoom and to change focus. The cameraman can freely observe his surroundings, because the camera rests on the shoulder below the line of sight. At present, the camera runs for two hours on batteries with an electronic system to make the motor run at sixty cycles. The Nagra tape recorder by another means keeps the same speed, thus insuring perfectly synchronized sound. No connection is needed between tape recorder and camera. The sound man ascertains the camera's activity by watching the lens. When the zoom is at wide angle, the sound man can see a "W" on the zoom. At telephoto, he can see a "T". The takes are numbered verbally on the tape, and a pad of paper with this number is photographed by the camera when shooting ends. The brothers are presently completing design plans on an even lighter camera, weighing less than fourteen pounds, that will shoot thirty-three minutes of footage.

In many ways, the Maylses' technique is similar to that of Drew Associates, for whom they worked from 1960 to 1962 on the Time-Life experimental film project. Earlier, in 1955, Al was teaching psychology at Boston University when he went to the Soviet Union to photograph a film about mental hospitals. Shortly thereafter, Dave began working for Marilyn Monroe Productions, Inc., as assistant to the producers of *Bus Stop* and *The Prince and the Showgirl*. After the latter film was completed in England, the brothers made a tour of Europe by motorcycle, spending six months in Poland where they shot a film, *The Youth of Poland*, about the 1957 revolution there. A portion of this was shown on NBC.

Working on *Primary* with Richard Leacock of Drew Associates was a turning point for the Maysles. Leacock, who had been Flaherty's cameraman for *The Louisiana Story*, derives some of his methods from the Flaherty approach—the non-structuring of action and the "non-preconception" of what is to take place. The Maysles also worked on *Kenya* and *Yanki, No!*.

Like Drew Associates, the Maysles use the hand-held camera and portable synchronized sound to film actuality, but their values are different. "The *Life* magazine philosophy influenced the picking of subject matter," explains Dave. "They wanted life-or-death situations and chose emotionally charged events to film." Frankly journalistic Drew preferred to record a newsworthy event for public information. In contrast, the Maysles feel that more subtle situations can be equally involving. They are mainly interested in revealing character.

Showman is more than the revelation of a single man's character, because by inference, Joe Levine illustrates something about America at large. Among the many European critics who praised the film, Peter Graham in *Films and Filming* said that "the film showed, I think, the tremendous possibilities of reportage technique. In contrast to Jean Rouch, the Maysles are more concerned with using their technical skill (which is greater than Rouch's) to record reality without tampering with or imposing on it. Louis Marcorelles write in *Cahiers du Cinéma* that *Showman*, "the least recognized and the least understood of the films shown at Lyon, seemed to me to be the most beautiful, the purest. I would easily rank it among the ten or fifteen great films that it has been my fortune to see since the war . . . a work that exists only through the cinema. . . . As for the Maysles, they create without theories, according to a glorious American tradition." Shortly after this was published, Barbet Schroeder, a *Cahiers du Cinéma* editor, brought Al to France to photograph a film he was producing with Jean-Luc Godard as director.

The following conversation with Al occurred after the film was completed.

HALEFF: *What film were you shooting in France?*
AL MAYSLES: It hasn't got a title to it yet. The film is made up of four or five stories shot in different quarters of Paris. Jean-Luc Godard directed the one that I photographed, using our own specially designed camera. It's in 16mm color with 35mm blowup, so it will be shown in movie theatres everywhere.

HALEFF: *Why did they pick an American photographer for a French film?*
AL MAYSLES: Well, I knew the producer. I'd met him. He had seen our work and he knew the kind of photography that I do was of great interest to Godard. There are very few photographers that can film the way his films have to be shot. Godard makes films very much out of personal feelings, and you might say intuitively. They're not closely cut out ahead of time. A good deal of what goes into the film comes from the actual shooting at the moment. Not improvising exactly, but shots are not planned. The script has been planned. The scenario has been planned, and the actors know pretty much what they're going to do. Even that is subject to change. Most of the shots were very, very long, and it demanded that the camera move a great deal, and the grace of the movements and the com-

plexity of the movements made it necessary that the camera be hand-held. To hand-hold the camera and still get a perfectly steady shot and to be able to walk around the room and follow actors and such continuously is rather difficult, but more than that it requires a kind of agility that you just have to choose the shot as it's taking place.

HALEFF: *It seems to require a combination director and cameraman.*
AL MAYSLES: I don't like to use the word director, because I don't feel that the way I shoot that I'm directing anything. Godard didn't tell me how to shoot, except that what I shoot depends on whom I'm shooting. Godard has selected the actors and actresses. He has given them their words, and he had chosen the direction of their movements. He has made the rehearsals, but he hasn't told me how to shoot.

HALEFF: *Did Godard let you use your own camera, and did you shoot with synchronized sound?*
AL MAYSLES: Yes.

HALEFF: *Because heavy equipment for sync sound causes a loss in mobility, do the French shoot with sync sound for location exteriors?*
AL MAYSLES: When the French work inside a studio, they use sync; otherwise the sound is very frequently dubbed.

HALEFF: *Is it unusual for a dramatic film to be made with your kind of mobile equipment?*
AL MAYSLES: It's the first time it's ever been done. We are shooting very long continuous shots and moving in and out of them without stopping the camera. There'll be almost no cutting to it. Godard said that he didn't expect a lot of editing. If you do a lot of editing to footage, the editing takes place two times, in a way. First, as it's shot—if you're told what to shoot—and then there's the editing when you get the footage later on. If you do a lot of editing, you can end up losing a certain amount of authenticity. What's more interesting to me is that I know we can achieve greater truthfulness by shooting continuously. This minimizes the amount of editing that you can do as you are shooting, as well as the amount of editing that's done after. You know, when a human being observes a situation, he moves from one thing to another without stopping. If you do it continuously and with one camera, then the opportunity for faking it up is so much the less.

HALEFF: *How does this method differ from the usual one?*
AL MAYSLES: What happens usually is this . . . a director chooses the

action and then says, "OK, now we're in this situation, we'll take this shot," and then even as the shooting goes on, he or the cameraman notices some thing nice, and he stops and takes that little shot, which will be inserted. When you shoot that way, with all those little bits and pieces and put them all together, you're fabricating something. OK, it's a fabrication to begin with, but the fabrication is doubled or tripled or quadrupled. There's much less of that if you shoot in a continuous shot. I know this as clearly as black from white, and you just have to see these films to see the difference. Take a film like *America, America.* That was directed by quite a different kind of director, Elia Kazan. It's not a believable film to me. I don't believe a bit of it. I'm always aware that I'm in a theatre, rather than watching a movie, when I see that kind of film. When you watch a film of Godard's you know you're seeing a movie.

HALEFF: *Isn't this sort of editing, or lack of it, the opposite of what Godard did in* Breathless, *where he used fast cuts to do away with all the intervals that were cluttering up his action? How did he evolve from* Breathless *to a film with such long sequences?*
AL MAYSLES: Well, that may happen in this film too; I don't know, since it hasn't been edited. But in those parts of *Breathless,* as in this film, where the action does flow continuously it will have the effect I'm speaking of.

HALEFF: *What is the story of the picture?*
AL MAYSLES: It's about a girl who writes two love letters to two different guys. She seals the envelopes, mails them and then discovers that she's sent the letters to the wrong guys . . . put the letters in the wrong envelopes. Then she goes to each one to apologize. The first one is an artist who welds his own metal sculpture and the other is a mechanic welding an automobile in his garage. The actors are unknown here. Serge Davri plays the mechanic, Johanna Shimkus, the girl, and Phillipe Hiquély, a sculptor himself, plays the sculptor.

HALEFF: *Do you use Paris exteriors?*
AL MAYSLES: A little bit. You know where you are. This was done in Montparnasse and Levallois. Most of it was shot indoors.

HALEFF: *Have you worked on a dramatic film before?*
AL MAYSLES: No.

HALEFF: *Did you find that it was much different from working with nonactors as you have done previously?*

AL MAYSLES: With non-actors, you have an opportunity between shots to surmise what's coming next. You have an opportunity to pick and choose more, but in this kind of filming, with everything so tightly scripted, you have to be shooting something that's meaningful every moment that the actors are performing. You know you have to use everything you shoot. If you're shooting this way, you're not interested in stopping the camera and shooting this little item or that. I was interested in doing the whole scene in one shot, if I could. I got close-ups by moving around and using the zoom lens on occasion. It's the same kind of shooting that I'm ordinarily doing, except this was without any kind of a break to re-focus or to do this, that or the other. I had the script, but it didn't really specify the location of people, except that it was in the studio or in the garage. The actors had their words to say, but their movements in the room were not outlined in the script. It didn't say there's going to be a close-up here or a long shot there, and the girl moves from right to left. None of that stuff is in it. They ran through it a couple of times, I watched them, and then we shot it. When they ran through it the first time, they had the lights low. I could have shot it then and probably would have done as well. We completed the whole thing in a couple of days.

I don't believe in any labels or styles of filming. Who knows, we may at any time develop into something else, and I don't care for these categorizations. If you have to use a label, I suppose direct cinema is the one that's the most meaningful. What we're doing is direct in every way. We're not using scripts which frequently make for indirection. It's a kind of barrier. For us it's another impediment between the moment that something is really happening in life and the moment that it gets recorded into film. This is especially true if you are not using actors, and with actors too, although there are many different kinds of filming. It's hard to imagine making theatrical films without scripts.

HALEFF: *You said that most documentary films are surface realism. What do you mean by that?*

AL MAYSLES: I think that describes them in general. Actually, I don't know much documentary film. Just what I've made and what I'm interested in. What kind of realism can you achieve in a movie when you can't even hear anybody talking? I certainly wouldn't include Flaherty's films. He did as much as he could without sound, and he wasn't against using sound. Many people who have been making films within these last thirty years wouldn't have used synchronized sound anyway, even if they had it available to them. Instead they were, and are to this very day, using narration and music to such a degree that they, as many of them feel, are putting out illustrated lectures.

HALEFF: *How did you get interested in film in the beginning?*
AL MAYSLES: I got a visa to go to Russia and made a film of mental hospitals and mental health in Russia, just to satisfy my desire to see them and to make a report of what I saw. I thought that making a movie would be the most authentic way to do it.

HALEFF: *Do you consider your films to be journalism, social comment, an art form, or maybe something else?*
AL MAYSLES: It's really not much more social comment than Hemingway. I don't regard our point of view as being very different from his. I don't think we've made enough films to claim that we're doing just what he's doing. As I see what we're doing, it seems to me that our approach, the feeling that we have when we get into a subject, is probably something like what his involvement is. Do you think he makes social comment? He is, more or less. It's a social comment, but not in an overbearing fashion. I think that in *Showman*, there's very strong social comment, but it's not based on our desire to destroy the world Levine lives in.

HALEFF: *Do you think most social comment is based on the desire to destroy?*
AL MAYSLES: A lot of it is that way. For example, Chris Marker. I would regard him as a propagandist. We don't take ourselves to be propagandists. Another example is that film, *The Most.* It's about Hugh Hefner, *Playboy* owner. Many of the films of the Canadian Film Board, they're propaganda.

HALEFF: *You stated that if society is going to understand itself, it's not going to keep people from telling their story. Isn't that what the Canadian Film Board is attempting?*
AL MAYSLES: Yes, they're trying to do that, but they're doing it with a heavy hand. For instance, that film *Lonely Boy* about Paul Anka. I don't think they liked that kid when they made that film, and it shows. Dave and I are trying to find out what's going on. We capture what takes place. Do you think there's a strong point of view in that selection of photographs, Steichen's *The Family of Man*? Well, that's the kind of strength we want in our point of view. A lot of people looking through all those photographs will say, "There's no point of view here." They don't find it in each individual shot, and they don't find it in the whole collection, either. I don't agree with them, but they think that doesn't make for a point of view. We've been criticized for not having a point of view. When

people see *Showman* they say, "You know there's no point of view." When they don't like it, that's what they tell use.

HALEFF: *Then you do have a point of view? You see something in what is happening and you interpret it by photographing it.*

AL MAYSLES: Right. Those same people will probably think that Hemingway doesn't have a point of view either, you know. The statement we want to make is a cinematic statement, and the statement that Hemingway wants to make is in the form of a short story or a novel, and that's different from coming out with statements or points of view as they're commonly understood to be. What he has to communicate, his point of view, comes across to the person as he reads it.

HALEFF: *You said earlier that the cameraman is like a director who influences the action as a non-directive therapist does. Is such a therapist influencing action?*

AL MAYSLES: He certainly is, because if he weren't, there would be no sense in a person going to him. They might just as well sit home and talk to the wall. When we photograph people, they're not talking to a wall. The camera's not a wall. The camera's like a non-directive therapist. It's not therapy, although maybe in some cases it might be, but the relationship is one of a real person listening. In a way, because the observation is one where the observer is really interested in what's going on, it makes him a kind of participant. So, in that sense, not all of it is just going in one direction—from the person who's being filmed out to everybody. There is a bounce-back, because the person is being filmed by someone who is interested in him.

HALEFF: *In other words, this kind of filming cannot be done by people who are not strongly interested in the subject being filmed?*

AL MAYSLES: No, of course not. I think you're involved in a different kind of film making when you say, "I think I'm going to make a whole film from behind a mirror . . . behind a one-way glass." I don't think you can make one of our films that way. I'm trying to describe to you how active a role we take, and I'd say that the role that we take in making the films and in our relationship to the people that we film is a very active one, but we don't direct them.

HALEFF: *So if you were behind a mirror you wouldn't get the same effect. You think that it's an advantage for a cameraman and all the equipment being openly visible where the action takes place?*

AL MAYSLES: That's right. It depends on how you handle yourself and how you handle the equipment, and how big it really is. We minimize the amount of equipment . . . make it very small, and we don't take over the situation when we come into it. But the main point is this: we don't stage them, and we don't tell them what to do.

A Discussion with the Maysles Brothers

JAMES BLUE/1965

WITH CHARACTERISTIC for spotting trends and pinning labels, French critics found a new cause and called it *Cinéma-Vérité.* It has been called Film-Journalism, Truth-Film, Direct-Shooting, Kino-Pravda, Candid-Eye, and One-Eye. But a rose by any name still smells sweeter in French. *Cinéma-Vérité* stuck. Under its banner were united strangely differing approaches to film making. There was, however, one common denominator: the effort to capture, with portable sound-film equipment, life as it is lived and not as it is reinvented by the traditional cinema.

As their efforts multiplied, these film makers grew critical of each other, but their differences underlined a more deeply binding tie: an unshakeable faith in a kind of objective truth rooted within the subject. Their effort would, they hoped, lead them into communion with this Truth. Something close to a modern religion was born. Although most of the participants would reject the comparison, the parallel, if not exact, is at least instructive. *Cinéma-Vérité* has its orthodoxies, its heresies, its unitarians, and its fundamentalists. At no time in the history of film art have mystical and moral considerations been so important in the formation of a film aesthetic.

In the mystique of his quest—to continue the parallel—the film maker subjugates himself to the world around him. He says to Nature: "Not my will but thine be done." What then is revealed to him has all the more value in that it comes from without rather than from within. It is an art of "selflessness." In some cases the act of shooting is, for the film maker, an end in itself. It is communion. A way of relating to the world without.

If "Truth" is the God of this religion, "Authenticity" is its Prophet. If the spectator cannot believe that what he sees has really happened, is "Authentic," then he has a right to suspect the "Truth" of the film. Every effort of the film maker, then, both in the shooting and in the editing, is directed toward assuring the spectator that what he is seeing is not the result of an imposed point of view. Here we come to the keystone and major contribution of this ethical-Aesthetic: in the traditional film, immersed as it is in artifice, things cannot be shown that do not grow out of the internal dramatic logic of the structure. Events must have a "probability" about them or else they may be "too much" for a spectator to take. If we see a defense lawyer cry for joy upon hearing news that might save his client from the electric chair, we conceivably would react badly, as an audience of a fiction film, to this overdose of sentiment and lack of restraint on the part of the director. If, however, this happens within a framework of "Authenticity"—as it does in Greg Shuker's *The Chair*, about the rehabilitation hearing of Paul Crump—we are forced to accept the act as having really happened, and we must revise our own feelings about what is probable in life. "Authenticity" permits life to reveal its own truth, its own poetry, free from the tyranny of dramatic probability.

In the lexicon of *Cinéma-Vérité* Creation as the artist's duty has been replaced by Revelation, Believability by Authenticity, Beauty by Honesty, and Preconception, in the making of the film, by Attentive Submission to the subject. The classical documentarist is drummed out for having "used" life for the dissemination of a "selfish point of view." The fiction film maker is castigated for his suspicious theatrical artifice. Because film is a photographic medium, its only proper material is believed to be life itself—not as it is recreated, but as it happens. To these men, all else is heresy.

Cinéma-Vérité, as it is practiced in Europe by such men as Jean Rouch, Mario Ruspoli, and—at times—Chris Marker, differs fundamentally in its approach from that of the American group. The Europeans are eclectic, unitarian. All ways lead to the Truth-God. They intervene, probe, interview, provoke situations that might suddenly reveal something. There is an attempt to obtain from the subject a kind of creative participation. The Americans are, for the most part, fundamentalists. They eschew all intervention whatever its goal. They cultivate an alert passivity. They seek self-effacement. They want the subject to forget that they are there.

This latter kind of cinema has its roots in the pioneer work of the great American film poet, Robert Flaherty. It was Flaherty who first taught the principle of rejecting preconceived notions so that the shooting might become an "odyssey" of discovery. Flaherty, however, once his notions were formed, went on to stage or to provoke whatever might satisfy the needs of his film, according to his own sensitivity. It is interesting to note that Flaherty—like the Europeans—often sought the creative participation of his subjects. The Samoans of *Moana* and the Eskimos of *Nanook* suggested scenes that were put into these films.

Whether people are for it or reject it entirely, *Cinéma-Vérité*'s effect has been to force a redefinition or clarification of film aesthetics. As the coming of photography made conventional portraiture intolerable in painting, so *Cinéma-Vérité* has made the conventional "realistic style" in the fiction film a thing of the past for many new film makers.

Similarly, the staged effects of old-fashioned documentary now seem utterly absurd. At the same time that photography upset a good deal of painting, it liberated it for more poetic pursuits. At the same time that *Cinéma-Vérité* is destroying some of the encrusted conventions of traditional film making, it is liberating it, forcing it into more highly creative areas. What remains to be asked is "where is *Cinéma-Vérité* itself going?" What is its future? To know this, one must first know what kind of thinking has been taking place. The following discussion with Albert and David Maysles is an attempt to begin this search.

New York commercial film makers turn red and clutch their drinks when you talk about the Maysles. In Hollywood, the prestigious members of the lofty Motion Picture Academy saw ten minutes of *Showman* and stopped the projection. Old-school documentarists call it "anti-audience," "anti-art."

Al has just finished shooting, in *Vérité* style, a sketch for Jean-Luc Godard. Godard, with his taste for the imperative statement, declares "Al Maysles is the greatest cameraman in America."

Al was first associated with Richard Leacock, Donn Alan Pennebaker, and Robert Drew. Together they shot the early classics of American *Cinéma-Vérité:* the now famous *Primary*, about the Kennedy-Humphrey battle in the 1960 Wisconsin primary election, and the controversial *Yanki, No!*, which dealt with rising anti-Americanism in Latin America. Greg Shuker joined them at the end of 1960, and together they shot a two-part story on Kenya: *Land of the White Ghost* and *Land of the Black Ghost*. Al left the group in 1961 to set up his own company with his brother David. Shuker, Pennebaker, Drew, and Leacock, under the business name of Drew Associates, went on to produce, notably, *The Chair, Jane, Eddie*, and *Mooney Versus Fowle*. Leacock and Pennebaker have since withdrawn from the Drew group and now are teamed as Filmakers in the same building. Their newest work is *Happy Mother's Day*, formerly called *The Quints*.

Since leaving Drew Associates, Al and his brother David, who records the sound and does the editing, have sought to make films about people in all walks of life. Rather than treat journalistic subjects as the Drew group had done, they have attempted to deepen their penetration into a person or a group of people, taken at certain moments in their lives. This quest has produced *Showman*—about Joe Levine—and, recently, *What's Happening?* (about the Beatles). Neither of these films has received public release; however, *Showman* has been seen in film festivals around the world, and it has provoked both earsplitting protest and thunderous praise.

Because of Al's avowed purpose to catch a kind of "subjective-objective" truth, his cinema is one in which ethics and aesthetics are interdependent, where beauty starts with honesty, where a cut or a change in camera angle can become not only a possible aesthetic error but also a "sin" against Truth. In things cinematic, Al Maysles is a religious zealot.

AL: When I went to Cuba to shoot part of *Yanki, No!*, I didn't know any more about Castro and Cuba than any other person. I don't think I would have done better if I had prepared myself. When I got off the plane, I went to a mass meeting where Castro was talking to the mothers, and my first shot was the big close-up of Castro. I could spend five years tracking him around the world and I never would have gotten a shot like that. The better you know somebody, the more you are at a disadvantage. You are no longer curious to put down things familiar to you. The essential you let go by, because you say to yourself: "everybody knows that."

JAMES: *How did you retain this freshness when you worked on the sketch with Godard? Didn't you have to "rehearse"?*

AL: Yes. We ran it through dry once. I feel, though, that if I had actually been shooting the first time, it would have been better—as far as my camera work is concerned, better as far as the actors are concerned.

JAMES: *How did Godard prepare the scene for you to film?*

AL: Gee, I don't know. I know that he hadn't even met one actor until three o'clock in the morning of the day before we shot him. We shot half the film that same day. One thing I was curious about was whether or not Godard had caught the significance of what we were doing—as I felt I had—because what we had done had not been done before, I don't think. In continuous shots like that. One shot lasted eleven minutes. So I went over to Godard and I said, "In a word, what does this all mean to you? What do you think is so different about it?" He used the word Truth. And that is exactly the word. This kind of filming is truthful. Because it's impossible for the cameraman who is shooting that fast to connive, to contrive. What takes precedence is not what is in the cameraman's mind, but what's going on that he gears himself to catching, to observing. Do you remember the shot in *Vivre sa vie* where the girl was sitting down in the lower part of the frame? That seemed to me to be self-conscious. There is none of that kind of thing in the stuff that I shot. What happens is this: you see little details, even as you are shooting, and you say "Boy, that's the stuff to get." But you don't get it. Because you know that the only way to get it is to stop and move to another angle. So you have to say to yourself, "No! I'm not going to do it. It's more important to keep the camera running." It seems a paradox, but you gain by not sacrificing the film to what I would call "Selfish Beauty." What you gain is Truth. What little things you have missed are more than compensated for by not stopping, by continuing the flow.

JAMES: *Do you mean that you gain the audience's confidence that what they are seeing has really happened, that there has been no "intervention"?*
AL: It's like some of the long continuous shots in *Showman*. Take that long one where Levine is talking to his subordinates in his office. You never see a front view of those guys while you are seeing Levine. The usual way to do it would be to say "we've got to get the reaction shot of the guys." But what we gain by keeping, the camera running on Levine, then finally at the end of the shot walking around and seeing the guys' faces, is much more important than cutting back and forth.

JAMES: *What you have said here indicates a choice on your part—ethical because it respects reality, aesthetic because it produces a calculated effect. One of the criticisms of* Cinéma-Vérité *is that it is not Art. The sketch that you shot for Godard was an attempt to come to terms with this problem. What happened?*
AL: An interesting thing is this: my French is not good. I truly don't know what people are saying from moment to moment. And when you are shooting in that kind of continuity, you either know the language well or you miss a lot. Even so, I felt that I was shooting the right thing at the right time. Exactly what they were saying did not make that much difference apparently. As I shot, I was basically aware of who the girl was. I was aware of the relationship between her and the guy, and the movements between the two people and the counter movements, and a kind

of a rhythm that was involved. And I was very much attuned to that, moving with them and against them.

JAMES: *When you saw the rushes, did anything seem different to you, compared to your usual work?*

AL: The shooting I usually do has less of that kind of continuity. In reality-shooting, you get something and you stop, when you kind of anticipate that something is going to happen, but you have plenty of time to move into position.

JAMES: *Did these people that Godard placed before you seem as real on the screen as, say, Joe Levine?*

AL: No. That is why I prefer to continue making films without actors. Let me read you something that Bacon said: "The contemplation of things as they are without error or confusion, without substitution or imposture is in itself a nobler thing than a whole harvest of invention." I just don't think that anybody—Godard, Shakespeare or anybody else, as much as they may try—can match, put a mirror to, nature. Still, it's a question of preference, and mine is to create something artful, coming as close as I can to what I see, and using it as it happens.

JAMES: *In what, then, lies the art of* Cinéma-Vérité*?*

AL: Did you see *Jane* by Pennebaker? That film proves to me forever something that I could not have believed before—that it is possible to film a person who is warm and come out on the screen with something that is freezing cold. When I saw the film, I said, "Jesus! How could people be that cold?" And then one night I met Jane Fonda in a bar, and I looked at her and in the first two seconds I was suddenly aware of fifty million times more warmth in her than I had seen in any frame—all the frames together—of that whole film. You see, with a photographer like Henri Cartier-Bresson, everybody's warm. With Richard Avedon, everybody's cold. So even though in this style of *Vérité* one is dependent 100 percent on what is before the camera—what's happening by itself—one is also dependent 100 percent on who is filming it. And it can come out hot or cold. Those people who are not putting art into *Vérité* films . . . something is holding them back from being like Cartier-Bresson. I know Henri—he's a very warm guy. Not enough people have been working at *Vérité* films to prove just how artful a form it can be.

JAMES: *But Art depends on something more than being a warm or cold person. It must come out of something that is done with the camera and the cut-*

ting. Before a given event that is taking place, what can happen that will produce art for one man and simple journalism for another?

AL: I shot something once on the train in Africa—a woman breast-feeding a child. I started with a long shot, and I began to zoom in her direction. I didn't get far before I stopped zooming. She was still way the hell off. Ricky (Leacock) saw that and there was great admiration and he said, "That's the way to shoot it. Moving in any closer would have been too much." But in *The Chair,* in the scene of the lawyer that Ricky shot, he bore right in on him, and then the camera began to doodle around the room as though the cameraman was embarrassed to actually see the thing (the lawyer crying). It was a double mistake—one to come in that close, then to be there and not continue to see the man. In *Showman,* when one of Levine's men has lost his job and phones a friend about a new job, we were right straight on that guy's face. We didn't doodle; we didn't dabble, we didn't burst in on his eyes—we just took it straight on. This was it. You got the feeling that we were just going to let it be just that way.

JAMES: The Chair*, by Drew Associates, was shot by several cameramen. Would another cameraman help you in any way?*

AL: We shoot everything with one camera. The Godard film was interesting because it was shot with one camera. Another person, other than Godard, might well have said, "Look, O.K., we're going to shoot this with one continuous run, but we need at least two cameras so we can get cut-ins." But we didn't do it that way. Then we achieved Truth. Because it was one camera, it achieved Truth and emotional involvement, too. You, as a viewer, become the one camera. You are not two or three cameras that are impossibly in two situations at the same time. When you go to a reaction shot, it's false. You, as a person, could not have jumped across the room. In my films, you rarely see any shooting from positions that are not natural to an observer of the situation. The shots are either from a seated position in a chair or from a standing position and not from crazy angles. In *What's Happening?* there is this disc jockey in a room and the Beatles are there and the camera is moving from one to another. It's some of the best shooting I've ever done. It could have been done by waiting for the best moment to shoot each one of them and then editing it together. But if you are able to shoot them continuously, from one to the other, the interrelation is not editor-made, and that moment becomes much more convincing to the viewer. It's much more honest.

JAMES: *Ethics plays a great part in the way you shoot. By shooting with one camera and linking things, you feel you are assuring the spectator that what he sees is really taking place and has not been created for his benefit. In this way, you feel you have obtained Truth. Many people feel, however, that this is not Truth at all. They say you are filming trivia. Mere surface appearance.*
AL: Life is made of trivia. In a sense, Levine is a trivial person.

JAMES: *They mean by this that you do not penetrate into the person.*
AL: Fiction film makers and writers think that they are catching important things by creating them. I don't think they are. I'd like to know what you would have an actor say or do in the role of Levine that would reveal him more. I'd like to see the subject done better. I don't think it can be.

JAMES: *There might have been other dimensions that you might have discovered had you allowed yourself to intervene or to "create," so to speak.*
AL: There is a hell of a lot more to him that we would have liked to have gotten. But I think that our approach is correct. I'm not making excuses, but the actual time with him in which filming was permitted was about fifteen hours.

JAMES: *Granted more time, in what ways would you have "dug deeper?"*
AL: By using the same technique: not telling him what to do. For example, the Hilke thing. There was a third dimension to that that we didn't get. At the Boston banquet to welcome Joe back to his home town, Levine addresses the group—talking about the old days, how poor he was, and how Hilke was the only rich kid because he had shoes. Then he asks if Hilke is there. Hilke stands up and says, "I'm here, Joe!" Later, there's the second dimension: Joe in his office back in New York is talking to his buddies—the continuous shot we mentioned earlier—and he says, "I'm going to have Hilke over to the house one of these days." The third dimension would have come if we had been able to be at Joe's house when Hilke did come—because Hilke did actually go to see Joe. We had asked to be allowed to be there but Levine didn't let us know. But we were talking to Mrs. Levine afterwards, and she said "Well, Hilke stayed too long. He was there about half an hour or so but he didn't know when to leave. He should have left sooner." Which was a revelation again. Levine is talking as though he cares so much about Hilke, but Hilke had to come to his house and then Joe was disappointed that he hadn't left sooner. If we'd gotten it, it would have been like that little story by Thomas Wolfe, about a railway engineer who runs a locomotive on a fifty-mile journey

everyday for forty years or so. Each time he passes some cottages, two women wave to him and he waves back. For all those forty years he says to himself, "someday I'm going to see those people." And it's like Levine. Levine says, "someday I'm going to see Hilke." In the short story, it's the day of his retirement. The engineer says, "I'm going to see those people," and so he goes down and knocks on the door. The two women come to the door. There's that same instantaneous familiarity in recognition, and beyond that there is nothing they can say to one another. He's kind of flabbergasted, and he walks away. That is the only kind of relationship these people are capable of. It has only been on a hand-waving basis. They can't go beyond that. Levine can't go beyond that with Hilke or anybody else. He's not that interested. It would have been marvelous if we could have gotten that. It's "trivia." But all that Thomas Wolfe is reporting is trivia. He's talking about a trivial thing: that these people can wave to one another but that's all.

JAMES: *Do you feel that in your films you get complete objectivity? Do you pretend to present "reality"* per se?

AL: Absolutely not. It would be deadness of some sort if we did that. We are filming human beings.

JAMES: *Your basic material is in the world around you. Do you feel that you are reorganizing that material according to an inward impulse?*

AL: Yes, but somehow remaining faithful, being faithful to what is really there. Now look at this photograph by Bruce Davidson. (A teen-age girl in blue-jeans and jacket holding a kitten and smiling at the camera; behind her in the street, out-of-focus reflections seem to dance about her head.) Davidson has caught the sparkle of those lights that are the sparkle of her eyes. You know that there is a great life in that head of hers. Confused by youth and, you know, probably misdirected—but it's there! In every one of Bruce's photos—the great ones—there is a juxtaposition of one thing with another. He is alert to these things—he puts them into his photo. People don't realize that one can be a documentary guy—apparently just recording, but projecting something of himself onto the thing and still remaining absolutely true to what is outside himself. The peculiar thing about this kind of photography is that it puts more of a burden on the viewer . . . a responsibility. Because, to most people without the eye for it, this is just another photograph. But if you have it in you, this can do much more for you than if somebody had taken this kind of subject and had set it up—had been more "artistic" about it.

The funny thing is: You are not at odds with the way God or Nature puts things. You're not at odds, it's not a fight against it, but it's the harmony between you and the world.

JAMES: *Why do you need so desperately to draw things out of Nature, out of the world around you? Why this need to know that what you are filming is authentic and not something that you have created?*
AL: My background has been more scientific than artistic. I taught psychology at Boston University. I was going to spend my life doing research. Scientific method was my main interest. Apart from that, I just feel more comfortable as an acute observer. I admire people who have a humble attitude to the subject matter and to the world around them. There is another thing: if you take this humble attitude toward something outside yourself, the chances are that you are rewarded. It satisfies a selfish need. It means that your work is going to become more permanent.

JAMES: *Because it documents something?*
AL: Because it depends, in the final analysis, on something outside of you. I know damn well what people will see in *Primary* one hundred years from now. In these last five years, people have come to see it all the more as a truthful film. If we had started out with some defined point of view, I am positive that film would be rubbish today.

JAMES: *You are accepting a tremendous moral responsibility. Some people point out that Mrs. Kennedy fares better under your lens than Mrs. Humphrey, who you've shown in more limiting circumstances. Although in each case you have "quoted" the world around you, choice is involved. How then can you say—"this is the way it was?"*
AL: I'm not keenly worried about if, after I film someone, I say to myself, "Gee, I got this person at the worst time. It makes this person look bad," because I know damn well that I wasn't trying to make it that way. What I got is an appropriate sample of the person. People do see that if we take Mrs. Humphrey at a moment when she is disagreeable, but treat her with Love, they will be getting the Truth, an unprejudiced truth of this woman. But if we dilly-dally around trying to create a situation for her when we're going to get her at both times, we are doing more harm to the film than good. Our obligation is to be honest with what we are filming. What destroys art, destroys documentary, is to be fair. We have faith that by filming a thing when it happens as it happens and without implicating our judgement, even if we film something that obviously shows the

person to be "bad," then, because we are letting it happen out of itself, everything from which to judge will be right there on the screen.

JAMES: *Out of this philosophy of self-effacement and rejection of a point of view, how do you find a structure for your film?*
AL: In the long run what works best—and we find ourselves coming back to it—is having it happen just the way it happened. Even the order of events. When we made *Primary* we tinkered with putting one scene before another, but by the time we were through everything seemed to fall back into the same time-sequence again. I'm not laying down a rule, but generally things seem to fall back that way. In *Showman*, however, several things are out of order. For example, the guy who loses his job is seen talking about Levine to someone on the street. The scene comes in the film before he loses his job. Actually it was filmed afterwards.

JAMES: *Isn't that lying? Once admitting this exception to your principle, where are you?*
AL: Now David did the editing. You'd better talk to him about that.

JAMES: *In literature, there has been a great deal done in the direction of reality. You have mentioned Thomas Wolfe. Are there other writers who have made you say, "That's how I want to film"?*
AL: Hemingway. I don't do too much reading. It's hard to say why you do it this way or that way. Everything really comes out of life, comes out of experience. So why not go to it directly.

I was talking to a photographer friend the other day and he said when you get enjoyment out of a relationship with a girl—sleeping with her—and it's *real*, boy, and you feel something real, well, comparable to that is when you take your still picture, and at that moment you know you've really got it, and you've got something you don't have to explain, you know you've got it right there. Something great. You feel it. It's something indestructible and no critic can tear it apart. I think you are on the right track when you start with your own experience and that which you are experiencing which is outside of you.

JAMES: *What you seem to be aiming at inevitably is to find that experience, undergo it and film it at the same time.*
AL: I tried something like that. It didn't work out well but I hope to get back to it. I want to make a film called *Coup de Foudre*. I want to meet a girl and film the very moment I'm meeting her and stay with her for awhile. An experience totally new for me, new for her, and be filming. I

have tried it with two girls. The first one was . . . well, she said nothing at all. The other kept talking all the time.

JAMES: *They were playing for the camera?*
AL: They were. But when you meet someone for the first time they reveal more of themselves than at any other time.

JAMES: *This desire to "have an experience" has led you into this long-run shooting technique, has it not?*
AL: Within that long run or long take of the camera, if it is continued, it works to the film maker's advantage in that the person has to break down and reveal himself within that long run. Whereas, in a short take, the person can put on his mask.

JAMES: *Do you really think that while you are having an experience yourself, you can depict it artistically?*
AL: There is an experience I had. There was a girl that I loved very much. I hadn't seen her for five years. In the meantime she had married, she had two children, and I didn't know that I was ever to see her again. But I came to Paris where she was living—just where she was I didn't know—I called her parents, they told me she was married, had two children, and the address. I went to the home, she wasn't there. I spoke to the husband. He said that she was at a museum. Well, all this stuff, so far, is stuff that I could have filmed. I went to the museum. I walked in. The museum was all on one floor, one big room. She wasn't there. But I thought that she would be arriving any moment. I sat down. There is only one doorway into the museum. I sat at the far end. I could see everybody walking around, conversing, and she would come in through that doorway over there. I sat and I could see all of this in wide angle. Every time that door opened, you see, I had a choice. I could zoom into that door. I would do that sometimes, I'm sure. Other times, I would just keep the camera rolling at wide angle. And we'd see a little child come in. And an old man came in. Each time, I was expecting this particular girl. Or I could walk in closely and take a close-up. There were all kinds of choices, but most of it I would shoot in very wide angle that corresponded to the mood I felt. I had the advantage of seeing all of these people conversing—a little group here and there. And that door, ever-present, bringing in another person who might be the girl . . . or might not be.

So for me personally, there was something very important going on and I was very interested in it. And taking those two things: "something important going on" and "personally interested in it," it's something I should film.

(I followed my conversation with Al Maysles by a chat with his brother, David, who handles sound, editing, and business affairs for the pair.)

JAMES: *Your brother has talked about the need of being honest, of gaining the audience's confidence in the authenticity of what is shown. He feels that he does this by linking scenes rather than making separate shots, by keeping the camera rolling, by submitting himself to the life going on around him. I wonder what principles guide you in cutting Al's material. In* Showman, *there are many places where you relate shots, cut back and forth, use cut-aways. I even saw places where you profited from the fact that we couldn't see a person's mouth move to lay in dialogue from another shot. Does this pose for you an ethical problem?*

DAVID: There is no such thing as being strictly objective in anything that is at all artistic. The objectivity is just a personal integrity: being essentially true to the subject and capturing it essentially. One of the places you are referring to is where Levine is on the phone and says Kim Novak is coming. We have that in the out-takes where you can see his lips moving, but it just didn't work in combination with the shot preceding it. He did say it, maybe not at that time, but to preserve a certain continuity we changed it. We wouldn't distort his words and change them around to make him look bad. When you see the film, you have an overall belief that you are seeing something real. You mentioned cut-aways—we used very few. There are mostly intercuts of different scenes. The vice-president giving a pep-talk, the salesman, then back to Levine on the phone.

JAMES: *This is a betrayal of "real" time, is it not?*

DAVID: I don't think we ever strive for that kind of reality. There is no worth in "this is the way it was—*exactly*." Then you'd have people picking their noses and everything else. It could be repulsive. There is nothing artistic about that. We try to keep people interested. We'd bore them very easily by just staying on Levine talking a lot of nonsense. We wouldn't have any audience and I wouldn't want to see it myself. You should, however, try to go along as much as possible with what you have. But there are times when you can't. For example, in cutting *Showman*, I was thinking of dubbing some stuff that you couldn't quite hear. We were in a room with Levine in Rome, the noisiest damned city in the world. So all you hear is noise and a lot of the lines you couldn't hear. As it turned out we didn't use the scene, but if we had, I wouldn't have hesitated to try at least dubbing. I would have been dubbing in the same thing that he said. I don't know if I'd get Levine to do it. He probably wouldn't cooperate. I'd have gotten an actor.

JAMES: *What do you do once you have material on film? How do you proceed?*
DAVID: I line it up exactly as it is shot—chronologically. Then I look at it a couple of times and make notes and try to put a structure down very very roughly on paper. And the theme, too. Then, with a couple of people here, we chop it down roughly into that version. We try to go for broke in the first cut. We don't make any two-hour assemblies when we know it's an hour picture.

JAMES: *You say you try to establish a theme. What thematic ideas occurred to you in making* What's Happening?*—on the Beatles.*
DAVID: I was trying to show how they typify a great part of American youth. I feel that there is a sort of restlessness. They want to find out what's happening in town. Where are we going to go? It's like *Marty*. They're always looking for something—for a "beat."

JAMES: *One of the criticisms made against your work—even by people who admire it—is that it lacks structure. What do you do to make us want to see more?*
DAVID: Ideally, we'd like to have a story that has a beginning, a middle and an end—a logical development. I tried in *Showman* to get a structure that gave it direction. The guy that gets fired—you see him at work and you finally see him fired. The build-up to the night when Levine gets the Oscar. The sequence about Joe's visit to Boston—wheeling and dealing and finally a very humble moment at home in Boston. I think you come out of the film feeling that you have been involved in something you didn't know about before. I think there is structure. We have learned one thing from hard experience: the quicker you shoot a film, the easier it is to edit it. There is a continuity in time.

JAMES: *What is the role of narration in your films?*
DAVID: Ideally, part of our whole purpose is to make the viewers their own commentators. Not to tell anything but to show. Narration is only a leg that you use for support if you need it. It picks up something that isn't in the picture that you missed. I want to make a film that doesn't need narration, that stands together as a film. I feel that the same criteria that apply to a Hollywood film should apply to ours as well. You shouldn't have to say, "Well, that's a documentary so you can have narration." I

don't want any of these allowances or apologies. What we're really trying to do is something that is not at all different from a conventional Hollywood feature. Only we're not using actors. We are trying to convey the same thing. Our purpose is to have an emotional involvement from the audience—an interest, an excitement. We want them to feel that it's worthwhile, what they are seeing, that they perhaps will learn something or get some insight. Our purpose is not to inform or to teach or anything like that, as has been the purpose of documentaries for years. We are not interested in showing slums among wealth. We are trying to do something no different at all from a Hollywood feature except that we are using real situations. That's our challenge. That's why we are so excited. We're trying to do something that's better than Hollywood can do with actors. We feel that we can get in film something no scriptwriter can invent. Things as they come in real life are much more exciting than anything that you could invent or stage. Writers try to emulate life. They feel they have to have it under their control. We feel just the opposite. We observe and shoot things as they happen. If we knew what the next scene was going to be—exactly how it was to be played out—we wouldn't have any interest in it. The excitement comes from seeing something revealed before our own eyes. We try to transfer that excitement to the audience. In most theatrical movies I don't believe what is happening. We accept them because of conditioning.

JAMES: *Did you see* Pather Panchali*?*

DAVID: Terrific film.

JAMES: *But these are actors. Ray has directed them in a "down" style where they do not enlarge upon life, but their effects are simplified and highly controlled. Let us compare a scene as it might happen in reality and as Ray staged it—when at the end of the film the father comes back with the shawl for the daughter who has died. He has been away in Calcutta and is not aware of his daughter's death. He says, "I brought this shawl for Duga." The mother takes it suddenly, bites into it, falls down crying, and at that moment the father without a word of explanation understands what has happened. He falls down accusing himself. He is in terrible pain. Now, in reality this scene might have been a wordy exchange over a period of time. It would not have had the poetry of this kind of selection. The scene, then, might have been less powerful or poetic if you had filmed it as it happened.*

DAVID: All film people are after the same thing: an emotional response. As you say, it might be a wordy thing, but I think we could cut that wordy thing so that it might be even *more* convincing and even *more* exciting.

Essentially we are allowing things to happen rather than controlling them. We feel that things that really happen are much more exciting.

JAMES: *What about the future of this approach?*

DAVID: Technically it can be perfected. The equipment can be smaller, lighter, and less obtrusive. We need improvement in sound quality. But the main thing is the film itself. The thing that nobody has hit yet—including ourselves—is a *solid* continuity, and a subject that isn't a political or documentary thing. A film that couldn't be classified. No more people walking out afterwards saying, "it's great but it's only Kennedy and Humphrey. It happened just that way, didn't it?" We want a more meaningful subject. Much more low key. Something that isn't public figures that everybody knows. It must have a lot of the qualities of a good Hollywood film. A continuity from beginning to end. No narration. It must have sympathetic people. We don't want people to say: "It's a documentary, isn't it?" If we reach that day, something will have been accomplished.

JAMES: *Do you think that the factual style corresponds to something in our society?*

DAVID: Yes. This society has become so fictional with the advent of television. Everything seems to be fictionalized. Fantasized. There's a need for straightforward, truthful reports.

JAMES: *Fiction tends to give us a point of view. This kind of film making leaves something open to the viewer.*

DAVID: It's more adult, isn't it? The spectator can make up his own mind. From this standpoint, *Showman* has been very successful. There is a great deal of controversy after the film is shown. "Do you like him? Don't you like him?" Some people think he stands for one thing, some another. Some intellectual will come up and say, "Gee, why do you want to make a film about someone as disgusting and as revolting and as greedy as that?" But a lower class person, like a projectionist at a film lab when I'm checking the print, says, "Isn't that guy great! Look at how he remembers his friends." There's always this controversy. We don't want to resolve it. I think that's part of the success of the film. Fifty percent feel one way, fifty percent another.

An Interview with the Maysles Brothers

JONAS MEKAS/1966

DAVID AND AL MAYSLES, together with Ricky Leacock, are working in that style of film-making which has become known as the direct cinema (in France it's called *Cinéma-Vérité*). Until now, whenever one wanted to explain what the direct cinema is all about, one had a hard time in doing so. But with Truman Capote's book, *In Cold Blood*, answers became somewhat easier. Direct cinema has now a parallel in Capote's nonfictional novel. That's what Maysles' *Showman* is: a nonfictional film novel. It isn't a perfect answer, but it makes the process involved easier to understand.

Hearing that Maysles Brothers had just completed another film, *With Love, from Truman*, I went to see them, and we had the following conversation:

JM: *You have been working together on films. Is there any "labor" division between you two?*

DAVID MAYSLES: Al is responsible for the development of the equipment. He has been working, for instance, for over three years now, building a new camera which will facilitate the film work that we do. He is also responsible for all the shooting. I am responsible for all the sound, the production, and the supervising of the editing. That is more or less the general line of things.

AL MAYSLES: When you say "division of labor," in our kind of work, it is a little misleading. Our work overlaps. We don't direct in the conventional sense. We both select, for example, and we arrive at an idea between us. While we are shooting, we have words back and forth—what we should film and what we shouldn't film. So it's direction by selecting.

From *The Village Voice*, 3 March 1966. Reprinted by permission of *The Village Voice*.

JM: *How many films have you made till now? Which ones would you like the public to know about?*
AM: There are four major works: *Showman. . . .*

JM: *You don't think you've done anything of importance before* Showman*?*
AM: There were contributions to the work of other people. I am talking about the films which are completely our own. The list,then, is *Showman, What's Happening: The Beatles in the U.S.A., Meet Marlon Brando,* and now, *With Love, from Truman.*
JM: *Looking back at those four works, it seems to me that it was natural for you to bump into Truman Capote: Your cold-blooded direct-cinema style is so close to what Capote is doing in his book,* In Cold Blood. *Do you see any connection between Truman Capote's nonfictional novel and your own work in the nonfictional cinema?*
DM: Yes, we are interested in poetry that comes out of nonfiction. Truman Capote's book is the closest thing to our own work we have ever come across. What we are doing is in direct parallel in motion picture form to what Capote is doing in the literary form. The only difference is that in this particular book, he had to go back before the events were taking place. In other words, the murder took place, then he had to find out what happened, how did it happen. He had to go back and to reconstruct—which we didn't do. But it could very well happen that the next nonfiction novel he writes will not be of murder but something that starts the moment he gets into it, and everything will happen as he sees it. He has said himself that our work is the closest thing to him. There is a common bond, in our styles and approaches.

There was one bit of conversation that we had that was particularly fascinating and exciting for us. When he was talking about the subject matter, and when we were discussing which story he would like to take next, what story he would like to do next, how does one choose the subject—he said that the subject matter of crime has never been of particular interest to him. It wasn't even when he engaged in it. What was interesting to me was that you pick up a subject matter, and at first you may not see much reason in choosing it—but as you begin to follow it, and as soon as you find something of yourself in it—you are in. What Capote found in his subject was Perry. Perry was just like Capote, he was very sensitive. In other words, you find something in the story, in the subject matter, that, unconsciously, begins to fascinate you.

JM: *Capote looked for his subject matter in the newspapers. How do you choose your subjects?*

AM: In the case of the Capote film, NET was doing a series on novelists, and we chose Capote because he particularly appealed to us. And it was a labor of love, because NET doesn't give any profit incentives, as you probably know.

JM: *By now, you have completed four films. Do you see any development in your style? With which of your films are you most content?*
DM: We are most happy with the *Showman*, really.

JM: *For what reasons?*
DM: I think for the reason, I say it now, because I am quite sure of this—that we went into that film like a writer goes into writing a short story. Its growth is more organic, multisided, and complex—many different feelings, moods, situations are reflected, the character of the man is presented in a more complex manner. The Capote portrait is much simpler, but we like it also. There is much feeling in it. We like all four, really. Each one is doing something else. But *Showman* still sticks out as the "accomplishment."

Talking about Capote's and our own techniques, there are other parallels. He, for instance, is very conscious of intruding upon his subject, of making any kind of intrusion. That's why he doesn't take notes. The same way that we try to build our equipment. We try to gain a certain kind of rapport, some relationship with the subject, as Capote does. To establish this relationship, we have perfected a camera that doesn't make any noise. It helps us to get that type of spontaneity, of rapport, without someone being self-conscious because of the equipment. Also, we work to establish a balanced human relationship before we can start shooting—you have to get the complete trust of the person you are filming.

JM: *Is anyone else, besides yourselves and Leacock, doing anything worthwhile in direct cinema, here or abroad?*
AM: Capote has inspired us more than anyone else. Or *8½*; or *Hustler*.

JM: *Why* Hustler?
AM: Its simplicity, perhaps. The story, really. The structure of the story was so simple. Something that we could do in a real life situation.

We don't see much of TV or cinema. We are all by ourselves. Really, it takes time to make films. It took us three years to get out of *Showman*, financially. We did it the way we wanted it, but we had to take the losses. It may be shown, eventually, but at the moment it doesn't fit the networks' appetite.

JM: *What happens to your movies after they are shown on television?*
AM: We own them all, but we have no official permission to show them in theatres. They are all in various states of restriction.

JM: *You shot your Capote film around New York. But there was one cemetery shot in it, from Kansas. Was it stock footage?*
AM: Oh, no! We went to Kansas just for that one shot. We felt we had to do it. As a matter of fact, while shooting it, to help ourselves, we had a small tape recorder on us, with Capote's voice on it, reading that part. For authenticity of feeling.

JM: *Are you planning another film?*
DM: We are still looking for a good story that would sustain itself for an hour and a half. We are going to make it as soon as we find it. It is funny—we are working the same way, Capote and us. We buy newspapers, magazines, we look through all the items. One thing is certain: This story will have something the other films we did till now didn't have—it will be because it is a good story, but not because it's about a "famous person." It will be a person and a story that nobody knows anything about.

An Interview with Albert and David Maysles

BOB SITTON/1969

BOB SITTON: *First of all I would like to congratulate you on a marvelous accomplishment—a milestone in film making and in recording the passing American scene. I'd like to talk with you about the* Salesman*'s subject matter and how you came to make it.*
ALBERT MAYSLES: It is just a kind of feeling and emotion we have about people. We had the idea we wanted to do a story about salesmen and the adventure of the road. And we had the wish to really make a film about everyday people.

BS: *What was it about Bible salesmen that interested you?*
AM: Well, Bibles are sold and the idea that a Bible can be sold is a jarring one. A Bible represents an ideology that is supposed to be American. The film is a collision between that ideology and our materialistic way of life. This collision is not enough to stop the Bible salesmen from selling their wares. That the purchasers do not see it as a collision is the story of our times. If everyone knew the consequences of selling in his life, and all its ramifications in our society, we would escape from many dilemmas and live different kinds of lives. *Salesman* shows us the difficulties of our lives through witnessing people who are nice guys doing bad things.

BS: *Do you think there is something wrong with selling Bibles? Any more than selling priests' robes or any other religious item?*
AM: I think there is something wrong with selling Bibles if you don't believe in it. That's why the film is so valuable for our time. The wrongness of it is not that apparent to everyone. It is in a kind of a borderland

From *Film Library Quarterly*, vol. 2, summer 1969. Reprinted by permission of the author.

which makes it so palatable to buyer and seller that they don't realize the terrible consequences of their activities. The salesman doesn't at any moment realize how tawdry his life is because it is dedicated to the sale. That's true of people in any kind of selling activity. No one's life is as fulfilled as it should be.

BS: *David, do I sense that you have a different attitude toward Bible salesmen?*

DAVID MAYSLES: Yes, because I think that they are in no worse predicament than the majority of people. Most people have no real goals in their lives. They are not really working toward the fulfillment of dreams. If you are not working toward some kind of dream for yourself, life is hardly worth living. That is the whole thing about tragedy. I think there is a great beauty in tragedy. In order to be really fulfilling, our lives have to be tragic. You can never fulfill your dream. If you could there would not be any challenge left in living. Still, people set their dreams at a much lower level than they should.

BS: *About the salesman in the film; I suppose the nearest comparison would be Willy Loman in* Death of a Salesman.

AM: One great difference is that when a playwright begins to set down his play he necessarily has to start with the general and then specify the particular. He has in mind a certain character, and in the descriptive process he fits in all the facts of that imagined person's life. The process with us is entirely different. We select particular people about whom we know very little. We are prepared at any moment to change our notions about them. In the process of watching and setting down the particulars maybe we reach generalizations: maybe we never do. But the filming is spontaneous. So I think we have a terrific advantage over the writer in that any generalizations come later on. In fact, the audience takes part in forming those generalizations as they see the film. In that way it's a more objective and much less contrived kind of process.

BS: *Yes, there is no question about that. I was going to say that in Miller's work it seems to me he begins with a noble character and then we later see that the character has particularity like other men. In your film you begin with particular things about the men and then at the end the overall impression is of some kind of heroic stature in the midst of smallness. That's why I am interested in your attitude towards the salesmen. Do you see them as noble people despite their shortcomings?*

DM: They are not much different from most of us. Ours are more O'Neill characters than Miller characters. Miller's characters are all more or less external. You don't get very close to them. You don't feel really close to Willy Loman. But you do feel a kind of nostalgia for the values he has—shining up his shoes, having the car polished, wanting his son on the football team. However, these things are not so common or important today. However, the tragic condition of O'Neill's characters is timeless. Their dilemmas are relevant to any age.

BS: *O'Neill, like the Maysles, puts people in an ethnic milieu. The characters in* Salesman *and in your film on Joe Levine are ethnic characters.*

AM: I think that our characters are more than ourselves, and O'Neill's and Miller's characters are less than themselves. Perhaps the characters of both playwrights are greater than ours. There is still that possibility, but since everything comes from the playwright's imagination and memory, theatrical characters can't be any more than that. By contrast, the characters in our film are what we could catch at a particular moment.

DM: Everything we do is an expression of an immediate feeling. You know we are not sitting around thinking what we want this character to do. We discover everything in the filming. We discover the theme and the point of view. We did not have any preconceived purpose in doing the film. We knew that we had warm feelings about guys who travel on the road, that it could be interesting and might work if we found the right person. But we never knew which way it would go. Maybe there would never be a sale in the film, or it could all have been about selling. It happened to be about Paul because he was the one that worked out the best and therefore the one we concentrated on. It was possible that the whole thing could have taken place in a motel room or in a sales meeting or anywhere else.

BS: *This is the kind of earmark that the film has that distinguishes it from other* cinéma vérité *films. I get the feeling of discovering the subject matter in the process of shooting and editing. Could we talk more about that? Now do you go about the business of shooting? Did you instruct the salesmen?*

DM: Absolutely no instruction. We just lived with them as if we were one of them. There were never any meetings or any kind of direction.

AM: It comes hack to what we were talking about before. We really do believe that the film is something greater than and outside of ourselves. We really want to see what is going on around us and catch it while it is going on. There's something in that, a truth that people are not aware of and we have to catch.

DM: We are looking for things all the time. For instance, we knew that

Paul spoke with an Irish brogue. We knew that he was a great story teller and that particularly thrilled us since our father used to talk with an Irish brogue and tell charming stories. My heroes, when we were children, were the Irish because they were successful. Paul's heroes, on the other hand, are Jews—Arthur Goldberg and Jacob Javits, for some reason. I was always telling him that the great writers were Irishmen.

BS: *Your last film,* Showman, *was also about a Boston salesman, Joe Levine. It too has an ethnic flavor.*
AM: We never thought of the connection until after we had made *Salesman*. Our films come from life and selling is a big thing these days. It has been claimed that the biggest industry today is not manufacturing automobiles or the telephone industry but selling.

BS: *But isn't that kind of dying out? In the film I get the sense of an era gone by.*
AM: The door-to-door salesman is on the way out, but there is still a significant number of them. One thing is sure, that no matter where you are involved with the selling process you cannot have a really free or candid expression of feeling. You have to please the customer, and the customer is also involved in being persuaded. So he also is trapped into a situation in which communication becomes a matter of selling or buying.

BS: *Some critics call this film* cinéma vérité, *but you don't like that phrase, do you?*
DM: Well, *cinéma vérité* means so much to many people. For example, it started, I believe, in Canada or France. It was used by the Canadians first in films that were based on interviews. That has nothing to do with the kind of films that we make. There is a spontaneity that comes out of letting things happen and just capturing them on film. That is what is meant by the term. But when you interview someone the mere forming of the questions gives you part of the answer. Besides, the claim to being truthful is misleading. *Salesman* most surely has an artistic truth, but a lot has to do with selection in the editing and it is our kind of view. It is the way we saw it and maybe no one else would see it that way. We feel the film is representative of what we saw, but someone else would probably get a different story with the same material. It is immediate cinema and we are discovering it while we are doing it. We are not directing, just catching things while they happen.

BS: *You did this film in 16mm. Do you think you could have done it the same way in 35mm?*
AM: No, you need the kind of mobility of 16mm.

BS: *When you blew it up do you feel that there was any loss?*
AM: No, it was improved. 35 projection is so much better than 16. The laboratory handling is much better. When you make a 35mm blow up you can control each frame. In 16mm you can only time scenes.

BS: *But the points on the screen are farther apart and the light becomes a little washed out.*
AM: Do you feel the film is washed out?

BS: *Yes, but I liked it. I thought that gave it a vaguely misty quality.*
AM: I would always prefer that anything we shoot be shown in 35mm because of the better light quality.

BS: *You talk about discovering the film in the shooting process. Could you weigh that a little? Do you discover more in the editing than the shooting, or vice-versa?*
DM: When it comes to the final film it is hard to judge. Mechanically you discover more in the editing. But if it is not originally on film you can't put it there.

BS: *What was your shooting ratio?*
AM: Something like 25-1 but that doesn't mean much.

BS: *But it does say that you threw away an awful lot of film.*
AM: In shooting the film the camera had to run a lot of the time when we didn't really want it to. We didn't want to miss anything. If there were an automatic way to turn on the camera and sound at exactly the right moment you could save a lot of footage. When you are shooting in 16mm the film is the least expensive thing. You keep the camera running so as not to miss anything.

BS: *Did you add any sound afterwards?*
DM: Very little.

BS: *One interesting thing about* Salesman *is that it is the kind of realistic film that does not pretend to be fictional. But at the same time it is not straight documentary. The camera is present in the action. This introduces a point that may jar some sensibilities. Some people may say, "These Maysles brothers are trying to put one over on me."*
DM: The way some movie makers answer that is to deliberately put themselves in front of the camera. We left ourselves out because we feel it is better that way. The salesmen we filmed have lived and worked together for seven years. They have a very close relationship. They must make sales or they get no money, so they were too involved with their

work to be concerned with us while they were selling. They have a passion for what they are doing.

BS: *How did they react to the film?*
AM: Well, they never made a big thing of it. They could never really comprehend why anyone would want to watch them for an hour and a half.

BS: *One criticism I have read is that you did not show enough of the home life of these men.*
DM: All you get to see is their life on the road, in peoples' homes, and in motel rooms. You don't have to see all of a person's life in order to understand what he's like. We spent time with Paul's family and that is not in the film. We went to a family wedding and we saw very quickly the kind of relationship he has with his wife and daughter. The relationship is like his relationships with other people. A man relates to all people in the same way. If you see a man in one close relationship, you know how he relates to other people. Many people expect a realistic film like ours to be a kind of TV survey. By that I mean if you do a study of a salesman in Massachusetts, you must also look at a salesman in Kentucky. But no one asks of a novelist that he fill us in on everything that happens to his characters from the cradle to the grave. He shows what appeals to him and no one questions his right to do so.

BS: *How have the salesmen responded to the film?*
DM: Only Paul has seen all of it. I knew he would like it because we all like and respect each other. It took us more than two years to make. Paul liked it, although he was discomfited by some of it.

BS: *In a way, we have talked about this all along, but I want to ask you directly: What makes a Maysles film different from other films?*
DM: They are personal. Our films are an expression of ourselves, the result of the way we grew up, the parents we had, and so on. Both of us are against materialism. We didn't set out to make a film on that subject, though it came out that way.

BS: *What would you say, Albert?*
AM: It is a kind of passion. An idealism about life. *Salesman* could have been merely about exploitation, about people hurting each other and doing unethical things. But our idealism consists in a childlike belief in life as it is. We derive what we say from watching people and discovering what is inherent in their lives.

DM: I should say, Bob, that it isn't just a Maysles film. Charlotte Zwerin was very important in the making of the film. We had the original concept and were the producers and directors, but Charlotte lent me an objective eye in editing the mass of material.

Salesman

ALAN ROSENTHAL/1971

ALBERT MAYSLES, or Al as he prefers, is one of the best documentary cameramen in the United States, "the greatest" according to Jean-Luc Godard. He is also, together with his younger brother David, one of the key North American figures in the development of *cinéma vérité* or, to use a term they both prefer, direct cinema.

Maysles was born in Boston and raised in Brookline, Massachusetts. During World War II he enlisted in the army and was assigned to the tank corps. Following demobilization, he gained a BA at Syracuse University and an MA at Boston University, where he later taught psychology for three years.

Both of the Maysles brothers started in film in 1956, but in the beginning followed separate paths. Thus, while David worked as a production assistant on two Marilyn Monroe pictures, Al went to Russia to make a film on mental health care.

Their work as a team dates from 1957 when David and Al decided to travel from Munich to Moscow together to make a film about the aftermath of the Polish student revolution.

During the early sixties both David and Al were associated in experimental television projects for Time, Inc., together with Robert Drew, Ricky Leacock, and Don Pennebaker. Al's main contribution to all this was the shooting of *Yanki, No!* and part of *Primary*.

In 1963 the brothers produced what was, till recently, their most famous film, *Showman*, a controversial hour-long portrait of movie mogul Joseph Levine. This was followed by films about the Beatles, Truman Capote, and *Meet Marlon Brando* (1966). In 1970 Al and David, and Charlotte

---

From *The New Documentary in Action*, University of California Press, 1971. Reprinted by permission of the author.

Zwerin also produced *Gimme Shelter*, which featured the playing of the Rolling Stones and an alleged murder by a member of the Hell's Angels gang. Apart from the "portrait" films, the brothers have also produced a considerable number of industrial films, and Al was invited to France to shoot one section of a four-part feature for Godard.

Salesman (1969) covers six weeks in the life of four traveling Bible salesmen. One sees them on a typical day pitching wares in snowbound New England and later swapping experiences in their motel. One follows them to a super sales meeting in Chicago, and later travels with them to Florida for more door banging, exhortation, and selling on the Catholic honor plan (an installment gimmick).

As the film progresses it increasingly focuses on the personal crisis of Paul, a likeable man of fifty-five. Paul has been selling for twenty-two years, but something has gone wrong. He is beginning to confront the failure of the dream of riches and independence, and it is agonizing watching him fall apart at the seams.

The film then is an intensely moving portrait of an ordinary human being, which also provides an insight into part of the American milieu. It's a slow and sometimes ponderous film to watch, but it illustrates some of the most interesting things about Al's work, such as his camera versatility and his extraordinary sensitivity to people and situations. It also demonstrates the fundamental difference between European and American exponents of *vérité*—the former being deliberate, obtrusive, and provoking and the latter passive and as detached from the action as possible.

The Maysles call the film "a nonfiction dramatic feature." Like *A Married Couple* it is a move in a new direction. Besides broadening the whole concept of the feature, it also gets away from the usual *vérité* emphasis on stars or major crises to concentrate on normal and uneventful facets of the human situation.

But it also provokes certain major questions. Would this idea of following the world of the ordinary really have worked if Paul's identity crisis hadn't occurred to give the film a focus. In other words, are the normal conventions of drama and conflict still essential to provide a structure for this more human and low-key movement of *vérité*. Maybe the answer will be seen in the next film of the Maysles which is scheduled to be a highly personal movie starring their mother, themselves, and the whole family.

Q: *What did you do before you started making films?*

A: I used to teach psychology at Boston University. I also had a number of jobs, including selling Fuller brushes from door to door. When I got out of college, I worked for several weeks as an encyclopedia salesman with the Encyclopedia Americana and discovered the whole canned speech that they used for their customers. I believed every bit of it, and it took me a week or two before I began to see that there was a basic deception involved in that kind of selling. So I quit in the third week, although I had made an awful lot of money. That adds some background to the film *Salesman*.

Q: *Who taught you the rudiments of film making?*
A: Nobody taught me anything about movie making. When I was a kid, I had a little still camera that I bought in a hardware store called a Univex. The pictures were so small that the film size was called "00" and cost ten cents a roll. After a while I vowed I would never take any pictures again until I could get decent equipment. That didn't come till 1954 when I took a friend's Leica out of hock for two hundred dollars; in turn for that favor he said, "Take the camera with you on your trip to Europe," so I had a chance to take my first pictures with a decent camera. The following year I went to Russia and borrowed a 16 mm camera from CBS. I told them I was going to Russia, could get into the mental hospitals, and might be able to make an interesting movie. Mind you, I had never taken any movies before. I met the CBS people a week before I departed and they gave me a hundred feet of film to practice shooting with. I shot some stuff, CBS processed it, and told me some of the things I had been doing wrong, which were fairly obvious to me; the fact that I wasn't holding the camera steady, the fact that I wasn't holding the shots long enough. That was my training and off I went.

My whole interest in making the film was as a discovery. It was something that nobody knew anything about; there was only one book in this country written on the psychiatry in Russia. I came back, showed the film to CBS, but they weren't very interested because mental health in Russia didn't have "political significance." I then finished the film on my own, got it shown on network television in Canada, and also sold it to a drug company. So I more than made my money back on it.

Q: *You've said on record that you consider* Showman *and* Salesman *the best films you've done. Was* Salesman *your idea coming from your experience selling encyclopedias? Was it David's? Or did the two of you generate it?*
A: We were always making lists of subjects for films, and one thing that had been on our list for a long time was a salesman's convention. But nothing got done about it. Then in 1966 David had a lunch conversation

with Joe Fox of Random House Publishing Company. We knew Joe, because a little while earlier we had filmed Truman Capote, and Joe was his editor. Anyway, David told Joe we were looking for a nonfiction subject to make into a feature. We wanted to do in film what Capote had done in literature, with his novel *In Cold Blood.* Now Joe used to be a book salesman, and when he said "why not film a traveling salesman?" that immediately sparked an interest in David; when David in turn told me of his conversation with Joe it immediately clicked with me as well.

Then David got to work writing letters to different kinds of selling companies—Geritol and the like—companies that sell you everything and anything. We thought of book salesmen too, although for my part I had been turned off the whole scene and would never have considered an encyclopedia salesman because the whole thing is such a low form of selling. Then David met a Jewish high school friend who was selling Bibles in Manhattan, and this turned us in a fresh direction. A Bible salesman was something different. Selling the Bible represented a metaphor of our time, which had ramifications reaching to every avenue of our culture. So that's how we happened to choose this subject.

Q: *In the film your principals are salesmen for the Mid-American Bible Company. Was this the first company you contacted?*
A: We hired a researcher to look into the various companies, and it was quite a long time before we found the right one. For one thing, although we would explain by letter or telephone what we were after, no one could really grasp the concept. They were used to scripted movies and so didn't know what they would have to do for this film. They were also very sensitive about how they would be portrayed, so it was very difficult to get them to cooperate or understand what we wanted to do.

Q: *How did you zero in on the Mid-American Bible Company?*
A: We got as far as talking to one salesman who we thought would be good. We went to Rhode Island, and he was terrific. He was a guy who had a confusion of roles. On the one hand he would talk about how the customer was a sucker; and on the other hand, he really wanted to be like his brother who was a high school teacher. He would have been great, but his boss didn't want to cooperate, and without this cooperation we were dead. So we decided not to film him. Also, he was the kind of salesman who not only sold the Bible, but also sold magazine subscriptions, *Look* magazine, all that sort of thing. It was getting too diffuse and detracted from the pure Bible salesman idea.

I don't know exactly how we heard about Mid-American. David had heard of a company in Chicago that had some ninety salesmen on the road selling Bibles; and he contacted one of the owners of the company in Chicago. This was Kenny Turner, who is in the film. We met Kenny, and as we were interested in going back to New England where we come from, David asked if Kenny had any salesmen in the New England territory. Kenny said, "Yes. We have four guys; they work together," and almost with that there was a keen interest on our part.

When we met the guys, we found out they went by names they had invented for themselves—the Badger, the Bull, the Gipper, and the Rabbit. That's very Irish, and even at that early point it warmed the cockles of my heart. This was because although my father was brought up Jewish, he lived in a totally Irish neighborhood and was probably as Irish as he was Jewish. This also gave a peculiar twist to the filming of *Salesman*, because traditionally the salesman is supposed to be Jewish, and someone from an Irish background like Paul would normally work as a clerk at the post office or as some other kind of government employee, which is what my father did. So there was a curious kind of reversal of roles which accounted for my special interest in the thing.

Q: *Did you go out with the four salesmen before you started filming? Did you get any feeling of their personalities in relationship to people, or their problems or hang ups?*

A: I would say that most of it was on a feeling level. We liked the guys, all four of them, and we could see the potential from the start. We looked into the Rabbit's face for example, and those eyes were so extraordinary; he just looked off in kind of a dreamy way. The four complemented each other. At first we didn't know for sure whether Paul would be the main character or whether it might be Charlie the Gipper; but we knew that one of them could and would be, so we were sure we had a major character.

Q: *What were the reactions of Paul and the others when you suggested the film?*

A: They were kind of amused; they didn't know quite what to make of it because they didn't think they were worth it. They couldn't understand a film being made of their lives, because they seemed to be so ordinary. I guess almost anybody would feel that way because the whole history of movie making has been to portray extraordinary things, and no one has felt that much confidence in looking at life itself and finding the extraordinary in the ordinary. But one person who expressed the idea sixty years ago was Tolstoy. His first reaction to the movies was when somebody came to his home in Moscow in 1906, saw him sitting on the porch, and shot some home movies of him. They showed him the stuff a few days later, and Tolstoy said, "That's it! We don't have to invent stories any more; we have an instrument now where movies can be made of ordinary people, of Russia, in ordinary situations; and we don't have to invent stories any more."

Q: *After the men had agreed to appear, what financial arrangements or general arrangements did you make with them? Did you tell them how long you expected to shoot?*

A: We figured we would need maybe two or three months, and we ended up using six weeks. We told them we would need to be with them for three months, on and off, and they agreed to that. I believe we paid them a hundred dollars each, and they signed a release; we also agreed that we would pay their expenses—not all their expenses, but things like the trip to Florida. Their expenses, in fact, came to something between $10,000 and $15,000, so it was a very sizable chunk. There were two factors; we didn't have much money to give them, but what was even more important, we didn't want to make an arrangement that would make them feel like performers.

Q: *Can we get into the actual filming and its problems?*

A: It's pretty simple. You just ask the guy what's coming up, and you look into his schedule. He doesn't know the kinds of things that are going to make good film for you; so to a certain extent you have to act intuitively. Each salesman would have a hundred cards of people's addresses that he would pick up at the beginning of the week, and he would say he was going to such and such a person today and we would go with him. We had a terrific advantage in filming four people rather than one, because we could break away from one person and give him a rest and pick up with another one.

Q: *How did you get over the problem of knocking on a door and suddenly confronting a stranger, not only with a Bible salesman, but also with a cameraman?*

A: You have to know and impress on yourself that it's not going to be a problem; you may be wrong, but you have to feel quite confident that your presence isn't going to adversely affect what's going on.

Q: *What did you say when you knocked on the door of the potential customer?*

A: The salesman would knock on the door, and I would have to make a judgment right then and there whether to start filming at that moment—which I did sometimes—or whether to put the camera down. Then maybe he would start chatting, and I would be filming. Then, not long after that, Paul or Raymond would introduce us by name, and we would explain why we were there. The explanation would usually run something like, "We are making a film for movie theatres and television about this salesman and the three people he works with. We're following them from house to house, and we never know exactly what's going to take place; but we are very interested in the job and find it very likable, and the purpose of the film is inventing more than just a human interest story." That took me maybe thirty seconds. Most people at that point would then say they understood, even though perhaps they didn't; but we would try to explain honestly what we really were about, and that was enough. Then when the whole filming was over, maybe twenty minutes or thirty minutes later, they would say, "Tell me once more what this is all about," and then we would explain and give them a release form which they would sign.

Q: *I am interested in the technical problem of filming a scene with just the one camera, and your difficulty in trying to follow actions and reactions. How do you approach all this?*

A: Well, I don't think in terms of actions and reactions. I don't think in technical terms at all, but rather of what I really want to get, and what I really want to get is a front head-on look at the person who is talking at the time. I'm not thinking of an artistic shot or an artistic composition of shots, though that's important. I suppose that approach makes the editing more difficult, but I feel that it is one of the reasons why the human content of the film is so strong and so totally convincing, because my concentration is on what I feel I have to get of the person, rather than some artistic thing I'm trying to prove. In none of the shooting, for example, do you have any views that are from high up or from low down. There is one shot where I'm looking down on a card table, but it was shot that way because that was the best way to get the coverage and not because I wanted to be artistic.

Q: *What was the size of your crew?*

A: The crew consisted of just David and myself. I did all the lighting and David handled the Nagra tape recorder.

Q: *How did you manage your lighting? Did you use a sun gun and bounce light?*

A: I have a light on the camera which is a sun gun with a 1,000-watt bulb in it. When I entered a home I would just plug it into the wall and flip it on. I also had a battery on me so that I could use the same lamp with a 250-watt bulb, and flip that on if necessary. You remember the scene where I follow the guy out of the house at night and into the car? Well, I couldn't walk out of there and still use the light plugged into the wall, so I flicked on my battery power, followed him out of the house, and as he pulled the car out of the garage I was still shooting with the sun gun. All of these things were one time efforts—never any reshooting.

Q: *What film stock were you using?*
A: Plus X and double X which I would rate at 125 ASA, which is normal for it. Very occasionally I would push it a stop. As for shooting ratio I think it was as high as forty to one.

Q: *What would you say was the biggest problem or problems in the shooting?*
A: The biggest problem was money, but more specifically, having only 400 feet of film in a magazine is a pretty big hang up. I should have had 1,200-foot magazines, but they get too bulky.

Q: *In this kind of intimate filming do you think the cameraman affects or alters the situation?*
A: I think he always does. The problem is to handle it so that it becomes more of what the scene is rather than something different.

Q: *Did your four salesmen ever deliberately play up to the camera?*
A: No, I don't think so. Certainly not while the camera was on, because the moment that occurred, I would turn the camera off.

Q: *I was wondering about Paul? He seems to have these monologues specially put on for the benefit of the camera.*
A: That's a little special. That's where I would say our presence made him more of himself; the monologues are the kind of thing he is doing all the time.

Q: *You said if Paul or the others tried to do something specially for you, you turned the camera off. Can you give me an example of that?*
A: To tell you the truth, I can't remember any time when they actually tried to do anything special. I would say that there were many times when I didn't film because it would have been in bad taste, for example some of their conversations about their wives or something like that.

Q: *On this question of Paul and his monologues, did you ask him questions to get him going or was it all purely spontaneous?*
A: If you knew Paul, you would know that he repeats himself a million and one times, and the one thing he would always repeat was his description of the other guys. The only time we may have prompted him was when we filmed him in the automobile. We started by asking him

about the guys, and then he took off by himself. It was when we were down in Florida with him, and all the filming had been finished, except for that. But that automobile conversation is the only exception. Normally, we completely left the scene alone.

Q: *Were there any situations you would liked to have filmed, but for some reason or other you couldn't?*

A: We once went out with the fellows before we began the film and saw them laying out their Bibles in front of a church. That was the only thing that the Bible company didn't want us to film. That forced us to make a decision—did we want to go ahead with that restriction and make the film. We thought quite long about it, and then decided that if it really was going to be the only restriction, then we would take it. However, not being able to get that, we had to get other material which made it quite clear as to how they got their potential sales leads, so that was okay. But visually, the scene in front of the church was fantastic, and I regret that we couldn't do it.

Q: *Were there any discussions before or during the film between you and David as to what should be in or what should be out?*

A: No. I firmly believe that a person is always revealing himself. What we get is an infinitesimally small percentage of any one man's life, so it is very selective. People say, "You're being very selective," as if to say that what we get isn't characteristic of the person. If that were so, if the handicap was so great that you could never really get anything characteristic of an individual, then you might just as well throw away every perceptive still photograph that was ever made. And here we are getting twenty-four frames a second—our images are far greater in number than in the still photographs.

Q: *We were talking earlier about your switching off when you thought it would show a certain lack of taste to continue shooting. It's a very stark film in that sense, but it doesn't really go outside the confines of these men selling the Bibles, it doesn't go into their personal history or background. Was this limitation deliberate on your part?*

A: We had an extraordinary entré to their lives, and we made use of that. We had footage of each of the men who is married, and of Paul who is separated. We had footage of them and their families, but we didn't use it primarily because it didn't help the film. In fact the inclusion of such stuff might have hurt it. Staying as small as we did made the film much tighter. Now some sociologists might say, "But we don't know that much about them," but they are wrong. By watching Paul on the telephone with his girlfriend you learn as much about how he relates to women, whether it's his wife or anybody else, as you would in all the stuff that we had of him with his former wife. Let me give you a reverse example. We were with Paul on the night that his daughter got married. We filmed the ceremony and all of the goings on between him and his daughter and his wife, which were very interesting; but the stuff that's in the film really is more revealing of him as a person with women and children than that material. So I think our decision to exclude it was correct.

Q: *Can you tell me something about your difficulties in selling the film? Have you recovered your money yet?*

A: If you have a very commercial film, you have no problem, that is if the person who is a potential distributor thinks that it's going to make a lot of money. A film like *Salesman* was more difficult because nothing like that had ever been done. Of course, that is usually what the distributors want—they want something new but they want something old. There's a paradox. There were all kinds of objections that the distributors raised in seeing this film—it was too depressing, too realistic for the public, and so forth. So we had to distribute it ourselves, in commercial theatres and at colleges—and we're doing pretty well.

Q: *What was the reaction of the four salesmen when they saw the picture?*

A: There was a lot of laughter, more so than from the rest of the audience. They saw it on the opening night in a full theatre, and a lot of the other people were annoyed with this group of people who were overreacting to the film. But there were other things. I know Paul cried at times when he saw it. My main impression is that they were amazed at the mass of material, and that there was so much in the film of their lives. It was very difficult; they had tried to imagine what the film would be like and couldn't. Once having seen it they were very much impressed with it. Whether it changed their notions of selling or not, I don't know. I don't think it did very much. In fact, after one of the screenings at the theatre, Ray the Bull walked out with the audience, and a man came over to him with his wife, recognized him, and said, "My wife would like to buy a Bible," and the Bull said, "You mean it?" When they both said, "Yes," Ray walked over to his car, pulled a Bible out of his trunk and got fifty dollars on the spot.

Q: *How did the Bible company respond to the film?*

A: I'm not sure whether they were pleased with the film or not. As salesmen, they like to present everything in a positive light, but when they saw the film they recognized a certain depressing quality in it. They thought it was too bad that Paul, the star of the film, wasn't a very good salesman. But then the other three were, so they were fairly happy.

Circumstantial Evidence: An Interview with David and Albert Maysles

ROBERT PHILLIP KOLKER/1971

"INTERVIEWS ARE superfluous . . . The film is our statement." I suppose David Maysles' comment would be fair coming from any artist. The Maysles brothers (Albert Maysles, cameraman, David Maysles, reporter-soundman, who with Charlotte Zwerin, editor, "direct" their films) have made or contributed to well over a dozen films since 1955, most of them television documentaries, including the first major film about the Beatles, made in 1964, and *Showman*, a portrait of Joseph E. Levine. But it has been their two features which have caused the most controversy. *Salesman* (1969) is a quiet presentation of four men who try to sell the Bible door-to-door. It reveals much of the pathos and desperation of "Middle America," and in its chief protagonist, Paul Brennan, presents the predicament of a sad way of life perhaps more accurately than does Arthur Miller's play. *Gimme Shelter* (1971), on the other hand, is a loud virtuoso piece recording the Rolling Stones' 1969 American tour, which ended at Altamont in the most horrifying public concert ever. People were beaten, a man was stabbed to death, and the Maysles got it on film.

Though highly acclaimed, both films have been attacked by some critics on the premise that they are false and manipulative; that, posing as truth, they are lies. The various problems raised by these works remain fundamental to the entire *cinéma-vérité* concept. What emerged from this interview, along with a solid, if necessarily defensive, attempt to put the critics away, was a definite contradiction between the Maysles' notion of spontaneity and the very formal structure of their work. I don't

From *Sight and Sound*, vol. 40, no. 4, Autumn 1971. Reprinted by permission.

know that the interview will put anyone's mind to rest about the problems raised by *cinéma-vérité* or "direct cinema," as they call it. It may in fact open up more questions than it answers. If nothing else, it reveals the attitudes and ideas of two very independent film-makers. —RPK

Q: *You both came out of University with degrees in psychology. Has your background influenced your ideas of filmmaking?*
ALBERT MAYSLES: John Lennon saw *Gimme Shelter* in Cannes and was quoted as saying: "My God, this was a *real* film . . . not any of that intellectual shit . . ." So when people ask me about my psychology background I have to say I don't think it has anything to do with our films. I think, in fact, that reasoning, intellectuality, is probably more than anything the enemy of art, and it would be the enemy of our way of making movies. People like Godard are good in spite of their intellectuality. He has been destroying himself as an artist by trying to lecture.

Q: *Does that mean you don't have any rational structure or ideas for a film beforehand?*
AM: Whatever structure there is in the films comes in the editing process, but almost in a secondary fashion. People have looked at our films and said—in *Salesman*, for example—that the cutting was fantastic between Paul Brennan on the train and the sales meeting in Chicago. Another sequence, when he talks about each of the salesmen while driving, is used as the structure for cutting in vignettes of the various salesmen. Those techniques are so unlike us. I took it as a kind of insult more than a compliment. Because the person who was observing those techniques didn't see that the real strength of the film was in its *not* having to depend on those kinds of editing techniques. They are artificial devices. If we had ended up with a film that had been edited in an Eisenstein style, those people would have said, now you're really getting into good moviemaking. Whereas we would have been disappointed to have had to resort to those techniques. It would mean that we didn't have in the material juxtapositions of events and people within, say, continuous shots.

Q: *But you choose juxtapositions, and if you have a juxtaposition of two sequences available, you'll use them.*
AM: Yes, but what I think Eisenstein took as the essence of film in the editing process would have destroyed the benefit of spontaneous juxtapositions that occur in filming—in life itself. I think the camera picking up material in an individual shot has great power. It has an ability to convey a truth that will allow the viewer more freedom to make a judg-

ment for himself, therefore to be given something that has a right to be more believable.

Q: *So then you withdraw yourself and allow the audience to make of it what they will?*
AM: No. At both ends we have a greater trust than someone like Eisenstein would have, a trust that the juxtapositions are there outside of ourselves. We have a trust that we are sensitive to pick them up. We have a trust that the audience somehow will find them there. We don't have to arrange it for them in such a way that they are funnelled into a more limited horizon.

Q: *But your films are very tightly organised.*
AM: These films *are* very tightly structured and composed. Now it's something I don't understand so well, because I am responsible for the photography. If I were very structured in my photography then the film would be a disaster, and I think that if in the editing the structuring took a traditional kind of importance, as it does in other films, then the films would be destroyed. Somehow or other between us, we preserve a kind of spontaneous quality of the diary and then make a novel out of the film—without committing it to fiction or an artificial kind of structure.

Q: *But a writer making a diary is quietly there in the background taking down notes. You are there with camera and microphone, and your presence must affect people's reactions. What we see on the screen is not what we see directly in life.*
AM: But it is what you would have seen if you had been there and seen it through our eyes. If you follow the arguments about how the camera affects those present, you would come out with the ridiculous notion that the way to make something the furthest from what actually happens is to go near it and film it, and the way to get closest to "reality" is to use actors and scripts. To film what actually happens, why not just go to it and have faith in recording events as they occur?
DAVID MAYSLES: I think audiences and film critics, in this country at least, are conditioned in such a way that it's very difficult for them to accept non-fiction. Non-fiction has usually meant a boring documentary, not a work of art. I feel certain that if *Salesman*, for example, was a hardcover book or presented as theatre there would be a totally different reaction. We are at the mercy of what really happens, which in a way is a limitation and in a way isn't at all. Our work is close to fiction because it's very subjective; it's a long way from newspaper reporting of an event.

AM: How could anyone we filmed in *Salesman* or *Gimme Shelter* be anything but what they really are? No one has told them to be different; we don't want them to be different. But we will be damned, and yet we won't let ourselves be damned, by critics who say that our truths are not truths. We won't let ourselves be forced into the position of saying that what we do is entirely objective and so deny ourselves the opportunity to express ourselves subjectively. The critics have this very simplistic thing: if you film a real thing, then it isn't real any more because you are a human being applying some subjectivity to it. Therefore, we won't allow ourselves to take the position of not being human beings. We are. But by the same token we are not going to let this subjective operation imply that we are telling lies. We are not. We express ourselves in an indirect fashion by expressing ourselves through what we find to be interesting around ourselves . . .

But isn't there a world of difference between the kind of subjectivity we employ and that of a fiction film-maker? Or of a documentary film-maker who believes that his idea, his subjectivity, consists in getting on to film something different from what he sees? His priority would be to show Paul Brennan for what *he* thinks Paul Brennan is. When he sees that Paul Brennan is different from what he thinks he is, then he either refuses to show that or he refuses to film it in any other way than how he wants to see it. We don't do that.

Q: *What is the difference between* cinéma-vérité *and your term "direct cinema"?*

DM: I think the danger again lies whenever you talk about "truth." When you are dealing with reality it seems to make everyone question it, where they wouldn't question a fiction film.

AM: Our films are spontaneous eruptions that we find ourselves catching with our cameras. To classify these things is some kind of sin. Nevertheless, people force us into giving it a name. So the name "direct" came into being—if only because people are set off on a rampage by the use of the word *vérité*. I think the word "direct" is more dispassionate. We go directly to things as they take place, and almost in spite of ourselves we are bound to come up with something that's more truthful.

Q: *Are you operating on some kind of "contract" with the audience? Something that implies you are present at an event, but that what is happening happens whether you are there or not?*

AM: I don't think it's necessary for the audience to be aware all the time of that dimension of our presence for them to accept the honesty or purity of what we are doing . . . I regard our films as the purest form of cinema I know of. As great as Bergman's films are, they seem more to me like theatrical pieces. And essentially what I see as cinematic—because only films can do it—is catching hold of reality in a spontaneous way.

Q: *Do you think a fiction film is a contradiction?*

AM: We would be short-changing ourselves if we called fiction films cinematic and ours not. It seems to me that the other films are departures from cinema, where we are right in the middle of what cinema really can do.

Q: *Let's talk about some specific things in your two features. It did seem to me that some of the scenes in* Salesman *were so smooth as to have been, if not scripted, at least laid out.*

AM: No one was ever told what to do. What I don't understand is why anyone would think we would want the people to be any different from what they are. Whatever refinements we make are in terms of cutting things down to smaller lengths. Not in the nature of changing names and places and events. We just don't think those kinds of improvements are improvements. One of the critics said that the greatest moment in *Salesman* was lost because during the silences, when Paul was in the restaurant for example, we didn't put words into his mouth, the words which we would have wanted him to say. But why would we want him to say anything, and what would we want him to say? It would have put a lie to the whole thing. One of the strongest moments in the film was provided there because you knew enough of Paul so that in his silence your own feelings and thoughts merged with his. Had he spoken, it probably would have broken the spell. Had we made him speak, it would have destroyed the whole effect of the film.

Q: *But when Paul goes about singing "If I Were a Rich Man" and the various bits of business he does in the car, aren't those prompted by your being there?*

AM: I don't know. But I know it's the kind of thing he's doing all the time. I don't for a moment think that he was a different person because he was with us. We won't accept the dubious honour of being labelled "directors" capable of making actors out of people merely by the presence of our camera.

DM: We don't impose anything on the people we film. We are the servants of our subjects rather than the other way around.

Q: *Tell me about* Gimme Shelter*, its origins, how you got involved in it, your intentions . . .*

AM: We didn't know what the film was going to be. We just had a childish faith that having seen the Stones and getting along with them, there might be a feature film there. So at our own expense and speculation we stayed with them.

Q: *The structure of* Gimme Shelter *is very tight and controlled. What were your editing principles, and at what point did you decide to use the device of intercutting the Stones' responses to what they were seeing on the editing machine?*

DM: We wanted something to go beyond just the concert and the tour, and we were developing different themes. One of them had to do with filming the detectives and the Angels and some of the aftermath of the killing itself. That material was rather inconclusive because the trial was still going on, for one thing. But as the film began to develop in the editing, we thought the most important thing was to keep it directly on the Stones' experience. We would try somehow to involve them in how they felt about it. Charlotte Zwerin suggested the Steenbeck editing console as a device. The Stones hadn't seen the material and when they asked to see it, it seemed like a good idea to film them reacting to the film rather than interviewing them, for example. A lot of the material of Mick Jagger viewing the film did work out well, so we used it. After doing all that shooting we thought the film needed a much more simple line. Within that line the Stones had in some way to express their feelings about what happened. They don't react with anything more than their expressions in a very simple fashion because they can't explain it any more than we can. Of course, their song "Gimme Shelter" at the end of the film is a very eloquent expression of their feelings.

Q: *In many ways* Gimme Shelter *is a film about a film. For example, near the end, when the killing is shown full screen, we hear Jagger's voice over saying, "Can you roll back on that, David?" and you show him, and us, the segment in slow motion and reverse two or three times.*

DM: No. Everyone seems to misinterpret that, to think it's two or three times. It's once at regular speed and then in slow motion; it stops a couple of times and then the scene continues at regular speed. So the killing is really only in the film twice.

Q: *But the point is that you made the film so that it builds step by step to the killing.*

DM: It does because that was the most important event of the tour. We weren't sure where to put the killing until the final editing. In fact, at one time we were thinking seriously of putting some of the footage at the very beginning.

Q: *Did you know a killing had occurred while you were filming?*
DM: No. That should be pointed out. The cameraman never saw the killing and I was right with him. I didn't see it, and the Stones didn't either, when it happened. The whole stabbing happens in less than three seconds.
AM: That's why it was necessary to show it in slow motion. If the cameraman himself didn't see it, how can the audience?

Q: *What was your relationship with the Hell's Angels?*
AM: They were helping us out. They were carrying some of our magazines . . .
DM: Oh? I didn't know about that. I knew they were guarding the truck I was on . . .
AM: Well, they would lift us up on the stage, for example. But we didn't have the choice whether to like them or dislike them, or accept help or reject help. They were there. If they hit you over the head, as I heard may have happened with one of the cameramen . . .

Q: *Does it concern you that, despite the fact that the film has much more to offer than the sight of someone getting killed, many people are going for the sensation of seeing a freaked-out audience and a killing?*
AM: Do they go and see it for that reason? I think more than anything that turns people away. Neither of us is an expert in that kind of thing. We wouldn't want to emphasise that part of it in the advertising because it seems as though people are afraid to see the truth, especially a tragic one. It might put them off seeing it.

Q: *Are you concerned that you may have been sensationalising a terrible event?*
AM: If we *had* been, I don't know how we'd feel about it. We didn't sensationalise it . . . I don't think Daniel Ellsberg feels guilty about having revealed the Pentagon Papers. Is he sensationalising something? There were some initial reactions to the *New York Times* publishing those papers, that it was sensationalism on their part. Most everybody was highly suspicious of the newspaper's motives for doing it because it was a scoop. And people were highly suspicious of us because we got a scoop on a killing. We did the right thing including the killing in the film.

Q: *Someone reported that you cut out Charlie Watts's comment about Altamont: "Maybe we shouldn't have done it."*
DM: That's one of the problems of discussing that kind of material, because it's referred to as "cut out." It could also be referred to as "not cut in." It doesn't sound so ominous. I could tell you a lot of things that are very interesting but not in the film. It's the same way with a writer. There's a lot of information in his notes that he thinks about putting in the final work. Obviously we're biased about what we do put in. Again, that's why I object to the word "truth."
AM: One could complain that the best photographed song, "Queenie," is not in the film.

Q: *Why did you choose not to use it?*
DM: I wouldn't put it that way. Why did we choose to use the other songs? We had so many songs and each is there for so many reasons. For example, "Satisfaction" just seems to fit in that particular place, it works there editorially. "Jumping Jack Flash" works at the beginning of the film. Editing is just what works and what doesn't work for you, and "Queenie" didn't work in the overall structure of the film.

Q: *What about the slow motion sequence to "Love in Vain"? That's a case of creating something that was not "actually" seen that way.*
DM: That too wasn't planned. Almost all of the slow motion stuff is not "Love in Vain," but we wanted to use the song and we had some nice footage to go with it. Also we wanted it to lead into the sequence of the Stones actually listening to the same song in their London recording studio, and so we put it together. If we had had really good stuff of "Love in Vain" the way it was played, shot at normal speed, we might not have used the slow motion footage. It's one of those things you find out about because you don't have the material. Although at one time we did think about slow motion—Charlotte and I thought about a lot of optical effects, but then we dropped all that. We had a hundred different formulas for the structure of the film at different stages. It just finally evolved into what it is. We could give you all the reasons why it is that way now, but we couldn't possibly give you those reasons before.

Q: *Tell me about the use of the footage by the California police to locate and try the Hell's Angel who stabbed Meredith Hunter.*
DM: We had the footage and were subpoenaed to show it. We also felt it was our duty to show it because they didn't have any other evidence. We thought at the same time we would film them working with it. Right

after the concert, people were sceptical about whether this guy would be apprehended or if anybody would bear witness against him for fear of reprisals from the Angels.

AM: In regard to the killing that the film caught, I'd like to see some of the people who complain about the presence of the camera and our own presence affecting reality argue that in court, as the trial was taking place. They'd be laughed out of court. With all the people who were at Altamont, with all that had been written about it, with all that had been known about it, it was that footage which was closest to the truth of what took place. And the court accepted it as such.

Q: *But the killer was acquitted.*

DM: The court determined from the footage that the killing was done in self-defence. It showed the gun [held by Meredith Hunter, the man killed]. There is no other evidence of the gun that we know about.

AM: So that footage, which the critics—as with all of our other footage—are so sceptical about, saved a man's life. It shows the end of one man's life and it saved the next man's life by showing what actually took place. Nobody in court could invalidate the footage. The self-defence plea was a complicated business, the footage was circumstantial evidence—it was as complicated as what is seen in the film. Compare what was revealed in that scene and told in all its complexity to what was told in *Blow-Up*. Compare two versions of fiction and truth.

DM: I again object to using the word "truth." There's so much behind it, the way Altamont was organised, who was responsible . . . But it was truthful to what went on before our eyes. We didn't tell any lies that we know about. Again the presence of the camera is the objection raised. But in the case of Altamont there were 300,000 people there. There were no set camera positions. It was such a chaotic thing. I can't imagine that anyone was conscious of being filmed, except maybe the Stones. But from what I can gather from talking to them, they say they are in a whole different world when they are performing and they are not at all conscious of a camera.

Q: *How is the film doing at the box-office?*

DM: It's not the overwhelming success a lot of people predicted. It did break records in New York. We'll have to wait for results from the rest of the country and from Europe . . . But the fact remains that we made it independently . . . just the way we wanted to. There is a great deal of satisfaction there.

AM: One of the subtle things that may be operating in terms of the success of the film concerns just how much the public, at any given time, is desirous of seeing the truth of their lives. I think that was true of *Salesman*. I think that people just couldn't take it. Right now, the rock scene being what it is, people may just think that *Gimme Shelter* is the voice of doom. Six months ago it might have been different.

DM: As we said earlier, our interest has been in making films as one would write a novel or do a painting or even compose a song. Evidently, from what we can gather, people don't go to the movies to experience anything but a very light kind of amusement. I don't think it's going to change us any. *Gimme Shelter* and *Salesman* are unique. There was absolutely no one to tell us how to do them. Every single inch of those films is exactly the way we wanted to make it. You have to pay for that, I guess.

Seeking to Take the Longest Journey: A Conversation with Albert Maysles

CALVIN PRYLUCK/1976

FEW ACTUALITY filmmakers are as controversial as Albert and David Maysles. One critic says, "They bring to their films a combination of originality, intelligence, and theatricality that is unparalleled in nonfiction filmmaking today." Another says, their films "raise the inevitable questions about cruelty, exploitation, greed, and exhibitionism." Their latest film, *Grey Gardens*, will do little to quiet the argument.

The subjects of the film are an unmarried woman nearing sixty and her mother, both of them named Edith Bouvier Beale. For more than twenty years, Mrs. Beale and Edie have lived as recluses in a decaying mansion. They also happen to be aunt and cousin to Jacqueline Kennedy Onassis.

A general discussion of ethics in documentary film was iniatiated in the Winter 1976 issue of the *Journal* by Calvin Pryluck's article, "Ultimately We Are All Outsiders: The Ethics of Documentary Filming." In the following conversation, Albert Maysles addresses some of the questions raised in the article which he had read shortly before its publication.

Inevitably, perhaps, Mr. Maysles speaks here of both his ethical and aesthetic perspectives. He also answers some of the specific charges that have been leveled against him and his brother throughout their careers.

The conversation was edited and rearranged by Professor Pryluck, with the assistance of the *Journal* editor, from the transcript of a longer and wider ranging discussion that took place in the offices of Maysles Films,

---

From *Journal of the University Film Association*, vol. 28, no. 2, Spring 1976. Reprinted by permission of the *Journal of Film and Video*.

Inc., in New York, on April 21, 1976. Mr. Maysles has read the edited conversation and made whatever corrections he wished to make.

PRYLUCK: *The notion that I've had of your films is that there was something cynical about the choice of topics. I'm satisfied that your latest film* Grey Gardens, *is treated about as delicately as it could be, given the subject. Yet . . .*
MAYSLES: Why do we pick these grim subjects?

PRYLUCK: *Well, you can put the question that way if you want.*
MAYSLES: I would say that the artist, if I may use that overworked word . . .

PRYLUCK: *You trying to figure out what it means?*
MAYSLES: Yeah. The artist seeks to take the longest journey, see? Sometimes it might be more interesting to do the Trans Siberian Railway than, say, the New York Subway, although the longest journey might be on the subway if you carry the viewer that much further spiritually, aesthetically, ethically, or whatever.

So, in *Grey Gardens*, we start out with two women—Edie Beale and her mother—whose value system and whose environment is so different from everyone else's. If by getting to know them and recording their experiences and getting all that on film somehow, you can move the audience that much further away from what their original impression was, then you've taken the audience on a long journey. You've taken *yourself* on a long journey.

I mean, it was a long journey for us. The Beales were aristocracy and we're from Russian Jewish stock. To make that close a friendship with people of that social level is a long journey. To gain that kind of acceptance of these two people could be a hell of a difficult thing. It's proven to be even more difficult to gain audience acceptance because of all these charges of exploitation.

PRYLUCK: *A couple of years ago, you quoted Arthur Barron asking about whether you were ever afraid of hurting people; and you said, "I don't ever feel that fear of exploitation myself. It's never occurred to me as something to be afraid of."*
MAYSLES: Right.

PRYLUCK: *But then at the premiere showing of* Grey Gardens *you were quoted as saying, "Exploitation is not an issue in this film."*
MAYSLES: Well, it's proven to be one with some members of the audience, but I didn't feel it was myself. Since they have raised it, it appears to be a problem for them; then it's something to talk about.

PRYLUCK: *Do you know of any films where you feel exploitation* was *an issue?*

MAYSLES: The one I think of is *Titicut Follies.* I could be wrong here, but I got the sense that the people who were making the film were abusing the subjects in the film because they were using them for some purpose that the people in the film may not have known about. They were abused because the film was done in such a way as to dehumanize them. You learn nothing about these people at all as human beings except that they're pawns of the system.

I know that makes a certain kind of point, but maybe in a situation like that the point is larger. I think you would find out more about the system, *pro* and *con,* if you allow yourself to find out more about the people. The film does the same thing as the system, in order to make the system look bad. That's bad all the way around. That kind of dehumanization is what pornography is all about. To me *Titicut Follies* uses people as so much flesh as one does in a pornographic film. I don't think we did that in *Grey Gardens.*

> The Maysles brothers have always been inveterate seekers after the phantom of documentary "truth." This quest has been hampered by the peculiar insularity of their vision and by its glib spontaneity. In *Grey Gardens* they do not mean to be cruel to the Beales, although they are. The movie has some slender justification as a piece of psychological reporting, about the ways two people rely on each other and torture each other. But all we see—perhaps all anyone could ever see—are the bitterness and the desperation, not how and why they began. Without the powers of art to enrich and transform, *Grey Gardens* remains an aimless act of ruptured privacy and an exploitation.
>
> JAY COCKS

PRYLUCK: *As I read the critics, those who don't like* Grey Gardens *seem to be saying it's exploitive, it's not socially useful, and besides it's not art.*

MAYSLES: But isn't that exactly the same criticism that photography has had all these years? I mean, I think it is only twenty years now or less that the Guggenheim grants have started to give money to photographers. Because it wasn't recognized as an art.

All these people understand is fictional film. They don't understand the potential of nonfiction film. They think the camera is an intruder by its nature. They speak about the merciless camera. It was merciless in *Titicut Follies,* I think. But is wasn't merciless in the case of the Beales in *Grey Gardens.*

PRYLUCK: *Let's look at the exploitation question a little closer. To use Molly Haskell's phrase from her review of* Grey Gardens, *"Aren't there times when we should close our eyes?"*
MAYSLES: I haven't found those times yet. When you begin to exclude things for somebody else's protection or for your own protection it becomes a habit like using marijuana or heroin or anything. But I give people credit for more than most people would in their ability to handle knowledge of all kinds, and I wouldn't want to restrict that. It's hard for me to imagine things that I would not film.

PRYLUCK: *Well, let's say I'm walking along the street, and there's a drunk who is retching in the corner: I'm not going to stare at him. It's not simply that I don't want to watch him so much as the fact that he's got a right to his privacy at that moment.*
MAYSLES: He's got a right to his privacy but, at the same time, the reason that he may be an alcoholic is that no one's paying attention to him. He doesn't need people passing him by; let the camera take part in the recognition. It needn't be bad for him. I assume always that when I turn the camera on somebody, it's going to be good. Good for the film, good for them, good all the way around.

> There are no simple ethical standards to apply, and because the situations are so fluid and variable, one has to be fairly knowledgeable not to get suckered into reacting to motion picture footage that appears to be documentary as if it were the simple truth.
>
> PAULINE KAEL

MAYSLES: I don't know of any single category of people who you shouldn't film. I mean, there are people who are eager to say, "Edie Beale: she's senile, and the other one is demented; they're incompetent, so they can't be filmed." I'm all for filming incompetent people. They're the ones who need it the most.

PRYLUCK: *There are real problems there . . .*
MAYSLES: Sure, there are problems, but if some psychiatrist told me, "Look, Mrs. Beale is incompetent; she was incompetent all the time you were filming her," then I'd say, "Gee, it's a great thing because we didn't abuse her incompetence!" I think what we showed in *Grey Gardens* were those areas where she is competent; she's a very competent person in the film. I think it's a very competent thing for her to have decided to expose the secrets of her life on film to everybody.

If you say the incompetent ones are not to be filmed, we're closing our eyes to it. Really, it's probably the incompetent people who need to be in a movie more than anyone, because they feel this sense of not being recognized, this sense of being nobody, the sense of loss of identity. They can feel it. If the camera is used to recognize their points of strength, they begin to develop a sense of identity, of recognition, of belief. Let's not deprive them of being filmed, because we are trying to protect them, see?

PRYLUCK: *Aren't there times when filming people could hurt them?*
MAYSLES: Yeah, there are some people; each case has to be individually examined. There are also some people running around with a camera I wouldn't trust and they shouldn't be trusted. I wouldn't want to categorize whom or whatever; it's an individual matter. I think they have a disrespect for people and they're hurtful to people. But I'm saying that to say also that there are people to be trusted. We're the good guys.

I guess the most important question is, "Would you let an incompetent run around with a camera?" Who's to decide?

PRYLUCK: *Have you ever* not *taken pictures because you thought it would be wrong for the subject, or in bad taste, or . . .*
MAYSLES: Oh, yeah. Many, many, many times when I'm filming, I put the camera down for one reason or another. I have to make judgments for the person when I'm filming. I have to say, "No, this would hurt this person, this is embarrassing, I have no right to do it." I'm sensitive to that problem, but it's not easy.

Once, as we were finishing a film, we discovered maybe two seconds that could have embarrassed the person. Two seconds, that's all; and we thought, "Well, what the hell, no one's ever going to notice this; we've been looking at this thing for two years and we never saw it." But we thought, "No, if one person sees it, it's not fair; so we'll cut it out." And we did.

PRYLUCK: *Earlier you said when you shoot something you assume it would be good for the people and good for the film. Are they the same thing?*
MAYSLES: There is some kind of a relationship between truth, beauty, and art. You tell the truth and it's good for somebody sometimes whether they know it or not; depends on whether they object to it.

You know, they say the truth will make us free. There's so much hypocrisy. The truth would make us free. If we don't have the truth, then we live by the falsehoods. Who's going to benefit from that?

We're left with the illusions that we have and we don't benefit from that a bit. It is strange that our society is so communicative on many levels; we have the capacity for enormous communication but there are areas that we are so scared stiff of, the most important are spiritual ones, that we just won't communicate, we deplore the fact that we are all alienated but we won't budge on it. We'll take the Woodward/ Bernstein version only when it's fed to us through Dustin Hoffman and Robert Redford. Everyone is rushing out to see that movie; is anyone clamoring saying, "No! we want the Nixon tapes?" No, we still haven't gotten those. We have a greater right and interest in those than in the movie.

> . . . the Maysles brothers recruited Paul Brennan who was in the roof-and-siding business, to play a Bible salesman for the "direct-cinema" *Salesman.**
>
> PAULINE KAEL

PRYLUCK: *Let me ask you about some of the things which have been floating around about the Maysles brothers. I think the most notorious is the business of you and Paul Brennan being in collusion.*

MAYSLES: Kael won't tell us where she got that information. If my memory is correct, she acted as her own researcher on that story, which is already highly suspect on the *New Yorker.* She is really malicious, and it's extraordinary that she's regarded as the dean of the critics.

One thing about Bible salesmen and other salesmen is that they sometimes go from one product to another. They'll sell a Bible one year and then go down to the West Indies and sell *The History of the Negro People*, or they sell encyclopedias for a month or two. Paul had been selling Bibles for years, and when we met him he was selling Bibles, and when we filmed him he was selling Bibles. It would have taken an extraordinary act of ours to get him to stop selling Bibles and do something else. After the film was over—maybe a year later—we know that he was selling siding. *After* the film was over, see?

PRYLUCK: *You did pay the expenses of the salesmen, didn't you?*

MAYSLES: Some of them. We felt that we should pay them something. We wanted to do it in a way that was going to least affect what they did; we didn't want them to please us or do anything. We were very concerned that if there's money exchanged it's not going to influence them in any way whatsoever.

---

*Maysles: This statement was omitted from the reprint of the review [of *Gimme Shelter*] in Kael's *Deeper into Movies* because we threatened to sue her if she republished it. In no subsequent issue has the *New Yorker* corrected Ms. Kael.

But some people use the fact that we paid their expenses as evidence that they went to Florida because we paid them and they would have not gone otherwise. That's not true. They were going down there anyway. It was their idea; it was always their plan.

> [*Gimme Shelter*] is into complications and sleight-of-hand beyond Pirandello, since the filmed death at Altamont—although, of course, unexpected—was a part of *cinéma-vérité* spectacular. The free concert was staged and lighted to be photographed, and the three hundred thousand people who attended it were the unpaid cast of thousands. The violence and murder weren't scheduled, but the Maysles brothers hit the *cinéma-vérité* jackpot.
>
> PAULINE KAEL

MAYSLES: Kael has this theory about *cinéma-vérité*, and everything she says is to try to prove that theory. I think the first time I saw it was in a piece she did on Norman Mailer. Then later she did a review of us, and everything she said there was a carbon copy of what she had said before about *cinéma-vérité*. She twists the facts to make the reader believe her theory. For example, she said that we set up the lighting for *Gimme Shelter*. Totally untrue. If we had set up the lighting so that we could make a film—which is what we would have done if we were setting up the lighting—then we wouldn't have had such a hard time getting our exposure. I didn't have the foggiest idea of what the exposures were going to be, and a lot of the stuff was no good because some of our guys didn't know what to expose for.

> Melvin Belli's bordello-style law office and his negotiations for a concert site are in the film, but it isn't explained that Porter Bibb, the producer of *Salesman*,** was the person who brought in Belli, or that Bibb became involved in producing the concert at Altamont in order to produce the Maysles film.
>
> PAULINE KAEL

MAYSLES: Porter Bibb was not the producer of *Salesman*; we were the sole producers. We never even met him until after *Salesman* was finished. If she had looked at the film she would have seen that he didn't have that credit.

**In the version reprinted in *Deeper into Movies* this statement was amended to read "publicist of *Salesman*" (Pryluck).

PRYLUCK: *Let me ask the question directly: What did you have to do with setting up the concert? Were you or Porter Bibb or anybody who might be interpreted as working for you . . . ?*

MAYSLES: Nothing.

PRYLUCK: *Your claim is that you were not involved in that at all, any part of it?*

MAYSLES: Right.

PRYLUCK: *The newspaper* Rolling Stone *claimed that the Stones wanted to beat the release of* Woodstock.

MAYSLES: The Stones never urged us to do anything. I don't think *that* was their concern. They didn't have that involvement in the film. Besides, they didn't have any okay in the film.

PRYLUCK: *That was going to be my next question . . .*

MAYSLES: The Stones gave us the release after they saw the film.

PRYLUCK: *Wasn't that the same with Levine and* Showman*?*

MAYSLES: We used to do that. When we made a film, we didn't ask for anybody's release until the film was finished and we showed it to them. That doesn't mean they had a veto over the film.

PRYLUCK: *What if they refused to sign a release?*

MAYALES: They didn't. So we haven't had the problem. It's so hard for me to imagine that what I'm doing might hurt people in any way because I'm not imposing any kind of thing on what they're doing. The editing is not of a kind that would place them in a context that I think would be embarassing to them or that they would dislike. And there is the record—we got the releases in both cases without having to change anything.

After *Gimme Shelter* was finished and in theaters a couple of months as an R rated picture, we wanted a PG rating so that kids under seventeen could see it. We had to change a shot of a girl without her shirt on; also, the word "fuck" was used three or four times. Other than that, there were no changes whatsoever. We've never made changes for anyone.

We certainly don't please the box office: We're known as the Cassandras of the trade. We collaborated on a film called *Yanki, No!* about Cuba and *Esquire* that year called us the Cassandras. In the last ten or twenty years, the times have been times for Cassandras, right? *Salesman* is a Cassandra story, *Gimme Shelter* is, and in a way *Grey Gardens* is, too.

PRYLUCK: *I'm still fascinated by your choice of subjects. What other projects were there that you might have gone into instead of* Grey Gardens*?*

MAYSLES: It wasn't between that and another one. Actually, I wasn't quite sure of doing *Grey Gardens*. But somehow I just knew that it had to be done. If you read the story in *New York* magazine about the Beales, you know what I mean about the fascinating story: an incredibly good film was there to be made, and I just had to do it.

I wasn't too keen on doing the one on the Stones [*Gimme Shelter*]. They are well-known performers; I thought I was getting away from my purposes which were to film more everyday kinds of things. *Salesman* is the closest to what we always wanted to do—and still want to do. It's about people who were not well-known until the film. Finding what we thought had to be known about these people and seeking to stretch the impression the audience could get from them: that's our keenest interest.

> Edie Beale dismisses the controversy. "People say we shouldn't have had the Maysles in our house," she says. "But they weren't holding a gun on us. . . ." The Maysles, she insists, were "factual. They get the pith of every situation. There is no difference in the way we lead our lives and what you see. Mother and I have sort of gone beyond time. We've always been objects of great curiosity, so I don't think this will make things any worse."
>
> The Beales, in effect, were two characters in search of anauthor, and now they have found one.
>
> CHARLES MICHENER and KATRINE AMES, *Newsweek*

Who's Who in Filmmaking: Albert Maysles

JUDITH TROJAN/1978

ALBERT MAYSLES is five years older than his brother and four years younger than his sister. He grew up in Boston, taught psychology at Boston University, and travelled to Russia where he examined mental hospitals with a camera he borrowed from CBS. The result was a film entitled *Psychiatry in Russia* (1955), hardly a blockbuster in the States during the witch-hunting Fifties. But Al was hooked; he never put his camera down again.

Joining forces with his brother, David, he became one-half of "The Maysles Brothers" filmmaking team—early practitioners of a form of *cinéma-vérité* they like to call "direct" cinema.

A middle child, Al also became the spokesman, on the road in college lectures and in print, for the team and the family. In the interview that follows, he discusses the Maysles family and their two "family" films: *Grey Gardens* (1975) and *The Burks of Georgia* (1976), the latter aired as part of the PBS series *Six American Families*.

Both films highlight "forgotten" people. Edith Bouvier Beale, age seventy-nine, and her daughter Edie, age fifty-six, lived for twenty years as recluses in a decaying East Hampton seaside mansion called Grey Gardens, but they are aunt and cousin respectively of Jacqueline Bouvier Kennedy Onassis. Once highly educated, coddled, cultured beauties (who in glorious old photos and oil portraits bear striking resemblance to Jackie Onassis), the Beales aged into flamboyant eccentrics holed up in a crumbling shell of a house. Mrs. Beale ate, slept, and literally lived

---

From *Sightlines*, Spring 1978. Reprinted by permission of the author.

in a bed covered with the debris of a lifetime—empty cereal and tissue boxes, cat food tins, newspapers, and an endless assortment of stray cats. Daughter Edie dreamed of a career as a dancer, but never left her mother's side long enough to pursue the career or the offers from the eligible, rich young men who tried to court her.

In the film, mother and daughter interact lovingly, and with hostility. They air individual heartaches, lament unfulfilled dreams, sing, dance, and in the process, reveal much about what is universally stressful and destructive in mother/daughter relationships and question the values and status quo of American life. The film looks uncompromisingly at two women who broke with the system at the top.

The Burks of Georgia, on the other hand, will never make it to the top. Grace, age fifty-six, and Arlon, age sixty-five, live on five rural acres near Dalton, Georgia. Of their thirteen children, ten survive, spanning the ages of fourteen to thirty-four. Most live with or within yards of Arlon and Grace. The Burk turf is covered with junk, cars in various states of disrepair, dogs, livestock, vegetables, and a tribe of grandchildren. Of limited economic means, and under-educated, they are often the subject of ridicule in their community.

The Beales and the Burks have a lot in common.

JT: *I've read that you and David are obsessed with family life. It's obviously a comfortable subject for you because you've managed a successful family relationship in business and film. Did your close family ties spur your interest in films like* Grey Gardens *and* The Burks of Georgia*?*

AM: I think it's just that we feel that almost any subject has never been dealt with properly until it's been dealt with realistically, that is, filming real people in real situations. And family has not, until recently, been dealt with—filming real people in real family situations. Since it's the most basic unit of all, it's offered us a tremendous challenge; it's been most interesting to us.

JT: *Can you explain why realistic views of families have been overlooked by filmmakers?*

AM: Because they think that they have to have some kind of purpose: a commercial purpose or an issue purpose, to put somebody up, or to put somebody down. They've always been purpose-oriented. Whenever they're filming a family or whatever, they make it entertaining, they make it funny. Consequently, the family has never been dealt with in movies, as, let's say, in literature.

And the family to most people would be an unattractive subject for filmmaking, because filmmakers are afraid of their own family relationships, they don't want to get into it. When they're going to spend half a million dollars of their own or somebody else's money to make a film, they certainly don't want to do it on the family which they would not think to be commercial. They think that when people go to see a movie, they want to get away from themselves.

JT: *Who, for instance? Even documentary filmmakers?*
AM: Oh, yes! There have been documentary films made about families. The Loud family [*An American Family*, by Susan and Alan Raymond] is one of them. The purpose there was to select a family that would somehow or other tell us all about the disaster of America. So, the first family that the producer saw, as he was going around selecting a family, had three suicides, And then there were the Louds, who were about to get divorced. It was with this kind of perhaps overly dramatic point of view that he thought he could prove some kind of a point. It's never really for purposes that are intrinsic to the nature of the subject or to the people in it that filmmakers would make a film about the family; it's always with some other kind of interest.

JT: *Do you think anything in your past life, your family life as a child, your relationship with your parents and sister affected your choice of career and style of filmmaking?*
AM: Yes. The main thing was that they inspired a curiosity about all kinds of people. I remember the first day that we met the Beales. A car went by with two girls in it; each one of the girls shouted one after the other, "You witches!" At that point, most people would have left out of fear or lack of interest. But, we felt that it was highly unlikely that the Beales really were witches, and we wanted to give them a chance in the film to be whoever they were.

Can you think of any other filmmaker who would choose to make *Salesman*, *Grey Gardens*, or *The Burks*? All three of those films are failure stories, in one way or another. In each case, the people are rejected by society. It was this kind of acceptance factor that my family instilled.

JT: *Were you raised in a wealthy family? Middle class?*
AM: Lower middle class. My father was a postal clerk. My mother was a school teacher.

JT: *Did the fact that both your parents worked make you more independent as a child, closer to your brother and sister and less dependent on your parents?*

AM: Actually, my mother worked before she was married and she didn't go back to it until I was about thirteen. She wanted to teach all that time, but in Boston they had a rule that they couldn't hire women who were married. Can you imagine that! Then, when we moved to Brookline, the problem there was that they had never hired a Jewish teacher. My mother went to the school commissioner and argued him into hiring her as the first Jewish teacher. I'm mentioning all that because that may, in part, explain why we've chosen frequently to film people who are not accepted by society.

JT: *What was your neighborhood like?*

AM: We were brought up in a marginal area of Dorchester; so, we were always in fights with the Irish. And in Brookline, on St. Patrick's Day, there were the usual fights. Boston in those days was a highly contentious city, full of ethnic conflicts. Then, it was every race, every ethnic group: the Irish, the Italians, the Jews, and so forth.

JT: *Why work with your brother? Why work as a team instead of forging out on your own?*

AM: Well, we see eye to eye, partly because of our family connection. When we first began, we had a lot of problems. But we saw that what we couldn't do apart from one another, we could do together.

JT: *Do each of you play different roles in the business?*

AM: Yes. Most of our filming is just a two-man operation. I operate the camera. David does the sound work. But, at the same time, he's in a better position to relate to the people we're filming because he can talk or see; his eye isn't partly hidden by the camera.

In business, I get a good deal of the jobs. David does some of the budgeting. And the two of us do a lot of persuasion.

JT: *Have you ever thought about making a film on your own family?*

AM: Yes, we started a film on my mother before she died. And then we couldn't quite finish it. But we got very good material, and we're going to use that at some time or another in a family film.

My mother was a member of an organization called the Saturday Evening Girls, a cultural organization that was organized by a very wealthy woman in Boston for immigrant children. My mother was only two when she came to this country from Poland. The women who were in that club scattered around the country, but my sister has tracked down all the ones who have survived—there are about a dozen of them left—and she's done video stuff of them.

When my mother died two years ago, my sister became fascinated with my mother's life and began to do a biography of my mother, which she's going to publish.

JT: *In both* Grey Gardens *and* The Burks of Georgia, *the mother is the controlling force in each family. Can you relate that to your own mother? Was she the dominant person in your family?*

AM: Yes, it's true. You know, there were six American families in that series, and one of the curious things they noticed after all the films were finished was that all the mothers were the powerful ones in the family. It may be characteristic of America more than we think.

JT: *Did your mother give you the impetus to push ahead in your career?*

AM: No. A lot of our ambition stems from the fact that my father was not very ambitious. He was a postal clerk, but he was, by the same token, very ambitious for us. So that, in a way, we wanted to achieve for him and for ourselves what he hadn't achieved himself.

JT: *Were most of your childhood friends Jewish? Did you stay within the Jewish community for social contacts?*

AM: Most of my friends were Jewish. I tried to get to know non-Jewish kids, but I was always disappointed because, sooner or later, the non-Jewish kids would prove to be anti-Semitic. But from the way my parents had trained us, we always saw the good in people. So that, as a matter of fact, was one of the reasons why we chose to do *Salesman* the way we did. We chose four Irishmen doing the job of what Jews normally do—which is being a salesman—not with the idea of getting even with the Irish or putting down Catholicism, but really with the intention of making a bond between ourselves and those people.

There were some people who saw *Salesman* and interpreted it completely the other way around. But that was their own problem. When Richard Schickel reviewed it for *Life* magazine, he thought the film terribly condescending. The fact is that he didn't have the kind of family that we had. His father was a salesman, and his problem had something to do with that, and nothing to do with the film.

JT: *You've been criticized a great deal for exploiting your subjects. In my mind, you do just the opposite: you allow forgotten people to have their day in the sun. Why not romanticize your subjects?*

AM: Because we think that being merciful to people is being truthful about them and with them. The common notion is if you're totally frank and truthful, you're going to hurt somebody, especially if what you're revealing is something that's not generally known about somebody. In other words, the idea that truth shall make us free is accepted, but it's not generally believed.

JT: *What do you think the exposure in* Grey Gardens *has done for the Beales?*

AM: David was just talking to the daughter [Edie Beale] the other day about Mrs. Beale's last few days. Edie revealed that when she was talking to her mother those last few days, she asked her, "What can you say about your life? How would you summarize it?" And Mrs. Beale said, "The film! The film is it."

JT: *So, the Beales have publicly stated that they like the film. And the Burks were given a chance to see and react to their film, and their comments were broadcast as part of the TV telecast. They also like their film. Apparently, neither family has the feeling of being exploited. How do you explain the contradictions between what the critics have said and what the subjects have said about their portraits?*

AM: We could talk a long time about that, but one of the main points is that you can't control an audience even if you wanted to. The audience brings its own likes and dislikes, its own prejudices, its own fears, and its own value systems. So, if you have people in the audience who are, and most of them are, from the middle class, the value system that they bring with them is cleanliness. Middle class people dream that they can get ahead and move up higher, have an automobile or two, and a house that's in a certain range of income. They all want to work. You could go on and on, and if I described all of that, I would describe exactly what the Beales put down. Their value system completely contradicts it.

It's not an easy thing for most people of the middle class to understand how somebody from the upper class would reject all of that. They try to deny it because it's a threat to their own existence as middle class people. And one of the mechanisms of denial is to say that there is something wrong with the Beales, that they're crazy.

Another mechanism of denial is to say that the Beales aren't really that way, but the camera *made* them that way. That's another sort of criticism we had.

But, they *are* that way! When the camera wasn't there, they were that way as well. The Beales, by their own statements, obviously believe in living just the way they have. But I think it's out of that unconscious defense of their own middle class way of life that the critics react to that so much.

Another element is that they feel that they have to defend themselves from the fear of death and dying. Mrs. Beale is eighty [in the film], and people have that kind of reaction to an aging person. As the daughter put it so well, when they were getting that kind of criticism: "Well, the thing is that they're afraid. They see my mother and she's eighty and she's that much closer to the Lord." People supposedly like the Lord, but they don't want to get too close to Him!

All of that stuff makes it all the more worthwhile for us to have made the film because we're getting into areas which illuminate certain areas of fear and the unknown which need to be illuminated.

JT: *Why do you think your subjects trust you, allow you to film these gutsy, revealing portraits?*

AM: That comes from our family. Both my parents were extremely trusting and unpretentious people who could make friends with anybody at any level of society. My mother knew Mrs. Roosevelt; at the same time, most of my mother's friends were as poor or poorer than she. She *wanted* to meet everybody.

She became a member of the American Jewish Congress, and so she had all of those friends, but many of them were somewhat narrow-minded, parochial. When she went on a tour with them to Israel, my mother spent all of her time meeting and talking with Arabs.

JT: *How did you come to film the Burks? Were you hired for this particular family film or did you choose the project?*

AM: We selected the family. The producers [Group W, Westinghouse Broadcasting Company] had it broken down so that they would end up with families representing different parts of the country and different socio-economic levels. But, by the time they had done five of the films, they discovered they hadn't done anyone in the South, and they hadn't done a lower income family or one in which significant people in the family were over sixty. So, those were the parameters. At that point, we talked to the producers. They told us that whatever family we chose would have to have those characteristics. But we were free to shoot anywhere in the South and pick any family. So, I went down to Georgia, and I found the family.

JT: *Why Georgia?*

AM: I knew a few people there. I knew somebody from Dalton, Georgia, and I knew a lawyer who through his experience with legal aid had connections with parole officers. I asked to get in touch with a parole officer in Dalton and he introduced me to the Burks.

JT: *What made you choose the Burks?*

AM: Well, for one thing, they were a tough luck family that no one cared that much about. They're likeable, but they've always gotten into trouble. There's always someone in jail at one time or another, but always for minor things because they can't afford to pay for a good lawyer. They don't get equal justice. I found out from the parole officer that apparently one of them had been in jail twice, and he was up on something for the third time. It would have meant twenty years in jail even for this minor offense because it was the third one. So, one of the other brothers took the rap. It's that kind of family; they are very, very devoted to one another, like my own family.

JT: *You got involved with the Beales through Lee Radziwill. You were initially going to do a film on Lee, weren't you?*

AM: Yes. It sounds funny that we would turn her down, but she introduced us to the Beales, and suddenly we began filming a great deal, even more than we were filming with Lee. Then about a week later, we looked at what we had. We cut it down to about an hour or so, and we showed her a rough cut. Lee saw that about 60 percent of the rough cut was the Beales. That wasn't the kind of film she wanted. But at the same time, we really weren't getting the kind of trust from Lee that we needed.

JT: *She didn't give you any financial help or support with the Beale film?*

AM: No. What happened was that we then gave this hour cut to her. She said she was going to see what she might do for television. Nothing happened for a whole year. Then we decided to just start our own film, on our own.

JT: *So you re-shot?*

AM: Yes. We didn't use any of that original material because it belonged to Lee. Then, when our film came out, she was quite angry. She thought we had used her material.

JT: *There are some very obvious parallels between the Burk and the Beale families—run-down houses with loads of junk strewn around, animals running wild, etc. Both families have been outcasts and subject to ridicule, but both are proud and there's lots of humor there, too. They're very closely knit, very interdependent families, with the mother at the center. Can you suggest why they might be so similar, coming as they do from different socio-economic and cultural levels?*

AM: By the same token, the differences are enormous. The Beales have travelled all over the world. Do you know that Edie says that she was engaged to Joe Kennedy, Jr.? At least, she had dates with him anyway, for sure.

JT: *With* The Burks of Georgia*, did you pretty much have total control over how the final film would look?*

AM: Right, but the producers did have some requirements; for example: playing it back to the family at the end. We really didn't want to do that. We wanted the film to stand on its own, and demanding that they see it and comment on it was kind of an awkward obtrusion.

The other thing we disagreed on were the subtitles. We didn't want any subtitles, because that's really a put-down of anybody.

JT: *You know, I saw the film without subtitles, and I had a problem understanding some of their dialogue. I could have used subtitles in spots.*

AM: Oh, it's a problem if you don't have subtitles. There are some things that you miss, but you don't miss much. You get the tone of the film, and that was what we were after. But they insisted on the subtitles. Speak to anyone in Georgia who saw it with subtitles, and they were really outraged because when you use subtitles, it looks as though those people are foreigners. It's a terrible put-down for them.

JT: *How would you compare the Beales' poverty with that of the Burks'?*

AM: The Beales' poverty was really not so necessary. They could sell that house, for example, and even for the land, they could get $100,000.

JT: *Where would they go? One might feel trapped in a situation like that.*

AM: Well, they could go almost anywhere. The two sons, who are not in the film, would actually have given them more money to get them out of there. But they would have had to live with more money, and that would have meant living in a different style. This style of life fitted them in many ways.

JT: *Do you think the Burks were ashamed of their poverty?*

AM: The Burks didn't regard it exactly as poverty. Poverty is a funny word. I learned so much about that word from having made that film. The writer of the series [Paul Wilkes] also wrote a book based on his experiences working on all six family films. And in this book, he devoted chapter to the Burk family. When we were with the Burks, they said there's one thing they didn't want and that was to be talked about as poor people. The writer was so insensitive. I saw the piece that appeared in his book. He used the words *poor* and *poverty* thirty-four times in talking about the Burks. I was outraged because he knew very well what their sensitivity was.

My own feeling about it is that there are different kinds of poverty. There's economic poverty; but John Dean, for example, has been described a number of times as a man of poverty of character. When we use the word poverty, it has all kinds of connotations, not just economic.

JT: *Did the Burks have a need for material wealth?*
AM: Sure, they'd like new automobiles. They have automobiles; I don't even have an automobile.

JT: *Did the Burks have any fantasy life at all? I noticed they enjoyed their television set. They even named a baby after* Baretta *star Robert Blake!*
AM: Right, but it was very hard to extract their visions of the world. Their opportunities are much more limited than what we're familiar with. Opportunities to travel. Opportunities to see other people.

JT: *And the Beales?*
AM: The Beales had a peculiar sense of time. They had an enormous interest in and preoccupation with their past.

JT: *Why do you think the Burks and the Beales walled themselves off from the rest of their communities?*
AM: I think a good deal of the psychology of both families is based on societal rejection. When you're rejected, your natural reaction is to exclude yourself from the people who reject you.

JT: *You've filmed two families who live in total disarray as far as most people are concerned. With your background in psychology, what can you say about people who live in this way? They're like pack rats.*
AM: For the Beales, I think it served a need to disgrace the rest of the family. Because they have this bitterness about the family not wanting them to be entertainers. In fact, the whole film is a kind of proud statement of who they are, but at the same time, there may be an element of revenge.

Mrs. Beale had quite a lot of talent as a singer, and all she wanted to do was sing. Her husband was very much against it; and the rest of the family was trying to keep up a front. They were in the Social Register.

JT: *Where did all their money go?*
AM: At the time of the Depression, Black Jack Bouvier, Jackie Onassis' father, allegedly invested a lot of money for the Beales and lost it. So,

they, in part, had to live without money. Which is true of the Burks, too. They're not skilled, they don't have jobs that pay much of anything. They work in the mills, but they're in the lowest paying jobs. And then, of course, they don't always show up for work, and they lose jobs, and they get drunk once in a while. There's very little money there.

JT: *The Burks' property looks like a junkyard.*
AM: It's hard for us to comprehend because our aspirations are so much higher, on every level. Everything falls apart at that level. If they're going to fix up the house, they'll probably cover the floor—which is partly dirt—with remnants of rugs. And that gets wet and dirty. One thing contributes to another. They don't have the money to pay for improvements; they don't know other styles of life; they have to use hand-me-downs and junk that they pick up here and there.

JT: *By keeping their adult children close by, didn't Mrs. Beale and Mrs. Burk maintain a certain level of immaturity in those children? Edie was socially fearful and used her mother as an excuse not to leave home. Don't you think Mrs. Burk fosters the same kind of dependence by having her children set up housekeeping within yards of her home?*
AM: There's a certain amount of independence that springs up in that kind of atmosphere. But when they have to settle things, it's a very autocratic kind of system. She's the one who arbitrates; the mother makes the most important decisions for the family.

JT: *How is Edie managing now that her mother has died?*
AM: I'm sure she misses her mother a lot, but she's putting together a nightclub act, and she's doing very well. Her voice is not anywhere near as good as her mother's, but there's a kind of sincerity that I think makes up for that.

JT: *Did your value judgments, if you made any, or your feelings about the Beales change during the filming?*
AM: They're always liberalized by that kind of experience. At the beginning, I was not as liberal about the way the Beales lived as I was after the film was finished.

JT: *When did your feelings change, specifically?*
AM: They changed all the way along, as we got to know them. For one thing, when we first began to film the Beales, we wondered whether they were competent or not. It was a very serious thing to find out. All that arose because of the Board of Health's attempt to get them evicted. If

they *were* judged to be incompetent, and we filmed them, then somebody, a member of the family—let's say, one of the sons who was against the film anyway—could initiate some kind of lawsuit against us, which they might win because the release that we would have from the Beales would be invalid.

JT: *Did you have them sign a release before you began?*

AM: No, but we actually looked into the matter as to whether they had ever been judged incompetent. We couldn't find any evidence of that. Now that I know them so much better . . . the Beales incompetent? I've rarely met such competent people!

JT: *How did you feel about the Burks? Were you really interested in them as people during the initial filming?*

AM: Yes. If anything, I was a little bit disappointed that we weren't able to get more of Mr. Burk because it was there if you could isolate him, but we didn't want to isolate him. When he's apart from the rest of the family, he's a rather different sort of person. He's as outspoken as Mrs. Burk. But when the two of them get together, then she takes over, and he sort of just disappears. At the very end, he has the last word when he says, "That's us!"

JT: *Were you bothered by their lifestyle?*

AM: It didn't bother me, one way or another, I think there's very little meaningful communication amongst them.

JT: *And between the Beales?*

AM: A lot of communication. That's where they were very different from the Burks. They really knew each other. They had a very strong hold on each other, a very strong love, a strong hate for each other, too; and it was all out in the open.

JT: *When you're about to film a new subject, someone who's unknown to you, do you find that beginning time to be the most exciting—when you're ferreting out all this information?*

AM: Yes, because we're filming it at exactly the same time. We don't do any research ahead of time.

JT: *What's the most fascinating thing for you about beginnings? Is it the mystery?*

AM: Yes, satisfying the curiosity. The first few days of filming are frequently the best of all, you get more good stuff in that first day or two because your energy is high. It's like having a romance with someone, meeting somebody for the first time on a train or wherever.

JT: *Is it because it's an unknown quantity? Some people don't feel that way at all. They're not in the least bit tantalized by the mystery of strangers. You're obviously interested in people and in digging out their stories.*

AM: That's right. And fascinated with this peculiar situation when you're with somebody who's really a stranger at that point, but you're more friendly with that person than you probably ever will be, because you're at the peak of curiosity. You know very well when you meet somebody for the first time, you ask questions, personal questions, and you give personal answers. After it's all over, you think, gee, I didn't even know that person, isn't that strange!

JT: *Some people are just the opposite, though, they withdraw at the beginning.*

AM: But they don't with us. They do trust us right away. And we respect them.

"Doco Direct" et al

JANE CASTLE/1986

THERE IS NOTHING worse than having to sit through a boring documentary. Deadweight commentary, tuneful music, and "talent" who walk from A to B, all have the effect of a good tranquiliser or perhaps a well trained sledgehammer. The first Maysles Brothers film I ever saw, at a Mike Rubbo seminar, was anything but boring.

Instead of feigning objectivity, the Maysles' camera saw as a real person would, objectively, reacting honestly to the scene. The characters of their films seemed to have more depth than those of any feature around at the time. They were real people, actually experiencing emotions rather than portraying them, as an actor, secondhand. Having begun their careers as psychologists, both Al and David used the filmmaking process as a means of indepth exploration into real characters. Instead of the action being choreographed for the camera, the filmmakers were totally at the mercy of their subjects. Instead of technical concerns taking precedence, the subject matter always came first and everything else would follow. In the hands of Al Maysles, the camera had suddenly been freed of its traditional aesthetic constraints and was now able to concentrate simply on what was happening in the frame.

The development of cinematic styles can often be linked to the parallel development of film technology. The Maysles' films grew out of a time when 16mm technology was rapidly being modernised; a crucial period which led to the radical evolution of the documentary film form. Cameras were becoming lighter, stock was becoming faster and lenses were going down to a lower stop than ever before. The step down from 35mm to 16mm meant that documentary filmmakers could now afford

---

From *Filmnews*, vol. 16, no. 3, June 1986. Reprinted by permission of the author.

to shoot at higher ratios, and a general change of attitude towards 16mm as a professional, rather than amateur medium meant that non feature filmmakers could be taken seriously at last.

Perhaps the most important development, however, was the advent of double system sound. All of a sudden the camera and recorder were able to move independently, never again to be linked by the archetypal umbilical cord (that is, until they invented the Betacam . . .). Filmmakers could now explore virtually any avenue which took their fancy with a system almost as portable as the filmmakers themselves.

The work of Al Maysles was once almost revolutionary. Today the style of documentary labelled "direct cinema" is taken for granted. Going to meet Al Maysles was a brainwave which came to me while contemplating a blizzard from a warm cafe on Fifth Avenue, New York. After their enthusiastic invitation to drop in, watch some tapes, and have a chat, my expectations were of a couple of slightly eccentric men pottering around amidst typical low budget chaos. Instead, however, the Maysles Brothers' penthouse was spacious, orderly, and alive with activity. The staff included production managers, editors, a publicist, a receptionist. While the two brothers still perform the key roles of "directors," cinematographer, and sound recordist, they now have a backup system to suit the seemingly constant flow of work.

What has changed is the type of films they make. People have to eat, and to eat they have to earn money, and the Maysles Brothers seem to have been able to find a satisfying compromise between making films and making money. Today they make films about artists, musicians, and composers—films assured of funding and distribution, primarily through the American networks.

A novel form of funding has been developed throughout the production of films about the conceptual artist, Christo. In order to finance his projects and the films that document them, Christo uses the money raised from the sale of sketches and plans to channel back into the productions.

They also make commercials. One of the Maysles' most regular clients is in fact the American Express Company which values the natural and spontaneous performances which result from their unobtrusive style of handheld camerawork. While the films they make are still out of the ordinary, Al admits that he would prefer to be making films like *Grey Gardens*—films which take risks with real people, founded on the basic principle "finding out."

Jane Castle

Q: *You have said that you had always wanted to try something new in documentary, even before you had started making films . . . You wanted to change the direction that documentary films were taking at the time . . .*
AM: Well, when I first got into it, I discovered as I started, that what I was trying to do was quite different from anybody else. But that's because my whole reason for making movies was different from even other documentary filmmakers. Here I was, going to Russia as a tourist and I thought—since I am going to be there for a month I should make use of the time, related to my own professional interest as a psychologist. I was a psychologist at that time. Psychologists, like anthropologists, like their observations to be untainted, and whatever they write down as observations should be rather pure. It seemed to me that if you film "directly"—without preparation, without a script, without much of any idea of what's coming up next, then the camera itself almost speaks as an instrument of objectivity. But, at the same time, the camera should be collecting as much information as possible, not only the images, but it should be the *moving* images and it should be the sound, but not just the sound that is edited in, but the sync sound. So, that's what I was aiming for the first time. I did pretty well, but because I didn't have sync sound we had to add some explanatory words to the film.

Q: *Do you think that when you go to make a film you're more of a psychologist/anthropologist than a filmmaker?*
AM: Well, you've seen *Grey Gardens*?

Q: *Yes.*
AM: That's anthropology. Nobody, no normal moviemaker in their right mind would leave the audience so open minded about these two women. You'd never otherwise expect to find that some people might prefer one woman over the other. It's so balanced, the view, and so open to interpretation.

Q: *Do you think that the "rough" style of* Grey Gardens *is perhaps misleading to the audience in terms of what they think is reality, whereas in fact the camera is influencing what is going on?*
AM: Well, does it?

Q: *Well, I think it does. Yet it's obviously hard to gauge and you could argue forever about it.*
AM: I don't think it does influence it that much. I've heard so many views on that. A good deal depends on who it is that's operating the camera, and who it is that is in the presence of the people. We don't even

use the word "director." Once you use that word, the relationship between you and the people that you're filming is an entirely different one. If you think of yourself as somebody who is controlling the scene, then you control it.

Q: *Do you think that your presence really affects the subject?*
AM: Well, you can either put them at ease, or you can make them nervous. You either control them or you don't. You either get them to like you or not to like you. You are either accepted by them or not accepted by them, by what you do, what you do with the factor of your presence. So the question as to how much you influence them is up to you. We see our influence as one where our rapport, as such, does not change the character or the situation or the people, but gains a kind of acceptance so they are still very recognisably what they are when we're not there.

I know all about the Hiesenberg Effect, which is a scientific notion where the introduction of any new element changes the notion of the whole thing. It's true, but it's what you make of it. Here I am, talking to you and having some effect on you, but you're going to walk out of here still pretty much the same person. And I will remain very much the same, so that in fact, if, instead of this discourse that we're having, you were filming me, I'd probably be pretty much the same. I don't believe that my opinion or beliefs would change very much.

Q: *Do you try to keep yourself as small as possible when you're filming?*
AM: I always prefer to film with available light than to add any light. I always prefer to handhold the camera than to use a tripod. We do a million and one things not to interfere with what's going on.

Q: *I see a link between the still photography of the sixties—people like Diane Arbus, and Friedlander, and a film like* Grey Gardens *where there's a psychological revelation rather than an aesthetic film. And also the audiences, in both cases, reacted quite strongly.*
AM: Actually, I found that got quite a different reaction from critics compared to audiences. Critics found that the film was completely exploitative. There were people in audiences who felt that way, but most people in audiences didn't feel that way at all. I think that maybe there's a connection between being a "critic" and a "cynic." To that extent cynicism prevailed amongst most critics but I don't think most people are cynical. When you saw it, you saw it with a group of students, do you remember their reaction to it?

Q: *Well they're all film students, but some of them thought that it was intrusive and exploitative. I think it's revealing, it's showing people bare, without any mask, but most people thought that it was fantastic.*
AM: We've been seeing a hundred years of dishonesty in movies, because the artifices of Hollywood are, I don't think it's too strong a word, "dishonest." I mean, I'm unusual that way. Most people go to see a Hollywood film and they don't think it's dishonest because it's "make believe." But no Hollywood film, no matter how well intended or how pure, can compare in its ethics with that of a documentary—an ethical documentary. There are some documentaries that are immoral in the way that they are propaganda. I think even propaganda in "cause" films is immoral. I consider advertising commercials as being really pure ethically because they present a very narrow point of view.

Q: *They're not pretending to be anything like truth?*
AM: Right. But when you make a film like *Grey Gardens*, you are either responsible or irresponsible, and that film demanded an incredible amount of responsibility on our part. I have no doubt that we fulfilled it. So we were rather astounded at the reaction of the critics. We couldn't imagine how in any way it was exploitative. We're not that sort of people. But, having read and heard the charges we began to figure out what basis there was to the claim. By any sense of the definition of exploitation, it means that somebody's getting hurt for someone else's benefit. Well I don't see how that film hurt them for our benefit. Indeed, I don't know how it hurt them at all.

Q: *Were they hurt by it—later?*
AM: In no way whatsoever. They adored the film themselves. So then I began to analyse what might be the motives for people making those charges and then I realised that even making a truthful film, a factual film on old age, will bring the charge of exploitation because people are so sensitive about the issue.

Q: *People might say "the subjects aren't responsible for what they're doing, so how can they respond, they don't know they're being made fun of."*
AM: Right, OK, but I don't see any element of ridicule or shame, so it has go be in the mind of the viewer. In fact, actually, I came to think after awhile that the film, more than any I know of, was (and this again goes back to my being a psychologist) a rather good test of one's emotional maturity.

Q: *The filmmakers?*

AM: No, the viewers. Of the viewers' emotional maturity. Psychologists have to suspect people seeing something and reacting with a great deal of over protection. It's a "highly suspectual" fact. I've been in audiences where psychologists get up saying "how exploitative" and how "offensive" it is. We're dealing with elements that get a very strong human response, and there are psychologists who in their practice are extremely protective—over protective. These women, as we know, are (as they say) very staunch characters—they don't need much protection. But people who are emotionally immature—who feel insecure about the delicate line, the balance between sanity and insanity, who feel insecure about getting old, who feel insecure about rich and poor, of their statue, of class statue—if they're insecure about all that, then this film becomes very disturbing, and so, being so disturbed about it, they'll either blame the women or the filmmakers. Being over protective of the women in order to protect this insecurity in themselves they will lash out at the moviemakers. One critic in New York, a rather well known one, ended her criticism by saying that the film never should have been made. "These are two women who obviously should never be filmed." There you really see the whole mechanism and its force, because it's not a genuine love or understanding of these women that precipitates that kind of reaction. If you're really protecting somebody you don't say that they should be banned or put out of sight.

Q: *Were there any criticisms of the film being too rough—the shooting style?*

AM: I don't see that at all. I don't know if your projector was jumping up and down—but if you had a good projector . . .

Q: *Well, compared to more "set up" documentaries, it's . . .*

AM: I think that from a so called "production" point of view it's got very steady shots and satisfactory lighting, good quality sound. The shots are well taken. It's as good a documentary as I know. It's much better than most. The colour is perfect. The lighting is very simple but . . .

Q: *But you have very long takes, and it's not shot to cut. Like so many documentaries are still being made. You might pan across to something and then pan back, instead of getting a closeup then getting a reverse.*

AM: Oh, we never think like that. That's not life. That's fake, that's Hollywood. The films that we've made over the last thirty years have helped to revolutionise Hollywood. Before we got into the act, Hollywood was never concerned about doing things on location. They were never concerned about making things real.

Q: *What sort of techniques do you think they've borrowed from you?*
AM: Well, they use and abuse, I would say. For example, we made a film in 1964 on the Beatles when they first came to America. The first Beatles film. Then a year later or whenever it was, *A Hard Days' Night* was made. *A Hard Days' Night* was thought to be a revolution in moviemaking. Did you ever see it? Because the camera was moving around, it was handheld, but that all came from seeing our film.

Q: *What other things did they borrow?*
AM: There was a whole television series, *The Monkees*, do you remember? Well, that whole series was based on having seen our film on the Beatles. I know because a couple of years later we got to know the producer, director, and author, and they said that they never would have done it if they hadn't seen our film, that it was an inspiration and that their whole style was based on it. But of course, it was all scripted and concocted. Through technical means they were trying to achieve the realism, which they achieved only as a kind of feeling. It's really just as fake as any other Hollywood film. There is a difference between doing something that's real which you can believe because it's actually taking place, uncontrolled and spontaneous. There's a difference between that and what has to be called make believe.

Q: *Do you think the audience can tell?*
AM: Not always, not always. It's kind of shocking. There were many people who walked out of *Salesman* and said, "Gee, who are those actors? They did a wonderful job!" The mainstream of the movie as an art form has been fiction and so that's what people know . . . they rarely go into a movie theatre and see a documentary film. So when they see one they still have the Hollywood mentality in their mind. It's a little bit difficult to erase it.

Q: *How do you think your shooting style has changed from the very beginning right up until today?*
AM: The technical part of filming, the equipment and all that stuff follows the intensity of your curiosity, the intense belief you have in recording reality. I can go with a camera that weighs ten times as much, that's bigger and a little bit noisier, but if I *had* to use it I'd still find a way of getting on film what I'm after. That camera right over there (points) is the one I used twenty years ago.

Q: *What's it called?*

AM: It's my own make, I built it myself. It looks rather strange, but actually in a way, in many ways, it's better than anything that's made today. The shoulder fits right in there and the camera's totally balanced so that you don't even have to hold the camera to be steady. You can drop your hands and it still just stays right on your shoulder.

Q: *Looking at* Grey Gardens, *you'd think that you couldn't do it without something light, like an SR or an Aaton.*

AM: I use the Aaton now because I like the magazines. They just flip in and out. But this is a much better designed camera because if you take your hands off the Aaton it would fall forward, and it's very tiring trying to hold it. And also to balance it. It's not balanced.

Q: *It sits on your shoulder, but . . .*

AM: It doesn't really sit on it, it sits in your hand. Believe me, I know. The SR is even worse that way, I think.

Q: *What about your approach to lighting, has that changed?*

AM: Well, obviously with the technology, it comes hand in hand. When you get faster stocks, you don't have to use as many lights. We now have faster stocks and faster lenses. I have a lens now, a zoom lens, that goes to T1.3. In those days it was 2.8. So that's almost three stops faster. The film that we use now is two or three times faster. So it's perhaps five or six stops more that we have to play with. It's great.

Q: *Do you use 94 much? And 91 as well?*

AM: Those are the films that we use of course. And now there's a new one—92. You may not even know about that.

Q: *How fast is that?*

AM: That's . . . it's about the same speed as the 94, but it's a little bit less grainy and a little better quality.

Q: *Do you think that there's more access to documentaries now because of TV?*

AM: Not yet. There will be, I think. Through home video. But then, unfortunately, people will be seeing *Gimme Shelter* or *Grey Gardens* or *Salesman*, or whatever, not on the screen but they'll be seeing it on this little box. Well, I suppose it's better than not seeing it at all.

Q: *What do you think about documentary filmmakers who use fixed, wide lenses for the whole film, for example* Demon Lover Diary *by Joel and Jeff De Mott, and* Death and the Singing Telegram *by Mark Ranoe?*

AM: Well, I'd have to see what they're doing to see how it's different from what we're doing. I can show you stuff that I've shot with wider lenses, I'm not averse to using wide angled lenses. There are certain things I like about a wide angled lens. As a tool for observation it again gives you much more information. If I'm sitting here filming you with a wide angled lens, I've got all this other stuff going on (in the background) at the same time and that's interesting, but then on the other hand I would like to zero in on your two eyes and if I got that close, right to here (close to face) to just your two eyes, I think the distortion would be too great and also it would be too much of an imposition.

Q: *You want to have a choice?*

AM: Yes. I have a new zoom lens now—I think I may be the first one to have it. It goes from 7mm to 58mm!

Q: *What sort of stop?*

AM: T2. The one that I use most of the time is the Cooke 9mm to 50mm. This is 7mm to 56mm! I can show you some stuff tomorrow where I used a 3.5mm lens.

Q: *Is that almost a fisheye lens?*

AM: Yes. No one uses it, but I'll show you some stuff that's incredible.

Q: *Do you use it for documentaries?*

AM: Yes, at certain times.

Q: *In what sort of situations?*

AM: Well, last year we made a movie of an orchestra conductor, Sergei Ozawa, he's a conductor of the Boston Symphony Orchestra. The film opens with a scene using a 300mm lens, and that's incredible. I got permission to film inside the orchestra itself, even during the performance, just walking around inside the orchestra. So I used an extremely wide angled lens. I would get right up on the podium *with* the conductor and with the camera right over the conductor's shoulder so that you could get the feel of his whole body as he's conducting, his face and also you can see the first violinist, Rudolph Circa, who was playing the piano at the time. It's only through that lens that you can get what it really feels like to be conducting. So, it works there very well, but if we're shooting the first scene with a wide angled lens having to be forty feet away from them it would be nothing at all. I don't believe in restricting yourself to one lens or another.

Q: *What do you feel about super 8 film and video?*

AM: Super 8 film I think you can forget about. I think super 8 video is going to be very interesting. I think what is going to happen eventually is that the amateur market, which is enormous now, is going to go through a phase where people go back, after a while, to still cameras because they gather so much information. For $10.00 you can shoot probably six hours, right? So having shot the six hours you just put it away and you never see it again because you don't want to go through it. It's too much to go through. The editing process is too difficult for the amateur.

Q: *What about for professional filmmakers? They can be really inconspicuous and it's very lightweight.*
AM: I haven't actually used it, but it's probably good enough for TV quality for many countries. I think it's wonderful. It's cheap and it's small. I think the quality is good enough for television. I don't know. Maybe the light has to be . . . I don't know what the parameters are.

Q: *Will you experiment with it?*
AM: Yes.

Real Artists Shoot "Real Farmers"

BROOKE COMER/1991

FROM A CRESCENDO of color in a sunset over the Missouri flatlands, to the earnest, weathered faces of farmers who talk frankly about their profession—involving God, family, weather, and politics—"Real Farmers" looks to join the many documentaries for which Maysles Films, founded twenty-eight years ago by principal Al Maysles and his late brother David, has received international acclaim. Director Henry Corra smiles, pleased with the work. The farmers aren't actors—they're real people. However, this is not another Maysles film—it is a TV commercial, using many of the same attitudes and techniques the filming team employs when making feature documentaries.

The Classic "Real Farmers" campaign brings *cinéma-vérité* to TV advertising. For years, fiction feature films have borrowed effects and ideas pioneered in commercials, and vice versa. And now a Du Pont campaign for Classic, a crop-enhancement product, employs a unique nonfiction film style to appeal to the target market: American farmers. "When Rumrill Hoyt first told us about this project, we were delighted. It was clear they knew how to use our company to its fullest potential," says Albert Maysles.

Maysles Films is known for its ability to put a cinematic finger on the pulse of human nature and bring those vital signs to the screen. Albert Maysles, who mans the camera on Maysles projects, has a specially customized Aaton, designed to fit the needs of the documentarian. Maysles, master of nonfiction cinematography, brought feature cinematographer Alex Gruszynski, to the "Classic Farmers" production for an unusual collaboration of talents.

From *American Cinematographer*, vol. 72, no. 7, July 1991. Reprinted by permission of *American Cinematographer*.

Gruszynski began his working relationship with Maysles in 1988, when the production company was hired to produce the HBO special *Sports Illustrated: The Making of the Swimsuit Issue*. Says the Warsaw native, "They were looking for someone to shoot the non-documentary, purely visual elements of the film." Although his father was in the film business in Poland, Gruszynski himself became attracted to the Scandanavian film scene, studying in Europe "because film schools there are more oriented to practical filmmaking, like independent craft schools."

Gruszynski was director of photography on *Almost You*, starring Brooke Adams; *Promised Land*, with Keifer Sutherland; *Tremors*, with Kevin Bacon; and *Brotherhood*, which Gruszynski calls "the *Easy Rider* the nineties."

Maysles and Gruszynski targeted their specific strengths to different aspects of the Classic Farmer production, creating a synergy that is evident in the extraordinary footage they brought back. Maysles put his eye to the viewfinder to capture the core of the message—the farmer's revelations, while Grusznynski covered the beauty shots—maximizing the impact of the rising and setting sun, across never ending cornfields under a vast midwestern sky.

Gruszynski is comfortable working with the Maysles team, which includes producer Doug Graves and editor Bruce Sinofsky. "Basically, they are documentarians," he points out. "They have a unique ability to capture the humanity and reality of any given situation. I knew on the Classic Farmers project that they wanted to capture more than the standard commercial images. For that reason, they're interested in cinematographers like me, who have a flexible background in both features and commercials. I set up the lighting, and shoot footage that captures a certain aesthetic, a backdrop, for Maysles' specialty, which is recording the human element in real people." He does not feel his own creative autonomy is threatened or compromised, but rather enhanced by the Maysles *Direct Cinema* approach.

Direct Cinema is a term coined by French film critic Louis Marcorelles to describe the Maysles' direct relationship with their subjects as they're filming them. It is most often associated with the Maysles' feature documentaries, which include *Grey Gardens* (1976), the controversial cult film that captures the haunting relationship between Edith Bouvier Beale and her daughter in their decaying East Hampton mansion; *Gimme Shelter* (1970), a film which has become a metaphor for the sixties; and many others.

When Maysles arrived in Missouri to film the Classic Farmers commercial he was armed with more than his crew and his Aaton. Co-filmmaker Henry Corra had already done considerable research during pre-production to understand how farmers perceive themselves. "Farmers consider themselves businessmen, entrepreneurs. They're taking risks, trying to get ahead," says Corra.

Before Maysles, Corra, and Gruszynski even arrived in Missouri, a good deal of important work was already done; a thorough search had been made to find the three "perfect" farmers to film for these commercials. Maysles' staff recruiters, Janice Isaac and Martha Wollner, "are highly specialized casting experts," says Maysles. They narrowed the search for three farmers from 400 to 150, and Corra made dozens of visits to Kansas and Missouri farms before deciding on the final three. "I'd look at them and think, 'Could this person be my friend?' I'd look for a charm, a sparkle, something winning about them, something meaningful," he explains. The final choices were reviewed with the agency, and the three filming subjects were selected.

The sparkle, or charm, that Maysles searches for is the core of the appeal that Classic Farmers generates. The natural warmth that comes across in the spots may seem easy to achieve, but there's much craft involved with eliciting and capturing this charm on film. One of the difficulties of *Direct Cinema* is that the essential tool—the camera—can be an intrusive obstacle in establishing the essential filmmaker-subject relationship if not handled properly.

Maysles follows its own "Seven Easy Rules on the Art of Real People Commercials," a commercial production primer which the film company published and shares with the community as part of its marketing campaign. Corra follows Rule Number Two: *It's all in the casting.* "Our goal was to honestly and truthfully capture a day in the life of a real farmer," Corra explains. "The media tend to glamorize farmers in our culture, or treat them as a kind of Hee-Haw parody, so understandably farmers are very sensitive as to how they are portrayed on television." The process had to be handled with great delicacy. Not only did the chosen farmers have to be affable, and insightful, they had to trust the filmmakers as well.

The Maysles Seven Rules are: 1. *Know Your Strategy*—No client's strategy exists without extensive research. Keep the key points in mind, and you'll know when to guide, and better yet, when to follow. 2. *It's All in the Casting*—When selecting real people, choose subjects who express themselves openly, and make sure they're people *you* like. Without the right people, your commercial is dead. 3. *Produce Small*—Put your subjects at ease by keeping their environment familiar; artificial settings and large amounts of equipment can intimidate anyone. 4. *Guide, Never Push*—Treat your subjects like friends and they'll return the favor; they'll come through with more substance and style than any script ever promised. 5. *Stay Spontaneous*—Every situation has more than one response so give your subjects the freedom to come up with their own. 6. *Be Patient*—Patience inspires confidence—and a confident subject is sure to give you the good stuff. Use time as your ally. 7. *Keep It Real*—Don't edit the life out of the spot once it's shot; leave room for the humor, the little comments and gestures that keep the real in a real people commercial.

Directing the action is always downplayed on a Maysles shoot and Classic Farmers was no exception. "Rather than waltzing onto their farms as directors, dictating their every move, the psychology was more that we were their guests for a day," says Corra. "The Du Pont client and Rumrill Hoyt's agency team understood this approach, and were crucial in helping us to create an environment where the production process became transparent." While filming, only the immediate filming team was present to allow the farmers to feel as relaxed and natural as possible. The agency creative staff and Du Pont client were stationed in Winnebagos away from the setup, watching the progress on a monitor, and communicating with director via a wireless communication system. In this way, the agency was able to provide its input without disturbing that crucial bond that was forming between Maysles, Corra, and the farmers.

The word "performance" doesn't exist on a Maysles shoot. "Our subjects never have to 'perform' for us," Corra observes. "We made it clear to the farmers that we only expected them to be themselves and allow us to tag along with them as they did their day's work." Everything we did was geared towards de-emphasizing the production process," adds Corra. "I recorded sound myself rather than use a sound man. Al hand-holds the camera rather than use a tripod. All this made for more mobility, more intimacy. This also allowed the farmers to move about freely wherever they chose. Neither the equipment nor the filmmakers dictated the actor. The farmers were allowed to just be themselves," says Corra.

"Another interesting thing that seemed to occur," continues Corra, "was, as the day wore on and the farmers watched Al and me lugging our equipment around, doing our craft, a kind of mutual respect seemed to develop. Hard work does not go unnoticed by these guys."

Albert Maysles, like many of his fellow documentarians, has always favored Aatons for, among other qualities, the portability factor. "If something unexpected came up, the camera is light enough so that I could run with it," Maysles notes.

Maysles' relationship with Aaton began over twenty years ago, when the camera's inventor and manufacturer, Jean-Pierre Beauviala, asked him to be a consultant on the design of Beauviala's first camera. Maysles recently met with Beauviala and joked with him about ignoring one of his original suggestions. "In the original camera, I very much wanted a magazine that holds eight hundred feet of film, rather than four hundred," Maysles explains. "It would give you twenty minutes instead of ten. This big improvement would add only two and a quarter inches to the length of the camera. I reminded Jean-Pierre that he hadn't yet come up with a camera that had eight-hundred-foot magazines, and he laughed and said it was worth reconsidering."

If he could design his dream Aaton, Maysles would customize it as he did with his own camera thirty years ago. At that time, he arranged for the eyepiece to come forward an inch or two, resulting in a camera that "balanced perfectly on my shoulder." To this day, no other such camera exists. "It was also the first movie camera with built-in battery power. Before that, the battery was on a belt, connected to the camera by cable," Maysles notes.

His self-designed camera was retired some fifteen years ago, but Maysles adapted some of his design innovations to his current Aaton. For example, he's installed a mirror and a light meter just above the front of the lens and "data rings" (which he was the first to conceive) along the barrel of the lens. "This way, while filming, I can measure the light and read the T stop and focus settings with my left eye open, without taking my right eye from the eyepiece," says Maysles. "So without interrupting the filming process I can instantaneously react and adapt to changes in light and focus."

At first Maysles and Corra were concerned that an over-emphasis on visuals might diminish the human aspect of the campaign. "When you shoot something for beauty's sake, the message is often lost. But, as it turned out, the agency wanted us to do what we do best—to unearth a real human spark, while Alex covered the beauty shots," said Maysles.

Gruszynski captured the beautiful times of day with a special Canon 150-600 zoom on his Aaton; the long lens was chosen "because you get these very phenomenal lines which are well suited to landscape photography." He observes that "it helps to compress the perspective, which creates stunning images that are completely different from the way the eye perceives them." He was also able to take advantage of the ability to shoot from distances of three hundred yards, which helped create poignant footage of the farmers from afar, off in their cornfields, richly adorned by magic-hour light.

With twelve magazines at hand each stock was always loaded, so that Maysles could adapt quickly to any light situation. Eastman Kodak's high speed 7296 caught the first moments of sunrise, and 7245 was used when the sun was bright enough, alternating occasionally with 7248. Maysles also chose 7292 and 7297 when shooting indoors.

With the shoot completed, the film processed and edited, Maysles and Corra are pleased with the results. The spontaneity they sought, without any contrivance, comes across on the screen. One of the keys to this, Corra believes, is to allow the conversation to unfold spontaneously, with little or no prescripted copy or questions. "I always have copious notes on possible ideas," he admits, "but I'll always let the conversation take its own natural course. It's a very open thing.

"The funny thing is," says Corra, "I was so taken by the love they show for their way of life that I've now decided to stake my life—my professional life, that is—on the subject." Corra has decided to make a feature documentary about the American Farmer, which will begin shooting in 1992. "The commercials took six days of shooting to come up with three great spots. It'll take several months for the documentary feature I intend to make on the life of a farm family."

The Making of Concert of Wills: Making the Getty Center

ANN HASSETT/1997

OCTOBER 29, 1997: In the blazing heat that late fall brings to Los Angeles, hundreds of construction workers are working feverishly to complete the $1 billion Getty Center for its long-awaited opening on December 16. And three thousand miles away, in a cold, dark editing room, three filmmakers fix their eyes on an Avid screen, racing to complete a film documenting the twelve-year creation and building of what is considered the most expensive American cultural project since construction of the Metropolitan Museum of Art in New York in the 1870s.

"I live in fear about what we're doing—we'll get our last architectural shots the day before the film is finished. It's going to be a miracle if it works!" said exhausted but exhilarated filmmaker Susan Froemke.

The Getty Center is a 110-acre cultural complex on a spectacular site overlooking the city of Los Angeles. Six buildings—more than one million square feet—house the Getty Museum and five related art institutions: the Getty Grant Program for the Visual Arts; the Getty Research Institute for the History of Art and the Humanities; the Getty Conservation Institute; the Getty Information Institute; and the Getty Education Institute for the Arts.

Fourteen years ago, as the project was being conceived, Getty executives decided to include in their plans the documentation on film of the entire process: conception, design, and building. "We wanted to document the process for historians. Hard as it is to believe now, in 1982 we didn't know when it would start, what it would become, when it would finish, or what the process would be," said Gloria Gerace, a Project

---

From *International Documentary*, vol. 16, no. 12, December 1997. Reprinted by permission of the author.

Manager of the Building Program. "At first we thought we would just shoot archival footage and maybe later there would be a film. We hired the Maysles because we saw in the Christo films (*Christo's Valley Curtain*, 1974; *Running Fence*, 1978; *Islands*, 1986; *Christo in Paris*, 1990) that they had captured a process, and we liked the idea of a film about how something was made. They were quality filmmakers, they were willing to come on board to a project that had no parameters . . . basically, they were willing to come on an adventure."

The adventure began in May, 1985—and twelve years later, on December 6, 1997, the IDA will host the first public screening of *Concert of Wills: Making the Getty Center*, a film by Susan Froemke, Bob Eisenhardt, and Albert Maysles. The film will air on KCET Los Angeles, Wednesday, December 17, at 8:00 P.M.

I wanted the filmmakers to share with IDA members a little about their experience. With twenty-three days (including weekends) left to finish the film, Susan, Bob, and Al took a rare break and reflected on the dozen years they've worked on this film.

SUSAN FROEMKE: In June of '85, we traveled with Getty Executives on a research trip to Italy—that was our first shoot. Our final shoot will be on November 20, 1997.

BOB EISENHARDT: After twelve years of filming, the very last shot will go in the day before the film goes to the Getty. [After a moment of astonished silence, all three broke into laughter.]

ALBERT MAYSLES: I mean, What's the rush?

ANN HASSETT: *What did the Getty have in mind for you to film?*

FROEMKE: Gloria Gerace called and said they thought it would be a good idea to document the process. They didn't know what else they wanted—they had seen the Christo films we had made and they loved them, but they weren't sure they wanted *a* film . . . they just wanted *film*. So for two years, we were just creating an archive.

EISENHARDT: In the twelve years, we've shot 150 hours of archival film.

HASSETT: *And when did the archival footage start to become a film?*

FROEMKE: Many times during these twelve—almost thirteen—years, Bob and I have stopped to analyze the footage and in early 1993, we began to see that there was a film that could be made. Two years ago we were asked to write a film proposal, and the project was green-lighted. Around October of '96, we thought we could even make a Maysles film. [Again, all three burst into laughter.]

FROEMKE: People will assume that since it's a film *about* the Getty, *commissioned* by the Getty, that it'll be a puff piece or a corporate film. In fact, it's a very real film, and that's what the Getty always wanted. They're very respectful of artists and the artistic process. Once it was decided that we would make a film, and not just shoot archival footage, they made it clear that they wanted viewers to see the real architectural and artistic debates, to understand the amazing process that created the Getty Center.

MAYSLES: What we have made is a documentary. I wonder if any of that language—documentary, corporate film—is valid anymore. We made a *real* film: everything in the film is authentic. It's not dramatized—it's the way it was. No attempt was made to make it different from what really happened. We had the privilege of being with some very interesting people when they were doing some very interesting things. Totally on our own—with more access—we might have gone deeper and further into the human elements—but the Getty wanted a film about the *Center.* There has never been a film about the process of making architecture like this. This is a film that dispels the "burst of inspiration" notion and all the bull about the artistic process.

HASSETT: *Since the Getty controlled when and what you could film, did access ever become a problem?*

EISENHARDT: We often longed for more access, but what the Getty gave us was remarkable. They provided us with an invitation to join them in the twelve years of extraordinary artistic debate—we saw things we didn't expect to see. You'll be surprised when you see the film.

FROEMKE: When you watch intelligent people who are not afraid to fight for their artistic points of view and you see how through this process the shape of the Center, the architecture, expresses these concerns, it's a view from the inside that is—as Al says—a privilege.

MAYSLES: In the early days, we would start filming, say at a meeting, and we would see a story line emerge, and we always wanted to stay and complete that story. But sometimes it was six months before we could come back, so we devised a system of what we called "updates." It's a little different from your usual interview, and it turned out to be an important—and very human—storytelling device.

HASSETT: *Everyone talks about the Getty's millions: did they give you millions to make this film?*

FROEMKE: The Getty is very careful about controlling how money is being spent—they're not throwing it around. You submit a budget and they expect you to stay right on budget. There are no overages. The hundreds of millions you hear about really went into the building of the building. We were their luxury, and the more the building cost, the tighter our budget became.

HASSETT: *You've shot an enormous amount of footage. How did you begin the editing process?*

EISENHARDT: We began going though the footage, editing the scenes, cutting together everything we thought had value. We took 150 hours down to 60 hours of selects. Out of that, it was a lot easier to see what stories were most important and what scenes best described the story points. Then, Phil Shane and I began to cut those scenes and at they same time, we began to structure the film. We showed Gloria seventeen hours of super selects. Out of that process, we created a four-hour film. That was six months ago.

FROEMKE: The last six months have been absolutely frenetic. Right now, we're living the finish. It's so difficult—all we can think about is that we have got to lock the film—we desperately want another few weeks! It's the most exhausting but the most thrilling . . . doing the music and seeing the titles—we're locking the picture before we even go out for our last shoot. We're terrified, but we're willing to take the risk because we want these last shots so much.

HASSETT: *As the twelve years come to a close, have you arrived at any conclusions about this experience and the film?*

MAYSLES: You know, I've been obsessing for a year or two, that there is so little on TV that is uplifting. And in this particular film, you are with one of the world's leading architects, along with one of the world's leading museum directors, and the viewer gets to be present with these remarkable minds as they solve problems. This film doesn't tell you what it was like—it *is* what *is*, and that's an important distinction—it's an inspiration. And when you see the film, you will be inspired.

Man of the People

BROOKE COMER/1998

IT CAN BE argued that no filmmaker has come closer to capturing the real lives of everyday people than Albert Maysles. His ability to bridge the barrier between documentarian and subject is not a learned skill or technique; rather, it is his keen interest in the lives of ordinary people that leads him to discover their extraordinary qualities.

It should come as no surprise to those who know Maysles' work that the "father of direct cinema" has been chosen by the American Society of Cinematographers to receive the organization's 1997 President's Award. Along with his filmmaking partners—his brother, David, Charlotte Zwerin, and Susan Froemke—Maysles produced a total of fifteen films; their output included the seminal documentary *Salesman* (1967), as well as fascinating pictures on such diverse subjects as the Rolling Stones (*Gimme Shelter*, 1970); an eccentric mother and daughter in their decaying East Hampton home (*Grey Gardens*, 1976); and the artist Christo (*Running Fence*, 1978, and *Islands*, 1986). Albert has also collaborated with several other giants of the documentary genre, such as Richard Leacock, D. A. Pennebaker, and Bob Drew. Maysles will be honored at the 12th Annual ASC Awards event, to be held on March 8 at the Century Plaza Hotel in Los Angeles.

"Al Maysles is an extraordinary man," says ASC member Conrad Hall, who used "real people" scenes shot by Maysles to amplify his much-lauded cinematography in the film *Searching for Bobby Fischer.* "He is one of the few people I'd call a complete filmmaker."

ASC President Owen Roizman agrees, stating, "We don't give this prize simply for cinematography; it's given to someone who's made a unique

From *American Cinematographer*, vol. 79, no. 1, January 1998. Reprinted by permission of *American Cinematographer* contribution to the art of filmmaking. I am delighted that Al Maysles was chosen this year, because his films include some of the most unique, interesting, and innovative works I have ever seen. He is truly a credit to our profession, and he is known and loved by many, many people."

Silence fed Maysles' passion for art. "As a child, I didn't speak," he explains. "It wasn't a deformity, I was just extremely quiet. No one knew if I was bright or dumb, so I had to repeat kindergarten. But my personality made me an avid listener, which served me very well."

He was seven years old when he bought his first still camera at a hardware store: a thirty-five-cent Univex, made of bakelite and small enough to fit into the palm of his hand. His first subjects were members of his family; his father, a postal clerk, and his mother, a schoolteacher, were Russian immigrants. His brother, David, would later become his filmic collaborator, and his sister, Barbara, pursued a career as an artist.

The young Maysles was able to capture the unique spirit of his family even in his earliest photographs, evoking a sense of reality and humanity which would become a trademark of his later documentary work. "I think photographers, like writers, consciously or unconsciously tend to go back to their childhood and use their early images and experiences," the filmmaker offers. "Perhaps one reason why books are so often more powerful than their translation to film is that during the filming process, [the material] inevitably gets detached from the author's original artistic cravings."

By the time he was ten years old, Maysles discovered *Popular Mechanics* magazine. Inspired by an article entitled "How To Build Your Own Enlarger," the young photographer made one of his own, using the lens of a Voigtlander Bessa camera he had purchased. But after several years without a proper still camera, he decided to suspend his burgeoning career. "I was extremely ambitious, and I felt that until I had a Leica, I'd put everything on hold."

In his early twenties, Maysles was teaching psychology as a graduate student at Boston University, and working as a research assistant at a mental hospital. He decided to use his summer vacation to motorcycle all over Europe with a Leica borrowed from a friend. It was during this journey that he shot what he describes as his "first really professional photographs."

Maysles and his requisite Leica crossed the Atlantic again the next summer, en route to Russia, where the budding artist shot still photographs inside Russian mental hospitals. He recalls, "I chose that particular subject because I was interested in what was happening in Russia, but

I wanted to get away from the solely political approach everyone else was taking, with everything going on in the Kremlin, but nothing close to ordinary people."

Before he left for Russia, however, *Life* magazine turned down Maysles' pitch to do a photo essay on Russian mental hospitals—not because the publication was adverse to the idea, but because its editors couldn't give the photographer the advance cash necessary to pay his way. As he walked out of the Time-Life building, Maysles looked up at a sign that said "CBS," and decided to give television a try. His cold call was a success; Maysles was ushered in to meet the head of the CBS news department, who loaned him a 16mm Keystone movie camera and agreed to pay one dollar for every foot of his film the network used, with the understanding that Maysles would retain the rights to all of the film he shot.

The wind-up Keystone posed various challenges; the camera was "so amateurish," says Maysles, "that you couldn't even focus the lens. It was no Bolex, and it was certainly no Bell & Howell. But the f2.5 lens allowed me to shoot in the dark conditions often found indoors."

CBS paid Maysles fourteen dollars for the fourteen feet of footage they eventually aired. The youthful cameraman used his remaining material to create his first formal documentary, entitled *Psychiatry in Russia.* He had hoped to sell the finished film to NBC, "but the program director at the network looked at it and turned the project down because it didn't have the kind of 'freak value' he was looking for," Maysles remembers. Instead, *Psychiatry in Russia* was scheduled to air on Boston's PBS station, WGBH.

As Maysles edited his project in a makeshift room in a warehouse across the street from WGBH, he was approached by Smith, Kline, and French, a pharmaceutical company that offered the filmmaker $2,500 for the right to make fifty prints of the film for their own use. "They'd heard about my project via the grapevine," Maysles says, "and thought the film would be of interest to American psychiatrists." *Psychiatry in Russia* ended up paying his traveling expenses after all.

Maysles was returning from his second trip to Russia, this time on a motor scooter, when he had a memorable stopover in England. His brother, David, had finished his service in the army and was working as a production assistant on *The Prince and the Showgirl* at Pinewood Studios in England. Maysles remembers arriving at Pinewood on his motor scooter and being ushered into Marilyn Monroe's dressing room. "She wanted to meet me because she heard I'd been visiting mental hospitals," Maysles recalls. "She was very interested in psychology, and the questions she asked me were rather clever; she even wanted to know if I'd ever been psychoanalyzed." He had not.

Encouraged by his sudden success as a documentary filmmaker, Maysles stopped teaching and spent another summer on a trip with his brother, traveling by motorcycle from Munich to Moscow. During their travels, they happened upon a student revolution in Poland, which they filmed. The footage later aired on NBC, accompanied by Chet Huntley's narration.

Maysles' nascent career took a crucial turn when he met documentarian D. A. Pennebaker, whose work would eventually include the 1965 Bob Dylan portrait *Don't Look Back* and the seminal concert chronicle *Monterey Pop*. When David Maysles showed Pennebaker *Psychiatry in Russia*, the latter deemed it the best first film he'd ever seen. Pennebaker then introduced the elder Maysles brother to Bob Drew and Richard Leacock, who were about to push the envelope of documentary filmmaking with a distinctly American twist on the French *cinéma-vérité* style.

The American approach "made you feel you were really there, as an observer behind the scenes," says Maysles, who prefers the term "direct cinema" when referring to his work with his brother. "Unlike the French version, nothing was staged. More than ever, viewers could feel what it was like to be in the shoes of the subjects."

Together, Leacock, Drew, Maysles, and Pennebaker made the film *Primary*, an insightful look at the 1959 Democratic primary campaign between John F. Kennedy and Hubert Humphrey. The film was Maysles' first sync-sound collaboration, and the filmmaker remembers a particular shot of John and Jackie Kennedy as they entered an auditorium and walked down an aisle through a crowd: "I stayed right with them. Pennebaker handed me a wide-angle lens, which was very daring back then, and I kept the camera over the back of John Kennedy's head as I followed him." The wide angle allowed Maysles to capture the crowds looking up at Kennedy as he moved through them. "I couldn't see what I was shooting, but I knew that the camera was seeing what Kennedy was experiencing."

Documentary filmmaking was forever changed after Drew and his fellow filmmakers received a grant from Time-Life to design a battery-operated double-system sync camera that did not require an umbilical cable link-up to the sound recorder. "For the first time, we were using sync-sound cameras portably," says Maysles. "The basic idea was really revolutionary, because we could suddenly get so much closer to reality without imposing on it. The new camera was created from parts of several existing models; it was part Auricon, and the tape recorder was a Perfectone. The speed of both the camera and sound recorder was governed independently by a highly accurate electronic tuning-fork mechanism in each device.

"Zoom lenses also allowed us a lot of flexibility, so we could be near or far without moving around and distracting people," he continues. "Suddenly, the camera became a servant to reality rather than a device used to manipulate it. Scenes filmed as they evolved could be as dramatic as in a preconceived film, but more compelling and engaging. Things that pass as totally credible in a documentary, because they are real, would seem all too implausible in a concocted, scripted feature film."

One of the Maysles' most commercial films was *What's Happening! The Beatles in the U.S.A.* (later retitled *The Beatles: The First U.S. Visit*). Albert didn't even know who the Beatles were when he got a call from Granada Television in England informing him that the Fab Four would be arriving at New York's Idlewild (later JFK) Airport in a few hours. Fortunately, his brother David did, so when the Maysles were asked if they would make a film of the band's arrival in America, the answer was a quick "Yes." They were soon rushing to the airport to film the band coming off the plane. Maysles, reports, "We stayed with them night and day, so we were able to capture exactly what they were going through in the thick of it, something that would have been impossible in a planned scene for a film."

Unfortunately, the brothers were unable to capitalize on their nonfiction feature about the famous quartet after completing the film in 1964. Maysles explains, "Even though Columbia Pictures offered us a million dollars for the film, we weren't allowed to show it in movie theaters because we couldn't get a release from the Beatles. The band had a project on their schedule called *A Hard Day's Night* which they were about to make, and United Artists didn't want another film to eclipse theirs, especially since theirs would be a fictional replica of ours." A shorter version of *What's Happening! The Beatles in the U.S.A.* did have one run on CBS, but only with the provision that actress Carol Burnett, whose own show's ratings were lagging, narrate the picture.

This would not be the last of Maysles' films to be withheld from audiences. One of his most famous works, *Salesman*, a portrait of four door-to-door bible salesmen, languished for twenty-five years before it was aired on the PBS television program POV. Maysles observes, "It's particularly ironic that *Salesman* aired on POV because we've always stressed that only by distancing oneself from a 'point of view' do you remain open to discovering the unanticipated."

Maysles himself had worked as a salesman during high school to pay his tuition through college, peddling Fuller brushes and then encyclopedias door-to-door. "On my first time out, I got so nervous after I knocked on the door that I couldn't remember my sales pitch. But the woman who let me in must have sympathized, because she bought a set of encyclopedias. Later, I came to realize that one of the most important aspects of filmmaking is liking, believing, and trusting in people. Making documentaries is such an odd thing; what you're doing, in a way, is just a surface phenomenon, because you're filming only what can appear before you—and yet, what you're thinking is so important. As Albert Fzent-Gyorgi put it, 'Discovery consists of seeing what everybody has seen and thinking what nobody has thought.'

"The process of discovery is an exciting adventure which becomes even more intense because you're recording your experience at the same time," he adds. "The experience is really of the other person you're filming, so you're also performing a service for them and for your audience, who may for the first time in their lives feel precisely what it's like to be a coal miner, a daughter, a salesman, a dying person, to be loved or hated. It's limitless."

Maysles credits much of his filmmaking success to his brother, David. "We couldn't have made all of those films without each other," he says. "There was no sibling rivalry because we weren't in competitive roles. We worked as a filming team, with me behind the camera. David also took control of postproduction, and we both found stories and made decisions. But above all, we held ourselves subservient to our subjects and the quality of our films."

In describing this symbiotic relationship, Maysles again recalls the motorcycle trip that the brothers took through Eastern Europe in 1957. "We were on back roads traveling an exhausting 200 to 300 miles a day, driving in turns. When one of us got tired, he'd move to the rear seat and rest his head on the shoulder of the driver and put his arms around the driver's waist. The driver then steered with one hand on the handlebar and the other clasping his brother's hands tightly together so that if he dozed, he wouldn't fall off. That's the image I have of how we worked together."

The siblings found their parents to be key inspirations. Albert explains, "My mother was a schoolteacher who took steps to better her life even as an immigrant child; she found a philanthropist, a Mrs. Storrow, whose dream was to inspire immigrant children, many of Jewish and Italian parents. She had a house by the ocean where the children would come to study music and art, and get exposure to a side of life they'd otherwise never have known."My father was a postal clerk, which is not a glamorous career, but he symbolized the greatness of the common man. Because of him, we usually chose to explore the lives of ordinary people instead of celebrities, which is exactly what we did in *Salesman*. Paul, the main subject in that film, turned out to be a lot like my father. They both had characters that touched the heart and soul.

The intensely personal direction that Maysles' films take "can seem strange to some people," he admits, "because secrets are revealed that wouldn't normally be disclosed. The more revealing and personal a film is, the more open you are to the charge of being intrusive. But according to those who know, such as health-care experts, it's healthier to disclose things than to keep secrets. A well-made documentary film serves the purpose of helping people disclose things they hold inside—as opposed to the tasteless displays on a Geraldo-type of show, which I deplore. "I can see the courage and the payoff on those occasions when people let loose their troubles, take a chance and expose their vulnerabilities. It's the talent and the responsibility of the filmmaker to discern an act of courage from an act of foolishness."

When Maysles was a child, he spent as much time at the Brookline, Massachusetts library as he did in his homemade darkroom. He remembers, "I'll never forget the day I found a book called *Architects of Ideas: Great Theories of Mankind*, which included Copernicus, Marx, Freud, and Einstein. The introduction asked the question 'What is the purpose of life?' As an answer, the piece described the flight of a bird, which comes up over the horizon. You observe it, it's beautiful, then it flies away and disappears over the horizon—to where, no one knows."

When David Maysles died in 1987, Albert spoke at his memorial service, and he recalled that description of life as symbolized in the flight of the bird. "When we all walked out of the chapel in South Hampton, a very strange thing happened. Just at that moment, an enormous flight of birds crossed the sky."

Coincidences have not governed Maysles' life, but enough have cropped up to astound him. "As Edie Bouvier in *Grey Gardens* says, 'Everything is time and place,' and I've been lucky to be at the right place at the right time." As an example, he revisits the moment when he and his brother met Pennebaker, who in turn introduced them to Richard Leacock and Bob Drew, with whom Albert launched his career: "I suppose I've I been fortunate enough to be better served by chance than control, by reality more than fiction, by a confidence in life whichever way it goes."

Albert Maysles: All You Need Is Love

JACKSON PELLOW/1999

ALBERT MAYSLES began his career in the early 1960s by teaming up with D. A. Pennebaker and Richard Leacock to make *Primary*—a close-up of the Wisconsin election between Senators Hubert Humphrey and John F. Kennedy.

Collaborating with brother David (who recorded sound), the Maysles Brothers forged a distinct style of documentary known as "direct cinema." Maysles films' were characterised by a fly-on-the-wall style that initially troubled audiences because their films rarely offered a directorial point of view.

This style projected a sense of timelessness, an independent record of life rather than an interpretation. They concentrated on character-driven works (a form rarely seen today) in favour of narrative.

After *Primary*, the Maysles brothers filmed a score of celebrity subjects-Mick Jagger in *Gimme Shelter* (1969), The Beatles in *What's Happening! The Beatles in the U.S.A.* (1964), and Christo in *Christo's Valley Curtain* (1974). But it was their touching insight into the lives of ordinary Americans—the Beales in *Grey Gardens* (1976) and the door-to-door Bible sellers in *Salesman* (1968)—for which they will be remembered the most.

Jackson Pellow caught up with Albert Maysles for a sneak preview of the issues he will raise when he comes to Adelaide in November for the Australian International Documentary Conference.

IF: *What do you think of the argument that when you add something (a camera and filmmaker for example) to a scenario it changes the whole situation?*

From *IF: Independent Filmmakers*, issue 19, November 1999. Reprinted by permission of IF Media.

AM: From my experience, that depends on the person making the film. You can end up with a film devoid of any emotion, even though there's plenty of emotion going on, because the filmmaker doesn't have it in him or her.

IF: *So it's very much up to the filmmaker, the way they behave and react that will lead to the subjects giving a lot of themselves?*

AM: Yeah. If the cameraman or camerawoman lacks the empathy and what I call the "gaze," that is how they look at the person they're filming, then it can come out cold.

IF: *You talk about this idea of the "gaze," yet your subjects very rarely acknowledge your presence. How do you reconcile that you're gazing at them, but they're not staring back at you?*

AM: Well, I'm referring to the initial contact. When you first see somebody, there's an exchange of looks, and if your gaze is appropriate and has this quality of empathy then you can establish immediate trust. Then things can continue to go on as they were.

IF: *I'm interested to get your take on the idea of the "seams" of the film. In your film* Salesman, *when the characters are in their motel room, the audience catches a glimpse of you and your camera and lights in the bathroom mirror. One gets a hint at the filmmaking process, the seams of the process are exposed. Was that shot deliberately left in?*

AM: No. It may have even intruded on the scene. It was there and we just needed the continuity of the shot. It wasn't intentional. Well, maybe this is part of the strength and beauty of documentary films. Because you're seeking a certain authenticity, there are things that the camera picks up that are significant and which, even after you've made the film, you may not have noticed.

I showed *Salesman* to a group of high school kids . . . One of the women got up and talked about the women in the film—she talked about how it was so intensely depressing for her to see in the women, what the role of women is in American society.

IF: *The women who were getting sold the bibles or the wives of the salesman back home?*

AM: Both. It was something she had never seen in a film before, and it so impressed me that we had caught something of feminist recognition. And until that moment we hadn't noticed it, and we got it just right. And we got it just right partly because it wasn't our deliberate intention.

IF: *Your first profession was as a psychologist . . . Has that helped you with your filmmaking, understanding the idea of the gaze and getting people to open up?*

AM: Well, I was able to put it into those words from having read an article that my wife (a family therapist) published. When I saw the two words (gaze and empathy), I immediately said, Ah huh, that's what it's all about. In the article she was explaining that too many psychotherapists know all the stuff by the book, but they don't have the gaze and empathy, so the quality of their work suffers. It would seem that by having those kinds of strong connections with the people you're filming, you're influencing things.

The thing that gives you fairness and objectivity is love. The love that you give to your subjects and your concern for the authenticity of what you're getting. They say that love is blinding . . . Oh no. It is love that opens up your mind so that you see all sides of things.

One of the destructive forces in journalism and so many documentary films is the good guy, bad guy approach. We have a tv series in America called *Point of View*. Nothing could be more destructive to the loving process, which gives you the truth and the subjectivity at the same time. Nothing could be more destructive than the good guy, bad guy, the point of view approach because everything is forced into a point of view, so you get to be one sided. They've tyrannised by trying to oversimplify things.

IF: *So by not stating your point of view the film can be open to a more complex reading?*

AM: That's right. A quotation I find so interesting is, "The essence of tyranny is the denial of complexity." So when you see a film like *Salesman*, oh it is so complex . . . It is such a human portrayal.

IF: *It's showing these salesmen as these people who have hearts and emotions, who are passionate.*

AM: Well, yes and no. The odd thing is that there is very little love expressed in the film. I'd say there's more love between the filmmakers and all the subjects in the film than what's expressed between the salesmen. I mean these guys are out to sell something; they can't let their humanity get in the way of it.

IF: *Would you describe the relationship between a documentary maker and their subject in terms of love?*

AM: Yep, love, acceptance, not trying to oversimplify. A word that I would use equally is taking the whole matter as a process of discovery. Not inventing characters, or making them any different from what they are, no better, no worse, no different.

IF: *And when can that love relationship turn to exploitation, do you think?*
AM: Very interesting question. With our film *Grey Gardens*, the question of exploitation has come up most seriously. There are some subjects, some people that are more vulnerable than others and therefore the question of exploitation comes up more readily, to the point where you have to ask, is it just in the nature of some people and certain situations that there's no way to depict them without exploiting. If you accept that, and I *don't*, that means that there are some people that you just shouldn't film.

IF: *I see, it becomes ridiculous to put up restrictions. When does it stop.*
AM: I guess the short version of my answer is love. If you really love those people, you can't exploit them. But in America we have television shows that are totally exploitative.

IF: *For someone who has shot so many hours of film, how did [your] experimentation [with video] go?*
AM: I'm beginning to use it now. Not for everything necessarily, but who knows, maybe I will end up using just video cameras. There are things that you can get with video cameras that you can't get otherwise.

IF: *What, for example?*
AM: Forty years ago I'm in Cuba. I was spending some time with Fidel Castro and Che Guevara. Fidel says he's going to go to the Chinese embassy that evening, there's a party, so I tag along. Throughout the evening I was standing shoulder to shoulder with Fidel, and of course I haven't brought my big camera, that would be too much. Anyway we're chatting, and a messenger comes running in and hands him a telegram and he opens the telegram and he turns to me and he says, "Shall I translate it for you?" He knows that I don't speak Spanish and I said, "Well please do,"—and at this point I would of had my little video camera at my chest and I would have gotten the whole thing I'm sure—and he translates it and it says: "Your State Department has just broken off relations with Cuba." And I missed it—because I didn't have a video camera.

IF: *What I found fascinating about* Salesman *were the moments that weren't narrative driven, purely character revealing, those little moments where you see the salesman singing in the car while he is driving along. You don't see that a lot these days in documentaries, they're mostly narrative driven. Why do you think there are fewer films now that are character studies?*

AM: Even documentary filmmakers, writers of books for example, publishers . . . everybody is getting more and more nervous about making sales of their product. So they're taking a safer course. Some things aren't narrative; they don't lend themselves to narrative and yet they can make excellent films. Forcing a narrative upon a documentary when it isn't there is very dangerous.

Stories That Tell Themselves

ANNE S. LEWIS/2000

ALBERT MAYSLES is one of the kahunas of *cinéma-vérité*—or, as he prefers, "direct cinema"—documentary making. In forty-five years behind the camera, he has made over twenty films, along with his brother David (until his death in 1987), including *Salesman* (1969), about a door-to-door Bible salesman (selected by the Library of Congress in 1992 as one of the twenty-five best American films ever made), *Gimme Shelter* (1970), about the violent turn of a Rolling Stones concert at Altamont Speedway, and *Grey Gardens* (1975), about Edith Bouvier Beale and Edith B. Beale Jr., former socialite mother-and-daughter cousins of Jackie O, who lived contentedly in flea-infested decrepitude in the Hamptons. A former psychologist whose camerawork has been hailed, and utilized, by no less than Jean-Luc Godard, Maysles is still making films at seventy-three. And still waxing reverential about the truths that reveal themselves without any prompting whatsoever, stories that simply tell themselves, in front of a hand-held camera and cable-free sound recorder—the technology he pioneered in the Sixties and which revolutionized documentary making. He's still unapologetically convinced that subjectivity and point of view have no place in a documentary. Don't even ask what he thinks about seemingly indispensable documentary tools like the interview or voiceover. Maysles has little use for the *gotcha!*, the in-the-subject's-face style of a Michael Moore, or the blur-the-line-between-fact-and fiction techniques of an Errol Morris. For Maysles, even fellow *cinéma-vérité* heavy Frederick Wiseman puts too much of himself into his films—he hasn't been able to watch a Wiseman film since that first, reputation-making *The Titicut Follies* (1967) because of all "that point of

---

From the *Austin Chronicle*, 11 February 2000. Reprinted by permission of the author.

view," although he'll allow that Wiseman's style may have matured over the years. Just let that sink in for a moment.

Maysles is bringing two of his early films to the Alamo Drafthouse this Wednesday, February 16, as part of the Austin Film Society's ongoing Texas Documentary Tour: *What's Happening! The Beatles in the U.S.A.* (1964), a "fly-on-the-wall-with-a-hand-held-camera's look at the Fab Four's first American tour" (and a foreshadowing of colleague D. A. Pennebaker's Dylan treatment in *Don't Look Back*), and *Meet Marlon Brando* (1965), the Maysles Brothers' riff on a Brando riff with the press during a film promotion. Outside of a retrospective last year, the Alamo screening of the Beatles' film will be its first-ever showing in the theatre, due to a long series of complications. Says Maysles, "When I saw the film for the first time on the big screen last year, I was on the edge of my seat the entire time—so happy—every single moment was just right, just right, just right! No greater pleasure for a filmmaker than thirty years later to look at something and see that it has held up."

Maysles concedes that both films are conceptual paradoxes for his style of filmmaking. The Brando film is, of all things, about Brando giving interviews. And in *What's Happening!*, the Beatles turned out to be merciless hams in front of the camera—anathema to a direct cinema filmmaker. "We could have told them to stop acting for the camera," Maysles recalls, "but they came to this country having been groomed to act for the camera; that was who they were at that point. We didn't want to shake them out of that. But there were some quite insightful moments that we caught, like Paul on the train, admitting that he was depressed and that the group was being turned into a product."

AUSTIN CHRONICLE: *Is your subject's awareness of the camera a problem for your style of filmmaking?*

ALBERT MAYSLES: This comes up all the time. People always say that the subjects wouldn't be that way without the camera. But I say, "You mean to tell me that with a camera, all of a sudden somebody is an actor?" In film schools today, the students are being taught all the wrong things. They're scared to death about not being objective enough because the camera is there; then they're scared to death that they're not being subjective enough.

In *Grey Gardens*, I'm confident that we captured the real Beales. The proof of that is that when the mother was on her deathbed, a year after the film, her daughter asked her what more she had to say, and she said, "Nothing, it was all in the film." Also, every morning during the six-week shoot, we would arrive a little earlier than we said we would so that we could spray ourselves with off to keep the fleas off when we were in the house. We'd do this standing just outside the house, so they couldn't see us, and we could always overhear the two women talking to each other. And it was exactly the same way they talked when the camera was running.

AC: *Do you interact at all with your subjects when you're filming?*
AM: We never ask questions. For example, in *Grey Gardens*, if we said anything, it was nondirective, as in that kind of therapy where the patient does all the work. If we spoke to them, it was just to reflect back what they were saying, to reinforce the likelihood that they knew we were paying attention. We tell our subjects when we discuss the prospective project that we would like to be with them and will be shooting whatever seems interesting. We tell them, if you want to talk to us, please do.

In *Gimme Shelter*, we were in Mick [Jagger]'s dressing room at the start of the shoot and he came over to us and said, "You know, I'm not going to be an actor in this film." We said, "Well, it's a documentary so we're not expecting you to do that." So then he said, "None of that Pennebaker shit." So I understood that to mean that this film was not going to be our kind of pure documentary. We could have just said goodbye and left at that point, but what we did was just wait, thinking we might get his cooperation. We started filming, and we never had a problem, somehow he just understood what we do.

AC: *Your skills as a cameraman have been widely acclaimed. How do you describe your style behind the camera?*
AM: My style is very natural, more like a good still photographer than a cinematographer. The cinematographer's job is to set the lighting; he may not even look through the camera. A good documentary camera person is subject to the whims of reality and has to be adept at any moment, like a still photographer, being ever watchful and listening very carefully so he doesn't have to ask someone to repeat something. I never have to say, "That was really great. Now, could you repeat that for the camera?" A good cameraman knows how to use a camera and at the same time be ever watchful. He knows what to shoot and how to give his subjects the love that allows that magical combination of full truth and full subjectivity. The cameraman has to have what I call "the gaze"—empathy—the way you look at the people you're shooting and how you establish their trust. Paying attention to people is an extremely powerful

force of recognition and of love. And that's documentary at its best. Without their trust, you're just a walking zombie with a camera and your subjects don't connect.

AC: *Why were you so pleased with your camerawork in the Beatles film?*

AM: My shooting was so good in that film. I was on the right person at the right time. I framed everything right, I was close up at the right time. The shooting was fluid. The shooting of that film was a complete revolution in filming technique—no one had ever shot a film that way before. The British press said it was a total revolution. We just tagged along with the Beatles; they didn't have to position themselves for us because the camera was no longer on a tripod as it always had been up to then. That meant the Beatles could just feel free to move around and be themselves. That new technology gave us the flexibility to catch a life as it was—without imposing on people. You didn't have to interview them, heighten the film with music, just real, straight, direct life experiences—a nonfiction filmmaker's dream.

You have the greatest force behind you when you're filming reality—if you just let it happen. But a lot of documentary makers force themselves into a mold to capture their own preconceptions, in other words as far away from fact as a fiction film. Errol Morris, for example, there are times when I feel he delights in confusing fact and fiction. I think you owe the public the courtesy of saying, "This is no longer a documentary. A documentary has to be factually correct, none of this hocus pocus, blending fact with fiction."

AC: *Are you saying that "direct cinema" is the only legitimate form of documentary?*

AM: Well, there are nature films that are probably factually correct. Those are not direct cinema, but that could still be called documentary. A documentary is fact in film. A good documentary is not just hanging a camera on the wall—there has to be a brain behind it. The brain calls attention to what's important.

AC: *Isn't that the dreaded point of view?*

AM: You could call it that, but if the POV is set up to give you a message—the hell with the facts—that's where POV gets into trouble. When you're getting into "purposes," then you're getting into POV. If your purpose is just to reveal the human condition, then that's okay.

AC: *How do you ever purge a documentary of subjectivity or POV?*

AM: Well, *Grey Gardens* was not a POV film, I would say, because we were fair to both the mother and the daughter. We had enough of each of them in the film for the viewer to understand both of them. I suppose you could call being fair to everyone in the film a form of POV. But if we'd tried to make the mother look better or worse than the daughter that would have been the bad POV.

Grey Gardens got ferociously negative reviews, by the way. Walter Goodman at the *New York Times* said that the Maysles Brothers should be disgusted with themselves for having made that film and taken advantage of those two women. No matter how good a film you make, you have to go through the perceptive process of the audience, and there are some people in the audience who just don't get it. You give them a wonderful gift, and they throw it away.

AC: *How do you see narrative in a documentary?*

AM: That's a very delicate thing. Sometimes you end up with a film that has no narrative and have to decide, well, maybe that's the way to show it.

AC: *Do you edit your own films?*

AM: No, I don't really take part in the editing, which may seem funny. My brother always supervised the editing and would give a lot of freedom to the editors. That works, both by virtue of the person we select to do the job and by the nature of what we've got to begin with. So far, our editors have, with the exception of the Christo project, produced the story that we wanted.

AC: *So what's next?*

AM: I'm off to Florida to do some filming of Edie Beale (the daughter in *Grey Gardens*) who's now living in Miami. She's now the age her mother was in the film and doing great. I'm also working on an ongoing project about meeting strangers on trains. And working on a profile of Mendel Beilis. I also do a lot of seminars.

I have an office of eight to ten people and some of them are working on commercials and infomercials.

Albert Maysles

LIZ STUBBS/2002

LAUDED AS THE father of direct cinema, an American parallel to the French *vérité* style, Albert Maysles is a landmark figure in nonfiction films. With the revolution of sync-sound and portable film cameras, Albert and his brother, David, shot films handheld, with very little, if any, interview interaction, simply allowing life to unfold before the camera, capturing more truth than would be possible if they attempted to "direct" subjects and situations. Their style and their films are legendary: *What's Happening! The Beatles in the U.S.A.* (1964), a look at a Beatles visit to the States; *Salesman* (1968) chronicles four door-to-door Bible salesmen and is often heralded as the classic American documentary, reflecting one of the richest portraits of the heart of America; the cult classic *Gimme Shelter* (1969), a portrait of Mick Jagger and the Rolling Stones on their American tour that ended with a killing at the Altamont concert; and *Grey Gardens* (1976), a portrait of a very unique, eccentric mother-daughter dynamic in their secluded, decaying East Hampton mansion.

Albert and his films have garnered awards not just for their merits but also for their contributions to their times. *Salesman* was honored by the Library of Congress in 1992 for its historic, cultural, and aesthetic significance. And Albert has been honored for lifetime and career achievement by such entities as the International Documentary Association, the American Society of Cinematographers, the Guggenheim, and, in 1999, Kodak recognized him as one of the world's one hundred finest cinematographers.

Albert heads up Maysles Films today and continues to be a prolific

---

From *Documentary Filmmakers Speak*, Allworth Press, 2002. Reprinted by permission of Allworth Press.

filmmaker—most recently with *LaLee's Kin* (2000) and a series of filmmaker portraits for the Independent Film Channel (2001).

LIZ STUBBS: *How did you get your start in film and documentaries?*

ALBERT MAYSLES: I'd been a psychologist, teaching at Boston University. I worked in a mental hospital as a research assistant, and I also headed up a research project in Massachusetts General Hospital. I mention all that stuff because in 1955—as I was still teaching and one has a summer vacation—I decided that it being only two years after Stalin's death, it would be very interesting to go to Russia. Maybe I could get some sort of impression, record my experiences in some way to fill an enormous gap that existed at that time. People had no imagery, no way of even comprehending in the slightest, because the media was so deficient in this regard—you know, what it was to be a Russian, just an ordinary person—we had no basis of common ground for understanding because everything was speculation about activities behind the wall of the Kremlin.

So with that in mind I thought I would go there and do something that I knew something about—namely, mental health. And I decided I would try to get into mental hospitals, which was a tall order, but I've always been an adventurer. And the more wild the adventure, the more interesting it would be. Every documentary is sort of an adventure into the heart and soul of certain people. At least, that's what it should be.

And so, it's a long story, but I managed to borrow a movie camera, a 16mm camera from CBS. I just walked in there, just a total stranger, told them I was a psychologist and I was hoping to get into mental hospitals, and they took me at my word. And they gave me a roll of film—at that time, it was just a hundred-foot roll, three minutes of 16mm film—and said, "Just shoot something and allow us three hours to process it and we'll give you a critique." That was my training. So up I went and two days after I arrived in Moscow I crashed a Romanian embassy party, met all the top Soviet leaders. One of them got interested in me. He came back to me fifteen minutes later with a telephone number for me to call. It was the head of psychiatry for Russia. Of course, he was notified I would be calling and that paved the way. So I made my first film that way; that's how I got into it. So my interest has always been in, I suppose, finding and recording how people tick.

LS: *How did your style evolve?*

AM: I have an interest completely different from Hollywood's way of doing things. I'm not at all interested in what's called high production value. It's the bane of our existence. To me, of course, the high value is not what makes it expensive, but the high value comes in capturing another person's experience as directly and as interestingly as possible. Now some people, perhaps even most documentary filmmakers, don't think you can do that with any kind of full authenticity. They'll say it's all a point of view, and it's a manipulation, and you're always selecting. I don't agree with the downgrading of the truthfulness of what one can do in a documentary. It's been thirty-odd years now since we made *Gimme Shelter* and it's a very truthful account of what took place—should be good for another five hundred years, I'd say.

LS: *Do you find the presence of a camera or camera crew changes people's reactions?*

AM: It can. But it depends on how it's used. In my own work I think that it's not a serious factor. That is, it's not a serious factor in making what I do any less valid, nor do I think that the fly-on-the-wall approach is at all useful, because the fly on the wall is an instrument without a mind or a heart to control it. But then, of course, people say, "Well sure, the mind and the heart already are getting into something very subjective and you're getting away from reporting reality." But the way I use the instrument, the way I use my emotions, let's say, is, I think, to get closer, to get closer to the truth rather than distant from it. And I think, perhaps, the determining factor is I empathize with the people I film.

Now, there are, in our culture, influences that would belie what I'm talking about. People say, "Well, love is blind." Okay, so in a way that's true and in a way it isn't. I mean, the more you love somebody, the more—if it's genuine love—the more you are open to discovering good, bad, whatever, without making any negative judgment. And if it's somebody that you can't find an affection for, you can still make a film of that person, and be fair to that person if at least you try your best to understand them. Okay. So if you're trying your best to understand them, that's another way of saying you like them. So much of it hinges on your ability to empathize. It's an essential ingredient, and if you don't empathize somehow or other, I can't explain it, but you can see it in your results. The photography lacks a heart, and too many people who are skillful technically in their camera work—too many of them—just don't give it the empathy that draws the emotions of the scene, draws it out, evokes it, and gets it on film. Without that process, you end up with a lifeless series of images. Too often, an Academy Award winner will make exactly that kind of film. Technically superior but without a heart and soul.

You have these two things. There's subjectivity and objectivity, and for me the thing that makes both possible is the affection, the empathy that you put into it. In true love, you're not trying to do somebody in. In true love, you're not trying to make the person look any different—better or worse—right? In true love, you fully accept the person exactly as they are. So I think it comes back to this empathy factor.

Another thing that goes along with that—we're talking about gaining access, as well, because if you haven't got the access then people will be put off by the presence of the camera. I find that I can gain access, more often than not, immediately upon meeting somebody. Another factor that goes into it is how you look at the person. It's called the gaze. So with the empathy and the gaze and good luck you can get access to just about anybody. You have another thing working for you, and that is, with that kind of access, with that kind of application of empathy and the gaze, you're able to do something for that person that would never otherwise happen. That is, you're paying attention to that person, you're giving access to that person, you're fulfilling for that person a very basic need that we all have, the need to be recorded exactly for what we are. So in a way you're doing a service of giving that person not a biography, but an autobiography, and again, there's so much misconception about that sort of thing, even among filmmakers. They give themselves director's credit? Come on give me a break—you start directing a person or the situation, and it's no longer a documentary. The very essence of the filming is not controlling, but uncontrolled, a lack of control on the part of the filmmaker. It's not just the fly on the wall. You are using various skills that allow you to do all this stuff, but you don't try to change anything.

LS: *Is anything verboten? I never hear your voice in your films. Would you ever do anything to create drama if you felt it was lacking? To what extent are you hands-off?*

AM: Just about 100 percent. But, it's funny—it's not quite 100 percent because, how should I say, you use your presence to allow that person to be an uncontrolled subject.

LS: *How do you choose your subjects? Do they come to you or do you do your own ideas for films?*

AM: It varies from one film to another. Like somebody might call me up and tell me of something that should be filmed that may not ever have occurred to me and I think, "Oh yeah, that's great, let's do it." That's how my brother and I made the first film of the Beatles. We got into that because we got a call from Granada television asking us if we wanted to make the film, and they had the money, and the Beatles were arriving in New York in two hours. We rushed out to the airport and four days later we had it shot. So that's how that happened. Each film happens in one way or another, usually in different ways. *Salesman*—we just got that idea on our own and went out and, at our own expense, at our own risk, made the film.

LS: *Let's take* Salesman, *as an example. Can you know before you start shooting what your story might be?*

AM: Well, two things. One is, you have some sort of an idea, but you're ready at the same time to abandon that if it doesn't happen or if something better, something else, comes along. When we made *Gimme Shelter*, we knew that the concert stuff would be interesting. What we didn't know was whether there would be more than a concert film. We didn't know, but we wouldn't have made the film just as a concert film. We thought some other stuff was going to happen. Just what that would be we didn't know. If you asked us to guess, we probably would have thought it would be more positive than it ended up being.

But we were determined as always, as John Lennon put it, let it be, which is in contrast with the way *Woodstock*, for example, was made. When they made that film there were a lot of interviews. We don't do interviews.

When you do an interview, the answer is your question, so it's a setup every time, and you're getting away from what documentary, I think, should do and what is its divine right or responsibility, which is to film people's experiences rather than set up an artificial situation where you're pumping them for information, information that is probably better recorded in literature rather than in cinema.

And so, when *Woodstock* was made, the filmmakers thought, "Oh boy, everything's coming up roses. Isn't it wonderful, the flower generation . . ." and you ended up with a film that wasn't really the way it was. There were all the seeds of Altamont at Woodstock—not all, but so many of those seeds were there. How many people were at Woodstock? Several hundred thousand? Okay, wouldn't you think that even now probably there are fifty thousand, at least, people from Altamont—the same number probably from Woodstock—who, even today, are still suffering from the effects of bad drugs? And that film, *Woodstock*, gave you no indication that anything bad was happening and it was only six months between the two, only six months after Woodstock that Altamont took place.

LS: *At some point in your filming do you discover your story, or is that something you discover in the editing process?*
AM: It can work either way. In *Grey Gardens* we were with them six weeks and we still were waiting for some culminating moment perhaps, but if it didn't happen, okay, well, it didn't happen. But it did happen one day when the mother and daughter were not in their bedroom, but they were in an adjoining room, which we called the pink room because the walls were pink, and it's when everything exploded. And there are little explosions and little manifestations of love as well as recriminations, but it culminated in that scene, and so, we had it.

In *Salesman*, it was a storm that was gathering all the time with Paul's evident decline, and it's interesting—the way the film was put together, you could read it in his face the first moments in the film. This guy had various human qualities that were very nice, but he was going to have a hard time making the sale.

LS: *Do you edit or do you hand over your footage to editors?*
AM: I don't edit myself. I've tried it and it's not the way I make decisions. With the camera I can make decisions, and I think the right ones instantaneously, but if I sit down and edit I can't make up my mind—and I'm not forced to do so.

LS: *So are you involved in the editing process at all—do you look at works in progress?*
AM: Yeah, but I'm really not on top of it that way. If it's something that I see should be done or shouldn't be done then I bring it up, but I'm very lucky that I've worked with the best. While my brother was alive he was in control of the editing. He supervised the editing, and we just about always saw eye to eye on everything.

LS: *How does the changing technology affect how you make films? AM: Oh, enormously important.*

LS: *Do you still shoot film or have you moved to DV?*
AM: I was just with Paul McCartney about a month ago. You know, Paul was heading up that event at Madison Square Garden—a bunch of rock stars got together to celebrate New York in consequence to events of the 11th of September. So it was a big event where they raised some $25 million at Madison Square Garden. And a week before it took place I got a call from Paul McCartney, whom I had filmed thirty-seven years before, and he said, "Look, remember what we did before? Let's do something now, and let's do it as we did before in black-and-white film." And

I thought, "Oh, okay, sentimental reasons if nothing else." Already, I was trying to wean myself away from film.

I had made with Susan [Froemke] a film called *LaLee's Kin*, and, in fact, I got the cinematography award for it at Sundance this past year. But even then I was beginning to think, "Well, what about this new video stuff?" And since then, I've made a series of four half-hour film portraits of filmmakers, all with a little video camera. The Independent Film Channel is showing these four film portraits. Scorsese was the first one, Wes Anderson is the second, Robert Duvall is the third, and Jane Campion is the fourth. And I did them all with the little video camera.

LS: *With a digital video camera?*

AM: Yeah. Mini-digital. Some of them were with the PD100, and later on I began to use the PD150 when it appeared on the market. I couldn't be happier with it. In fact, even when I was shooting the [September 11 concert for] Paul McCartney I was thinking to myself, every time I picked up the camera, "Well, now, if I had the video camera . . ." So during the course of that week I sat down and I made note of what I thought were the advantages of the PD150 over the 16mm camera. I came up with twenty-seven points. And all these points are very, very important.

LS: *Do you prefer to shoot with digital video?*

AM: No question about it. I can serve all the purposes that I've always had much, much better. Like we spoke of eye contact. Okay, well, when I'm filming with the PD150 I can look at them and they can look at me and that's very important. And that gaze and being able to continue that gaze at any time, it's very important. You might be filming a moment where . . . it's kind of touchy, like maybe a moment of embarrassment or whatever, and so it's quite natural for the subject, perhaps, to look at you for reassurance and there it is—they can look right at you. Your eyes tell it all without saying a word. Twenty-seven points is quite a big advantage.

LS: *Digital video is much more inexpensive than shooting with film. Do you shoot more because of that? Is your ratio higher?*

AM: You do shoot more. But then, of course, we've all heard, editors especially complain about that. And then there is the notion that since you're shooting a lot more, you're not being as selective, right? And so, my answer to that is Henri Cartier Bresson. Would he have been any better off had he shot with a Rolleiflex, which has twelve pictures, rather than the Leica, which has thirty-five? Because the Rolleiflex gives you a higher production value—it's a bigger image, 2¼ × 2¼, right? But you can't hold it up to your eye. You gotta hold it below so the camera is always looking up, and Henri Cartier Bresson wanted to make every picture count. And if you looked over his contact sheets, you'd see that each one was maybe not the best, but it was important that he got that one. Each one was right for him at the time, and so he had three times more chance of not running out of film. And in the case of the digital camera—sixty minutes versus . . . well, you can shoot it with sixty minutes or forty minutes with the same tape. But even with the forty minutes, you've got four times less likelihood that you're going to run out of film or tape at an important moment, and that's crucial.

LS: *What keeps you coming back to making films? You mentioned being an adventurer, so that's an appeal. What is it for you that keeps you enmeshed in film?*

AM: I remember addressing a group of filmmakers, and as I was thinking of what I should say I suddenly thought my first words were going to be, "Oh, what a terrible thing, what a terrible thing, what a terrible thing." I repeated it three or four or five times and I said, "The terrible thing is that there are so many people who never found in their work what they really want to do." And it's not likely to be that way if you're making documentary films. It certainly hasn't been that way for me. I have felt always that I was doing some good.

And also, the thing that drives you on is that there's no end to it. Each week many films are being made—and still, it's infinite. The well is not gonna dry up; there's always another one to do. And I don't think any of us feel that we've made the perfect film yet. There's a film that I've wanted to do for some time, which I think will be my best and I'm still hoping to do it. I've begun to do it, you know; I hope to get it done one of these days.

LS: *And what is that?*

AM: I get on long-distance trains in different countries. The reason I want to make it different countries is I want it to have a kind of epic quality, not just one country or culture—it'll be cross-cultural. People of different walks of life will be in this film. It'll be four or five or six major stories that will be spontaneous. So what I'll do is I'll get on half a dozen trains in different parts of the world and I'll roam the train until I find somebody where there's a story evolving, usually by virtue of why they're on the train. So I get off the train with them to film their story.

I took a trip across the country going from Los Angeles to New York several years back, and as the train pulled out of the Pittsburgh station with a new group of passengers, I was in the cafeteria coach when I noticed a young woman sitting alone at a table and looking kind of nervous, her two kids across the aisle. I could read her face; something was going on, so I asked if I could join her. At that time I had the 16mm camera on my shoulder, my soundman next to me. And I said, "I'm making a film of people I'm meeting on trains. If it's okay with you, maybe I could film from time to time." She said, "Oh, sure, that's okay." I started filming right away and she began to tell me her story. When she was three years old, her parents broke up in an ugly divorce and her father got custodianship over her, which is unusual, but, anyway, that's what happened, and he vowed that her mother would never see her again. And she's never seen her mother since then.

The night before she got on the train she got a call from a woman in Philadelphia. And this woman said, "Look, there's no time for me to send you a photograph or for you to send me a photograph of yourself, but get on the next train and I'll be waiting for you at the train station in Philadelphia." I got all this stuff on film. We got off the train and I continued to film and she looked around and there was no one at the platform. And then, as she walked up the stairs, there was a woman at the top of the stairs, a woman who threw her arms around her, and they talked. And then, finally, the woman, who was her mother, put her head over her daughter's shoulder and turned to me and said, "Isn't she gorgeous?" Well, that's why I make movies, and that's why I make them this way. It's the truth, so you have to believe it. Anyone seeing that stuff is not gonna have a shadow of a doubt that this was the real thing and I'd gotten very, very close to the experience of these two people. So that's just one story.

I have no idea what else I'm going to encounter. I took a train across Russia all the way to, almost to the Chinese frontier and returning from Novosibersk, which is very far, the east end of Russia. Again, I walked through the train and noticed through the compartment window what appeared to be a family. And I was with somebody who was translating for me. We knocked on the door and they allowed us in. It turns out that it wasn't a family. It was an aunt and uncle and two children, niece and nephew. And as I discovered, the reason they were on the train was that the two kids had just lost their mother, who had been killed by their father. And the aunt and uncle were taking them to their home way the hell out in the western end, in the Ukraine. That's why they were on the train. So that's another kind of story.

So I haven't decided just where; I'm very likely to go to India. The fanciest train in the world is the Blue Train, which is in South Africa.

But most of it is just ordinary people chosen only because there's a story that's taking place that's interesting.

When we made *Salesman*, we'd broken through into new territory. I think it's safe to say that *Salesman* was the first real feature documentary film. And so, if you take literature as a parallel arc, there's the nonfiction novel that Truman Capote made and then around that time, maybe a year or two later, we made *Salesman*, which we could call a nonfiction feature film. Now, what other parallels are there to literature that would inspire us to do something in another form, but still a documentary? There's a collection of short stories, okay? And usually a collection of short stories is by one author, okay? Okay, so that's the case here, there's one author and what makes it so, well, what appeals to me so much is that it's not just a haphazard throwing together of stories. They're all unified by the metaphor of the train itself. Which is a metaphor for life as the train goes from station to station. And also, it overcomes the problem we have in documentary in that it's very difficult to film anything but what's contemporary and so you don't go back. It's hard to go back into a person's life in filming actuality—get photographs and maybe home movies or whatever, but that's not the same as the material you can get that's contemporary. So this is an epic film, the train film, which doesn't go back in time or forward in time, but extends itself laterally by being in different countries, different cultures.

LS: *Do you have favorite films that you've done?*

AM: Yes, yes. Well, there are the three that I've made into DVDs, *Gimme Shelter*, *Grey Gardens*, and *Salesman*. My brother and I, because I wanted to do the train film, my brother wanted to do one of the family. Actually, really of my father and a cousin of mine. Both of these people, my father was a postal clerk and my cousin was a fighter pilot in the Second World War, so they were both heroes, although of different character. Both of us, my brother and myself, we went as far as to make a fifteen-minute piece sort of as a trailer . . . so people could see what the film was going to be about. But then my brother died, and I don't know, someday I may go back to that, as well. I have several other projects, too, that are very much from my heart.

Unfortunately, the way things go in documentary, if you're going to get money for something it usually is from somebody that wants a particular idea for a film. It's an issue or something of topical interest or whatever. Who the hell would ever put up money for *Salesman*? Nobody. And, in fact, even after we made the film nobody wanted to show it. It took over thirty years to finally get the film on television. PBS—I remember we used to go to PBS. One day I remember they had a new guy in programming. So I called him up and I said, "I'd like to show you a film," and he said, "Yeah, I've heard of you. I'd be glad to come over." So he comes over, we put *Salesman* on, and I go into the room to change the reel and I can see he's been crying and he says, "No, I've seen enough." And I thought, "Well, this guy's so moved by what he's seen that it's a sale without even seeing it all." And he says, "No. no, it's too depressing. My father was a salesman." So there is an association somehow between a film that is a meaningful, profound engagement with the viewer that is depressing, or there's some kind of resistance, especially on the part of programmers, to show that kind of thing. You think we had an easy time with *Grey Gardens*? No one showed it. It took us twenty-three years before it finally got shown on the Sundance Channel. No one would show *Gimme Shelter.* But with commercial television it has to be theirs or it's not gonna show. And not like with the Independent Film Channel, when they said, "It's all yours." As I say, that's not the way it usually works.

LS: *Is funding easier to come by since you've become established?*
AM: I don't think it's any easier for me than anybody else. I haven't gotten a cent yet for the train film. You see, part of it also is the criteria for news or entertainment—it's almost necessary that someone get killed. What I mean to say is, look at television. What is it, something like twenty thousand or forty thousand people get killed every year on television? How many times have you seen a story like the one I described to you of that woman finding her mother? And if I took that stuff and went to television they'd say, "Well you know, Al, it's not exactly entertainment and it's not news. You know, we don't do that stuff."

LS: *What about the Independent Film Channel, Sundance Channel, Bravo?*
AM: My understanding is that so many of the cable networks, they have their own format. I wouldn't want to submit *Salesman* to Bravo's format, or even Lifetime. The heart of the matter is that the best way for an artist, documentary filmmaker, or whoever to work is to come up with a film that comes from the heart. Some early images, or cravings, maybe of another person, but it really turns out to be a story of your father or a relationship that you've got to get off your chest somehow or another that lead you to put it into some artistic form.

Can you imagine Shakespeare as a documentary filmmaker? He'd go to CBS and he'd say, "Look, I've got this great idea. The guy's name is Hamlet." And they'd say, "Well, Hamlet. What kind of a name is that?"

"Well, it's Danish." "Well, we don't do foreign stuff. You know, you have to have subtitles, we don't do anything from another country." "Yeah, but this guy's so interesting he can't make up his mind." "He's interesting and he can't make up his mind and you expect people to watch some kid not making up his mind for an hour and a half? How long is it going to be?" "Well, maybe an hour and a half, two hours, you know, it's a great story." "Yeah but, no, no, no, it's not for us."

There's another thing, too. We spoke of the nonfiction novel and the nonfiction documentary, then we spoke of the short stories that are documentaries. What about poetry? I'll give you an example: I'm sitting on a bus. The same bus I take to work every day. It's a ten-minute journey. I have seen things on that bus that are the most beautiful, potentially video pieces of poetry. For example, I saw a very, very heavy black woman. She must have been a good three hundred pounds with a big hulk of a head on her shoulders. And I got to looking at her, but in a way that was somehow kindly and understanding enough that she wasn't put off by it. She had no reason to feel that she was some kind of an object of my staring. But I got so taken in by this woman and maybe some kind of anticipation that something was going to happen, I don't know. Anyway, I nudged the woman next to me who was white, middle-aged, and now the two of us were looking at this woman.

And suddenly the kid sitting next to this woman, this kid had to be her daughter, she gets up, slips around in front of her mother and nestles her head in between her mother's enormous breasts and falls asleep. Well, it transformed everything, as a poem can do, without any purpose . . . it's a poem, that's all. It doesn't have to justify itself. And if I'd had my little video camera in my hand I would have gotten it. But as it stands right now, there'd be nothing I could do with it.

But, you see, I'm getting into another problem that we have and it's very crucial, and that is, too much of what the media wants is not what's in our heart. They want stuff that has, if it's anything like what I'm talking about when I say poetry, they say, "Come on, but that's not what we do. It's gotta have a purpose. Is it on abortion? Is it news? Does it have anything to do with September 11? I mean, how can we justify showing it?" And some of the most important subject matter—just nice people doing nice things, but not just doing nice things, basically acts of good will and acts of kindness—that's all off-limits somehow.

LS: *Do you think that's changing since September 11?*

AM: It changed at least for the time being on two pages of the *New*

York Times. Even in the Sunday paper nowadays I believe there are one or two pages that have ten or twenty portraits of families that suffered from September 11. So it's a portrait of the guy and his family, or the woman and her family. Suddenly, in the *New York Times*, suddenly these human portraits burst forth. Except that this happened with September 11, you'd never hear anything about those families. But now, suddenly, you're hearing all the human stuff that went on and was disrupted by this event. That's probably just a temporary thing. But it does show you that that kind of information can make good material for a newspaper, but it's quite an exceptional case.

When my daughter was four years old—she's now twenty-five—I used to take her to pick up the *New York Times*. And so, one day we walked down the street, got to the newsstand and the paper hadn't arrived yet. I don't know, maybe the truck had broken down, or there was a strike, I don't know. But my daughter turned to me, age four, and said, "Daddy, the people haven't been killed yet." That tells it all.

I sat in the audience where there was a panel discussion amongst important filmmakers. Actually, they were all fiction filmmakers. The topic of discussion was violence and sex in the media. And so, when the panel was over, I was the first one to raise his hand, and I told that little anecdote of haven't been killed yet and a ripple of "Oh my God" went through the audience. I then elaborated on it and pointed out how there was a gap in content and surely people can complain about violence and sex, but nobody is getting to the goodwill and kindness that exist in people. And so, a panelist said, "Well you know that stuff is not dramatic. You have to have a conflict, and if you don't have conflict then you don't have drama." And do you think anybody else on the panel differed? No. They all accepted that. I was the only one that disagreed.

LS: *Have you ever done or thought about doing fiction films?*

AM: No. I have been approached. In fact, my brother and I met up with Orson Welles. We met him at Cannes and then he invited us to spend a week with him in Madrid. And we made a little film of him talking about a film that we would make together. It would be somewhere between a documentary . . . as he said in the film we were making, "I know exactly what the film should be. I have a script and everything, but I'm throwing away the script." And so, I mean, I'd be able to make a very good contribution to it, there's no question of that.

And then, on another occasion, I filmed a twenty-minute sequence with Jean-Luc Godard called *Paris Vu Par*—Paris as seen by several French film directors. So he set the scene and I didn't even know what was coming up, and I just filmed it the way I do a documentary and it worked just beautifully. So I can see applications. And, in fact, as I was making these half-hour film portraits of filmmakers and one of them is Jane Campion. I filmed her as she was preparing to make her next film, and she asked me if I would like to do the cinematography for her next film. Some of what I've done has been seen by fiction filmmakers and some of them have taken that and gone somewhat in that direction. I know that, for example, remember that television show the *Monkees*? Well, Bob Rafelson was the producer of that and he's an old friend of mine. And he said, "You know, I got the whole idea of doing that from having seen your Beatles film." So the whole style of that filmmaking came from the Beatles film.

LS: *What would you do if you didn't make films?*
AM: If I didn't make films, well, I've never had that decision to make since I started. I'd do something where I'd be able to care for people. I think that when you make a documentary, people are putting themselves in your hands and you have a responsibility to take care that that responsibility is met. And not everyone feels that way, you know, but I feel it very strongly. And it's interesting, I've noticed. I have three children and I've never told them what to do professionally, but this is a very strong factor in what they do—take care of people. One of my kids, she's twenty, she spent four months recently in Nepal taking care of Tibetan refugee children. There's all kinds of ways that we can take care of one another, and so I'd find another way of doing it, I guess. Maybe, I don't know, maybe as a therapist.

LS: *Well, your background is in psychology . . .*
AM: I guess I must have cared for people to begin with. And also, I was very lucky that I came from a family where my parents gave my brother and myself a great deal. They were immigrant children. And around the turn of the century, as a child, my mother somehow found an organization in Boston. It was called the Saturday Evening Girls. And the woman, a philanthropist, the woman who headed it up and paid for the whole thing, wanted to make poets and writers, artists out of Italian and Jewish immigrant children around the turn of the century. And so, my mother got a lot of inspiration and training in those areas and became a schoolteacher and a very ardent social- and civil-rights person. It's funny, one of the people she always wanted to meet was Eleanor Roosevelt, and I don't know how she did it, but just like me, she managed somehow or other to get to her and she spent a whole day with her.

And then, many years later, after I came back from Russia and made my psychiatry film, I read in the paper that Eleanor Roosevelt was going to go to Russia to look into social services there and she was hoping to visit mental hospitals. But she had heard that they didn't exist. So I called her up. I don't know how the hell I got her phone number, and I said, "Well, I made this film," and she said, "Oh, I'd love to see it." So I brought my projector and film and showed it to her. That was 1956, I think, and I hadn't yet got my hands on a sync-sound camera, and I was completely out of any money, so that by the end of the day she said, "You know, I'm leaving in three weeks. You're most welcome to come along." But I couldn't because I didn't have the equipment or the money. But she was taken that much by what I had to offer.

LS: *Did you or do you still have any anxieties about the process of filmmaking?*

AM: Well, what happens with me is once I get going on it, as soon as something happens, then it's just out of this world—a scene that is so telling that it propels me through the rest of it. I think it was a year ago; we had a screening of the Beatles film at the Film Forum here in New York. Because I had to introduce it and give a talk afterward, I sat through the film. I hadn't seen it in a long time, and I noticed that I was moving around in my chair as though I was operating the camera all over again, and I was zooming and switching shots. But I can tell you that if my way of doing it were any different, you know, then I would have felt, "Oh my God, I didn't do it right that time." But all the way through I felt, "Oh yeah, that's right. I got it right. I got it right. I got it right." So the satisfaction never ends.

You make a film from a script, a fiction film, and in a way that's the end of it because those lines never existed in reality anyway. But the lives of people in documentary, they still go on, and if you've done a decent job of it, they're still with you. And I get letters and telephone calls, which I return, from Little Edie Beale all the time.

And with *Salesman*, as you can imagine, Paul became a lifelong friend. One of the reasons we did *Salesman* and did it so well was that in many ways the whole thing stemmed from our heart. We were Jewish kids brought up in an anti-Semitic environment. We were in fights with Irish kids every single day, so the time had come to make a reconciliation. It wasn't just by accident we chose these guys who were from Boston, all of them Irish. And so it was a turnaround that sort of had to take place at some time, some way, and that's the way it was with that film. With someone else doing it, it could so easily have been a diatribe, piece of propaganda, pro-Communist, pro-capitalist, goodness knows, anti this, pro that. In fact, I like to tell this story: When we finished the film, we made it primarily to get it in movie theaters, but no exhibitor was interested. So we knew that the only way to get it into the theater was to rent a theater. So we needed money for that, so we had screenings where we hoped to get people to contribute to our fund where we could rent a theater. It ended up actually that we had to rent it from our own money, but in the meantime, we had all these screenings. Maybe a hundred people would come. At one of those screenings I noticed that as people filed out and congratulated us, there was one woman who was still seated, the last person to leave the theater. And as she got up and turned in our direction, I noticed that she'd been crying. And I also noticed that she was really quite attractive. And I elbowed my brother and I said, "She's for me." And that's my wife—that's how I met her.

And also, there's another thing that my parents gave me—this very romantic and positive view of life. My mother told me the story of how when she and my father were engaged they would meet for lunch at a certain street corner in downtown Boston. And my mother would arrive at noon, and my father would arrive five or ten minutes earlier and place himself across the street behind a window and just look at her. And then he'd slip around back and come down the street. So he could do this every day. And when you have images like that, really indirectly somehow or other—I mean with images like that who knows? Maybe that's why I looked at that black woman anticipating that something beautiful might happen. That's the instinct that you have to follow. The market, the money be damned. You've got to do that to do your best.

The Force of Reality in Direct Cinema: An Interview with Albert Maysles

SHARON ZUBER/2002

> Of all types of documentary, direct cinema is most prone to the mistaken notion that documentary films imitate or copy reality.
>
> —Carl R. Plantinga

WHILE RESEARCHING the connection between Direct Cinema filmmakers and New Journalist writers, I discovered that the Maysles brothers had made a short documentary about Truman Capote, *With Love from Truman: A Visit with Truman Capote* (1966, 30 minutes). The Maysles chose Capote as their subject because of "the perceived parallels in artistic approach" (Vogels 68–69). At the heart of the "perceived parallels" was the desire to capture reality. The Maysles brothers' work with Capote led to an ongoing friendship. This intersection of founding Direct Cinema filmmakers and a defining New Journalist writer provided the perfect opportunity to discuss the Direct Cinema filmmaker's claim to "capture reality" that has led to their being criticized as naïve and idealistic in a postmodern milieu. In August of 2002, I had the opportunity to interview Albert Maysles at Albert Maysles Films, Inc., his Manhattan office.

SHARON ZUBER: *I'd like to start by talking a little bit about your work with Capote and your relationship to New Journalist writers.*

ALBERT MAYSLES: All this talk about New Journalism but never the documentary filmmakers . . . it's crazy. I never thought of going so far as

From *Post Script: Essays in Film and the Humanities*. Vol. 26, no. 3, Summer 2007. Reprinted by permission of the author.

to say that we had influenced them but at least there were parallels, if not one influencing the other, but it was always the New Journalism and the printed word.

SZ: *I want to explore how both movements seemed to emerge at the same time, from some of the same motivations.*

AM: You may want to reach out beyond that, and now we've got all this reality stuff, so-called, which is bizarre. In fact, in a way the reality stuff is more like *Chronicle of a Summer*—the French—and has nothing to do with the American movement in the written word or in cinema. Interesting, huh?

Actually, it really goes back before that. The spark that *In Cold Blood* provided us with was the very notion that literature, the novel, became nonfiction, and that this could be translated into the documentary becoming a feature. The feature film, until *Salesman* [1968, with Charlotte Zwerin], was always a dramatic, fictional entity. We aspired to carry that feature, dramatic form into nonfiction the way Truman had done in the novel.

The first insight into that probability came to us from a friend of ours, at a cocktail party, who said she had just read a book called *Of Whales and Men*. It was kind of a modern-day, nonfiction *Moby Dick*. A doctor went on board a whaling expedition—he was Scottish, I think—and the whaling expedition began from England, I think, in the 1950s, at a time when English-speaking whalers existed. After that it became just Russian and Japanese entirely. So this doctor went on board and got to know each one of the men right from the start, because he had to examine them. And it turned out that the harpoonist was a Chicago taxicab driver. It utterly fascinated us. This was before we knew about Capote's book. We thought maybe a film had already been made on this sort of thing, and we found there was some sort of a short. And through that we found a man who had just lived down the street here, an American who had been on a whaling expedition. And we chatted with him until 3:00 in the morning. The first thing he said though was, "Look, if you're thinking of taking me with you, forget it, because I still can't stand the smell of those whales." By 3:00 in the morning, he turned to me and said, "When are you leaving [on the whaling trip]?"

Whaling had such a fascination. It turned out that when we read the book in 1964, maybe ten years had gone by, and there were no English-speaking whalers, so we dropped that possibility. Then Truman came along and revitalized us, and when we finished the film [about Capote],

David had lunch with Joe Fox specifically to talk to him about what we might do. Joe came up with the idea—what about door-to-door salesmen? We talked about it and thought it was great because we both had experience selling door-to-door. Separately, I sold toilet brushes and the *Encyclopedia Americana*, and my brother sold Avon products. We were enchanted with all the possibilities, but we just had to find the right guy or guys. So there were several months we spent researching this because there are all kinds of salesmen . . . but none of them had that greatness that we were looking for. And then a researcher discovered a company in Chicago, the Mid-American Bible. And they had four salesmen doing the New England territory. That gave us the Bible, sold as a product—so American, right? It's like the difference between doing a film with turtles or with whales. This was the whale and not a turtle.

And then, coming from Boston and being Jewish and being at odds with the Irish kids, who liked to pick fights, we never really quite resolved our problems with the Irish. In a way, the fighting—fist to fist (errgh!)—at least gave us physical contact with the people. But there was no cultural, social contact with each other as kids. And we missed that. These guys were Irishmen selling the Bible and from Boston. I've come to think that many a great work of art almost has to be autobiographical, because it taps into the need for self expression. There are things in one's life that are unresolved . . . that are seeking from your heart and soul to express themselves, and this was one of them.

So with Mid-American Bible supplying us with these guys, we looked them up and went out one evening with each of them and decided, yeah, this is it. There was still a lot more to be discovered [after selecting the subject]—we didn't know if the film would be about the four men and their manager or that one of them would become a central character; we certainly didn't know who or what would be behind the door each time they knocked, but we had high hopes. . . . In fact, after we made the film I remember browsing through Bartlett's book of quotations, and I came across a quotation by Charles Lamb, the English poet, "There's no sound more beautiful in the world whether in the country or the city than the sound of the knocking at the door." And of course in reality, when it's a salesman knocking on the door it's not all good.

SZ: *You've often mentioned how important it is to have a relationship with the person you're filming. What kind of relationship did you develop with Capote when you made your film about him for television?*

AM: First of all, we didn't have the prejudice against homosexuality that was rampant at that time in American life. We were told after the film came out, when it got shown on PBS at that time, that at least 20–30 percent of the public, upon watching it for two or three minutes, turned it off because of his feminine voice. I am hoping that wouldn't happen today, but that's what it was at that time. And that didn't turn us off at all. We certainly had an open mind about that stuff.

SZ: *There is an Arts and Entertainment special about Capote [on video] in which they scan the* New York Times *guest list to the Black and White Ball. Your name and David's name are on it; did you go?*

AM: Yes, yes. It was funny; there was a big spread in . . . *Cosmopolitan* magazine? Or maybe even it was *Look* magazine. I think it was the inside spread, both pages, and you saw so many people there. In front was a table where you could pick up an appetizer, and my cousin, who was about twenty years old at the time, said, "Oh! there's Albie looking for a snack, David must be looking for the women" (because he wasn't in the picture). It was taken to be, at that time, the greatest party of the century. Still is. So many of his celebrity friends were there, journalists, people in politics and entertainment, and it was to celebrate Katharine Graham's birthday.

That [the invitation to the ball] attests to the fact that we became good friends. And I remember very distinctly that after we finished the film, he was one of the first to see it. You never know for sure how he is going to react to it, because, certainly, there are times when the film is very personal. I remember him having seen the film alone. As he walked out of the door of the screening room, crying, he said, "This is the best film of its kind." He loved us, and he loved it. My only regret came when we heard that he had passed on. I thought we should have made some effort to have seen more of him. Not that we're great therapists or whatever. There was something special that my brother and I had with him. I think that companionship would have helped him to see through those tough times.

SZ: *What was your brother's involvement at Drew and Associates?*

AM: He wasn't involved as much as I was, because what they needed desperately was cameramen, and I was a key cameraperson. But they needed to find good stories, and so David was put on to find a good story. And he found one, but we would have to look at a list of titles. I remember he went with Pennebaker to Virginia, and David was the correspondent. You know we used two people. There was the sound guy—he was sort of the *Life* magazine correspondent—and the cameraperson.

I worked on *Primary, On the Pole, Yanki, No!*—I did all the Cuba stuff. You know that little family, the fisherman and his family? That's one of the best things I've ever done. It proves that the photography in documentary can be outstanding and can, in fact, vie with the best still photography. [looking at filmography] . . . *Adventures on the New Frontier*, there was a sequence there that I think was something I shot. *Kenya*, that's half Ricky [Leacock] and half mine.

See the name Petey Thomas? David found that one. *Petey and Johnny*. That is really his sole contribution to Drew. He went out on that one; he went out with Pennebaker. And Penne—they both got along very well—David said that right in the middle Penne had to pull his whole camera apart to repair it. I spoke to Penne about it, and Penne said, "Yeah, I had to do it, but I didn't lose anything."

SZ: *On the commentary for* Gimme Shelter, *you mention that you weren't a great editor but, because of ADD, that you were great as a cameraperson.*

AM: The weird thing is that having this Attention Deficit Disorder, when you put your mind to focusing on something at that moment you can draw yourself to something in a way that nobody else can. You can penetrate into the essence of something. You notice things that other people don't notice. So in an odd way, it works to your advantage. It's totally to your disadvantage if you're trying to edit because there you have the liberty to put off a decision, so you're impossible as an editor. But you could be very, very good as a cameraperson.

SZ: *Did the new technology of the sixties change the way you thought about the shots you were filming?*

AM: You'll see in some of the films, in *Salesman* for example, you'll see Paul sitting in the cafeteria, and it's quite a long sustained shot of him just looking off into the blue. Now, I would venture to say that any other documentary filmmaker would have thought it smart to say, "But Paul, what are you thinking of? We want to know what you are thinking." You probably would have needed cutaways, because there would be questions and answers, and you can't just go along continuously that way. So, you'd have cutaway shots, food on the table or a waitress walking, or whatever. Instead, in our film, the audience is totally absorbed in that man's thinking, whatever it is. And you don't know exactly what it is, but you can pretty damn well guess. In fact, in that guessing process you become all the more engaged, because now, more than ever, the process of identification is taking place. You are identifying with that person. You are in that person's shoes. You are with him, heart and soul.

We all like to criticize television by saying it is too much entertainment, the problem is not with the word. If you look it up in the dictionary, you'll see that the first definition is the problem one: "diversion." The second definition, in *Webster's Dictionary*, is "engagement." So you can be very much engaged by entertainment or you can be diverted by it. The films we make—*Gimme Shelter, Salesman, Grey Gardens*—are very much engagement films. You leave those films and all you want to do is see it again. Rather than say that's it, now I know how to escape from life, and it's pure fantasy. Or in the case of a Wiseman film, I agree or disagree. You've had that portion of it that has
been selected for you.

To make the point of that shot even stronger, when we finished *Salesman* we had no way of showing it. Television wasn't interested, PBS wasn't a bit interested, no one was interested, and cinema exhibitors weren't quite getting on to the notion that a documentary could be a feature. We decided to rent a theater. We didn't have any money, but somehow we'll. . . . So we had screenings, and maybe a hundred people would show up for these screenings. And at one of these screenings, as people filed out they congratulated my brother and myself; I noticed that, through a crack in the door, there was one person left in the theater. And as she got up and turned in our direction, as everyone did to leave, I noticed that she had been crying. As she got closer, I thought she was quite attractive, so I nudged my brother, and I said, "She's for me." That's my wife.

And it was that scene, I know, within the context of the whole—if you just had that scene alone it wouldn't do it—but that one, I'm sure, was the most tearful.

SZ: *In an interview, you mention that when you first meet a subject you have a way of looking at them. You called it "the gaze."*

AM: I came up with that term from reading a paper that my wife had written for publication. She was a family therapist. Somewhere in the course of that paper, she came up with the notion that so many of her fellow therapists know all the techniques—they've read and studied—but unless they have two qualities, they aren't going to get very far. One is "the gaze," and the other is empathy. And it's through those two, essentially, that you establish rapport. And it can be instantaneous, the first moment you look at somebody you can establish a rapport, especially if there is some kind of empathy that that person picks up from. I am very good at that, and so I can cite instance after instance of getting some immediate rapport. If you look at a lot of stuff that we shot, I started shooting right away, like for example with *Grey Gardens*. If you look at that material, there's just as much rapport there, it's just as good, just as useful as anything, anywhere right up to the last day of shooting. It's sort of love at first sight. Maybe each person may do it his own way, or her own way, and maybe as effectively. But that's how I see, I've come to realize that I have unusually good access to people.

This is so weird. I got a call from somebody who needed me to film Britney Spears. So, a couple of weeks ago I went to Mexico City to film her behind the scenes. They wanted me to shoot a film of this transition she is going through. She is giving up her performing life to do something else, maybe go to school or whatever. So, I had the task of getting access to her, and they said she is going to be difficult, she is a very private person and so forth. I got to her, very quickly, to the point where she was about to be visited by a psychic, and I said, "Look—I was told that she doesn't want to be filmed, and he [the psychic] wouldn't allow it either," but I asked her if it might be okay for me to do it. She said, "Yeah, it's okay with me." Then he came in, went around with his incense, this, that, and the other, they began to talk; I got a lot of that stuff. I said I would like to stay and film, if it's okay. He said, "No, I can't do it with you here." I asked if it would be okay if I just set up a camera and let it run. He said, "Yeah we can do that." So, I got it that way and a lot of stuff before and after.

I was a psychologist early on, too. That didn't hurt any. I have a great deal of confidence that I can get access, and that I really belong there, and that what I'm doing is a good thing for people. Why is it so good? It gives recognition for them as what they really are. Of the two instincts, people would rather disclose than to keep a secret. So I'm confident that I belong there, that I even belong at moments where it would be a trespass. I'm confident that I know when it would be a trespass and not to film at that time. But I also know there are times of— what I would call— vulnerability, which are not really hurtful, although the word means that, somewhat painful perhaps, but nevertheless would belong in the film.

It has to do with my family background, in the greatest measure. My mother told me that when she was engaged to my father, in those days they called it "seeing one another," that they would meet each other for lunch at a street corner downtown in Boston. What my mother didn't know was that my father would arrive maybe five or ten minutes early, place himself across the street behind a window and just look at her.

SZ: *The gaze!*

AM: Yeah. Very important. Observer.

SZ: *Did you and David begin your own production company because you wanted to push toward a feature versus just TV news?*

AM: That's part of it. Basically, no matter who Drew was or what his plan was or way of doing things, there's the necessity for any artist to go on his own. From that point of view, we felt a great contentment that we split. In addition to that, we had some basic differences. Drew was always looking for a crisis and was more attuned to larger scale events, like the Indianapolis race, the do-or-die crisis situation. Whereas, I'm sure coming from a lower/middle-class family, my mother a schoolteacher, my father a postal clerk, our identification was with common people.

My mother, as she was dying—she was a very poetic sort of person—thought for some days what she would want on her grave. She said, "Now I have it, I know what it is." She was quoting someone else, "Count on me, one who loved her fellow man." I don't have it on me, but when my father died, I wrote a letter to my closest friend. My mother happened to see that letter and took a sentence out of it and she said, "This should go on Dad's grave stone." It was something to the effect that he was a laymen, a simple laymen but rests in . . . some kind of greatness involved in being what he was. Both of them kind of elevated the status of ordinary people, and I wanted to keep that going. My brother had the same feelings. Most characteristic film was *Salesman.*

I am making a film about a woman who for forty years has been a nun. She is still a devout and loyal Catholic, but she has been working with homosexuals. The church, the Vatican, has put a silence on her. But she's fighting it. In making that film, I went out to the Bishop's conference in Dallas, Texas, with her. I met Garry Wills. When Garry and I met he said, "I know your work. I must tell you that somebody who has you as a great hero is Studs Terkle."

In a way we are still doing that, I am still choosing subjects where I can, where the ordinary person is caught up in some sort of drama. I am making a film of ordinary people I meet on trains. I meet them in different countries, on long distances trains, and I am convinced that as I walk through that train, I will find somebody where there is a story unfolding. So I get off the train with that person, get the story, because the story is usually off the train, but I get to her through meeting her on the train. The train itself is sort of a metaphor for life as it goes from station to station. But again, this is not Truman Capote in this case, it is not the nonfiction novel. It's the nonfiction short story, or collection of short stories. Many short stories are nonfiction, but they can be fiction too. This case, it's documentary short stories, connected by the train. And all of these are just ordinary . . . you know I am not looking for celebrities.

I have done a couple of trips, at least one across America and one across Russia. When I was traveling from west to east and passing through Pittsburgh, the train stopped, picked up passengers, and I walked through the train. As I was walking through the cafeteria coach, I saw that there was a young woman sitting at an empty table with two kids across the aisle. There was something going on in this woman's mind. I already had my camera, the sound-man was with me, and I asked if I could join her. She said, "Oh, please, great!" Then she took us aside and said, "I've got to tell you a story, what's going on. When I was three years old," she says, "my parents broke up in an ugly divorce and my father got custodianship over me. My father vowed that my mother would never see me again. Twenty-three years later and I still have never met my mother. Last night I got a call from a woman in Philadelphia who claimed to be my mother. She said, 'Look, there's no time to exchange photographs, you don't know what I look like, I don't know what you look like. Get on the next train, and I will be waiting for you in the train station.' " We got off the train—I am filming all of this—and she looks around and there is no one there. As she is walking up the stairs, there is a woman at the top of the stairs. As she comes closer the woman flings open her arms. She looks at me over her shoulder and says, "Isn't she gorgeous?" When you get stuff like that, why bother with trying to invent stories? So this may be a new form too, the collection of short stories.

SZ: *Mentioning different literary forms gets us back to the question that we started with today—the idea of reality. If you had to—this is a terrible question—how would you define reality?*

AM: Well, first of all, we're so mixed up about this; our society is so mixed up about this, so it shouldn't be a surprise that filmmakers are confused. Think of it, a judge turns to a prospective witness and says, "Will you tell the truth, nothing but the truth, the whole truth and nothing but the truth, so help you God?" I mean, an honest witness, if he had the guts, would turn back to the judge and say, "C'mon, gimme a break, you can't do that either!"

But I'll make every effort to. And what I tell—I have no understanding or ability to tell the WHOLE truth—but what I tell will be the truth as best as I know. And I think that someone determined to do that . . . it's in the capability of a human being to come very close to that mark. And I have more confidence that I can do it than perhaps most documentary filmmakers, in all honesty, will admit to. If you read quotations from Fred Wiseman, for example, he's practically a fraud. When he says, "Well, it's all in manipulation and selection. . . ." Come on, it's not the truth. And I dare say that most documentary filmmakers have come to think less of their ability to tell the truth and therefore, don't feel that much obligation. That's bad, that's bad. I feel very much obliged. When I read—you may have come across Pauline Kael's review of *Gimme Shelter*—well, hers makes a complete sham of *Gimme Shelter*. She makes it, I mean, what it's not. And I am sure that anybody looking at . . . because her theory was that it's all Pirandello, and in fact, nothing would have happened except for the fact that the film was made. [She believed] everything was designed for the film, even perhaps, the murder. AND, most devastating, was a statement that, in *Salesman* for example, Paul Brenner really wasn't a Bible salesman.

Distinguished critics like Pauline Kael have this habit of wanting to look very, very intelligent, very clever. Certainly, you read that article, not knowing that she was falsifying everything, and think "Gee what a brilliant idea—no one ever came up with that, gee." This I think was her first review of a documentary, *Gimme Shelter*. She didn't review *Salesman* or any of that stuff. It wasn't until she could say something kind of definitive, bold, and wildly eloquent. Anyway, finally, there was a book, *Imagining Reality*, that published her piece and our answer to it. And then, just recently, a magazine called *Moviemaker* published just our answer to it, described her article, and then did an interview with me. So, some of that is being clarified. . . .

By the way, Capote had the same problem that we've run into sometimes. And that is, people criticizing, "Why didn't you do everything you could to stop the execution?" And so, this latest film of ours, *LaLee's Kin [The Legacy of Cotton*, 2001 TV]. There's a scene in the film where one of the black children can't go to school because she doesn't have paper and pencil, and Grandma is talking to her. The urge of anybody watching this is, "Oh, please, somebody give this child . . ." Grandma doesn't have it, and she's got to go look for it, right? Somebody had heard about that in the film and wrote me this e-mail saying, "I don't understand why you didn't give that child the pen and paper?" I answered it as best I could; it was very important not to interfere with what was going on. And that somehow or another it would work itself out, and in fact the Grandma did find the paper and pencil, and they were okay.

But I could see that a viewer would be disturbed and that somebody, a cameraperson, has got to interfere to stop this thing from going on so badly. After I got that e-mail, just by chance the next day, I got an e-mail from a woman in Georgia who had heard about this. Not about the letter, but about this incident in the film. And she said, "I know about that; I'm just about to get into my car with four of my friends. We're going out to Mississippi to visit the family and to see what we can do to help them out." Just from hearing that little segment of the film. That's a factor in all of this. And people say, "Why didn't you stop the killing in *Gimme Shelter*?" THAT we would have, if we could have, but we were some distance from it to begin with.

SZ: *How could you? It happened so fast.*
AM: Yeah. . . . In fact, my brother wasn't even sure that we actually got it. We had to look at the footage later on.

SZ: *The structure of* Gimme Shelter *reminds me of* In Cold Blood, *with the opening sequences revealing the ending. Was that intentional?*
AM: You'd have to talk to Charlotte about that. Or to David, you know, if he were around. One wonderful element in the structure of the film, of course, is them [the Stones] viewing the scenes. And that came about when Charlotte or David thought we might get that stuff. We'd already known from the Stones that they wanted [to view the footage] . . . so we took advantage of their suggestion and said, "Yeah, we'll show it to you and film you watching it." That became a wonderful device for the structure of the film and also for letting us know what we wouldn't have otherwise—what was their reaction to all of this stuff.

SZ: *Yes. Tom Wolfe has said the one thing a filmmaker can't do is get inside somebody's head. And yet, in that scene with Paul . . .*
AM: Yeah, see this is a problem that many documentarians think that way, the way Wolfe does. And the only way to really get into this guy's heart and soul is to interview him. So, they respond to that need by copping out on what Virginia Woolf would have liked to have known in 1926 when she asked the question, "What devices are unique to cinema?" So, I would say the device that is unique to documentary is to directly film someone else's experience. The interview is an angle from literature and from an earlier form of documentary that didn't take advantage of what was so special about the documentary.

SZ: *Is documentary form evolving, and not just from the technological standpoint but from the standpoint of a language?*

AM: Well, the train film, for example, I think will be a step forward, in that it resembles literature, in that it's a collection of short stories. But even more significantly, one problem with the documentary is that the best that we can do is to film something contemporary, something that is actually taking place right now. Otherwise it's a re-creation, or a use of archival material, or interview. You know, it's sort of second hand rather than what Virginia Woolf was looking for. So we can't go back into history and still make use of the best of documentary, and you can't go forward, film something that hasn't happened yet. But in the train film, the train film will have an epic quality because instead of up into the future or down into the past it's going sideways. It will be half a dozen stories in different countries, in different cultures.

I'm hoping that it will have an epic quality because it will be multicultural, different countries. And some of it will have a little bit of the past and present because that thing that I shot in Philadelphia, that's already twenty years ago. What's happened to her and her kids? I know how to reach her, I'll go back.

SZ: *Has anything about the style of your filmmaking changed with the shift to video?*

AM: Someone asked me for what I would regard as the commandments. You know, Dogme has their stuff, so what are my commandments? My commandments are quite different from the Dogme. Although I might agree with most of them, they don't get to the heart of the matter. And that is, that is one of my commandments, for example, is "love your subjects." No mention of that, no mention of the connection that you should make with the people you are filming. That's true, of course, whether it's a documentary or a fiction. So, I'll give you that. And I emphasize in the documentary, the commandment is to be experiential, that you film experiences. And shy away from narration, hosts, interviews, and so forth.

Rules, of course, are made to be broken, too. So, it's not absolutely firm, but it clearly is how I do things.

SZ: *Are there other connections between the Direct Cinema movement and journalism or the influence of print?*

AM: Bob Drew was trying, with his Neiman Fellowship, to find a way to turn *Life* magazine articles into movies. Just as in *Life* magazine, there'd be a correspondent and a photographer. The ideal thing in making a documentary would be two people: the correspondent doing the sound, the cameraperson being the photographer, and then overlapping somewhat in their roles. That's what started it all.

Before that, five years before that, I was already making documentaries. I was teaching at Boston University. By the time I was twenty-eight, I was a research assistant in a mental hospital in Boston. I'd headed up a research project at the Massachusetts General Hospital and served as teacher at Boston University for three years. My twenty-seventh year I traveled all over Europe on a motorcycle; my twenty-eighth year I thought, "Wouldn't it be interesting to go to Russia?" This was 1955, during the whole course of that year there were only four hundred Americans in Russia, all that year. So, I was something of an anomaly. But before going, I had to think, "Well how am I going to pay for this? What could I really do if I had the opportunity to do so?" And I came up with the idea of making a film in mental hospitals in Russia. Actually, I thought of taking photographs. And so I hitchhiked to New York and actually showed someone else's photographs in a hospital, a professional photographer's, to *Life* magazine. And they said, "Well, your photographs are good, but we can't give you an assignment. When you come back, we'd love to see the photos." So, that wasn't going to help me any.

As I was walking down the street I saw a sign that said CBS. And I walked in. With my usual Boston naiveté, I asked to see Edward R. Murrow. And they said, "Well, why is that?" "I have a visa, a one-month visa for Russia, I'm a psychologist and I am hoping to visit mental hospitals." "Oh well, I'm sure he'd be delighted to see you, but he's on vacation. You should see the head of the news department." So I did. I ended up borrowing a movie camera and film and off I went. Through my special ability, at access, I crashed a Romanian Embassy reception, met the top Soviet leaders, and one of them gave me the information. And then I was on my way to my first film.

SZ: *What was the relationship between what the news departments were broadcasting at that time and the kind of films you were doing? It seems like there was a little bit of competition.*

AM: It's the same today. The news people don't want anybody to do the news except themselves. This is a very, very, very firm policy, and there's no way to get around that. Except that Bob Drew managed, because he got the support of Bell and Howell who would pay for the six television shows on ABC; he got ABC to agree to let him do these films. They still had to approve of them and had some ideas on changes and so forth, but the head of the news department, in fact, was so furious that he resigned.

SZ: *Was that Daly?*

AM: Could be. But, I'll give you my own experience in that way. About six or seven years ago, the Rockefeller Foundation asked if I would be interested in going to North Korea to look into making a film. They said, "We'll pay for the whole trip, and we have contacts so that you can get in there." So I came up with a proposal, which the North Koreans agreed upon. I would film an extended family in their daily lives. But then when I was on my way to North Korea, and stopping off in Beijing about to take the final flight, my interpreter friend was in contact with the Rockefeller Foundation, and he said he had just spoken to them, and they said that Tom Johnson, who was the president of CNN, that he will be on that same plane, and we might want to talk to him. So when we got to the airport, I looked around in the waiting room and everyone was there to get on the plane, including one other Caucasian. I went up to him and I said, "You must be Tom Johnson, I'm Albert Maysles." He said, "Oh, I know your work." But then he never said anything more. I said, "Aren't you interested in what I'd be doing?" He said, "Yeah, you're probably going to look into making a movie there. We can't do anything with outsiders. That's a firm policy of CNN."

And the weirdest thing of all, as I discovered sometime later, [was] that he had been recently appointed to this job as president of CNN, [and] his previous job was at the Rockefeller Foundation. So if he had stayed on, he might well have been the person to have sent me there.

SZ: *So what's the best hope for distribution of documentaries?*

AM: Last week I was in L.A. as a keynote speaker, and what was the conference all about? DVD. One of the panels that I was on discussed this very matter of how you market. What are the new marketing opportunities for DVD? I can't really answer that, but at least we will be able to turn from technology to content. And I spoke endlessly about the kinds of films that we could now do that we'd never thought of doing. The short stories, the poetic moments, and I gave those kinds of examples. We can do poetry, great poetry, with the video camera.

There was a time when sex was forbidden on television, in cinema, right? It had a high time in literature with all that stuff. Now there's no problem that way. But, more important than excessive sex or violence, you know, is showing good stuff. Edmund Burke said that "evil will triumph as long as good people do nothing." So when I think of the lousy television, which is dominated by lousy people doing lousy things, right, I think of that quote and I think, well, let's get going. DVD gives us another opportunity to self-express in areas where we think we can say things that are worth saying, where we can engage people with real life. So, the field is wide open if we only take advantage of it.

This idea, that understanding the real world allows us all the better to love one another. That idea came from the Italian screenwriter who did *Bicycle Thief*. . . .

SZ: *Zavattini?*

AM: Zavattini!

SZ: *You know, there's a connection there with Capote too, because Capote lived in Italy, worked on some scripts with Houston and Humphrey Bogart, and was exposed to the neorealist filmmakers De Sica and Zavattini. He greatly admired them.*

AM: Zavattini wanted to do just exactly what I'm doing now, only he couldn't talk Rossellini into it. My brother and I were at some event at the United Nations in Paris, and Rossellini was on the panel. They showed *Showman*. . . . He just couldn't understand why we would make a film like that. So, he really basically didn't quite understand the power of or potential of documentary, I think.

Anyway, Zavattini had this idea of making a film or series, maybe more than one film, it would be called "My Italy." They go into a town, and they'd say effectively, "What's going on?" "Well, so and so is having a child." "Let's go, we'll film it." That's it, that's what we're talking about. But he never did it. I had lunch with him once. He's an inspiring guy, a wonderful guy, Zavattini.

SZ: *You mention that Vertov's brother, Kauffman, didn't like this Direct Cinema stuff. That he was sort of against what was going on. Yet there is an interesting connection to Vertov in Direct Cinema.*

AM: Ricky [Leacock] could answer this better. He looks down on Eisenstein and, but even more pertinent, Vertov. He doesn't think that that's the real thing at all. And the little I've seen of it is hardly what we're doing now. For one thing, he didn't have the advantage of sync sound. How can you depict life without sound? Then wasn't it Soviet propaganda? What was his expression? The cinema of truth or something?

SZ: *Yeah, Kino Pravda. Cinema truth.*

AM: Cinema truth, and it wasn't. It was far from, far from what can be done now.

SZ: *Would you say that documentary filmmaking, like writing, is a process of discovery?*
AM: That's the word. "Serendipitous" is another way of putting it. Or, connected with "discovery" and "serendipity," is the idea of uncontrolled. If you're a good parent, you may be a good filmmaker, documentary filmmaker. If I'm correct, the word "education" is a very good word. If you look up the source of it, from the Latin, "e" is to take out of, and "duc" means to lead. You lead a person from out of that person; in other words, there is something in that person that you draw out. Rather than the idea of putting thoughts into people, you come up with ways of drawing them out. It's another way of truly respecting a child or individual that you are filming. We don't want to impose.

SZ: *Capote was criticized for calling* In Cold Blood *a new genre, the nonfiction novel. Did he really do something new?*
AM: Literature is not my area of expertise, but it seemed to me that he had gone a step further.

SZ: *One of the things about your mission statement is this idea of faith in reality. Many people today, particularly in academia, say, "Well, there is no reality out there" or "all reality is constructed."*
AM: Especially those who are . . . what's this whole new philosophy? Where you really don't know anything for sure at all? It's rampant at schools like Brown University.

SZ: *Postmodern?*
AM: That's it! So this postmodernism has corrupted our confidence in gathering truth.

SZ: *In the 1960s the postmodern French theorists were being translated into English. That's when their philosophy really began to take hold in the U.S. Yet, one of the characteristics of your style of documentary and the New Journalist style of writing is that you maintain a connection to reality, a faith in reality "out there."*
AM: Yes, that's very important. Along with that, for us, is being nonjudgmental. We're not trying to prove a point, we're trying to get very close to the actual.

SZ: *In some of your interviews you've talked about how there is a subjectivity, there is a point of view—I guess I am playing off this word "point." You're not trying to force a point, but there is a point of view?*
AM: I think the first commandment is "distance yourself from a point

of view." That's the key, that's the key to it all. . . . Some of these new journalism authors are . . . point of view and some of them aren't point of view authors, to use that expression. There's a whole scale from 1 to 10, or whatever. Some of them have an axe to grind; others are willing to tell the story without judgment and without preconception or formulation.

SZ: *"Without preconception" is a term that is used a lot when referring to Flaherty and his films. He took time to get to know the people and established a different kind of documentary method.*

AM: He would have, perhaps, been where I am right now if he had sound. I know that Ricky Leacock worked with him and has great admiration for him, and Ricky's a guy who is a purist, like myself. As you know, Flaherty was criticized for staging things a little bit. It was hard for him not to when he didn't have the kind of tools that we have today.

SZ: *But I think people who watch him realize he did get at a reality about Nanook even though he had to stage things. But what about people who do [stage things]? . . . I'm thinking particularly of Errol Morris and* Thin Blue Line.

AM: I had a bad experience with Errol. He worked in here—I think it was his first film—and he rented an editing room with all the editing equipment for three months, and then he just ran out and never paid his bill. To this day he never paid it, and I've reminded him a few times. He makes a lot of money on commercials, he could easily have . . . well. So that must have something to do with it. Now he has this contraption . . .

SZ: *The "interretron."*

AM: I don't know it well enough to fully criticize it, but it seems to me that it's a bundle of nonsense—that in fact, if he's looking to have the camera look right into the eyes of the person, and the person look right into the eyes of the camera that I've been doing this all along without any of that contraption. I get far enough away from the person—when I have to do an interview, let's say, for a commercial or whatever—which means maybe seven feet away, let's say, and the person who's interviewing gets as close to the camera as possible, right up next to it, so as far as the camera's concerned, that person's looking at the lens. And I'm better off, perhaps than his contraption, because that person is actually looking at a person. . . . But see, if I'm doing an interview I'd much rather do it with the person in loco.

SZ: *You mentioned that in* Grey Gardens, *in the bedroom scene, you had to add light. Usually you use just ambient light.*

AM: I just set up two lights, bounced them off the ceiling and that was it.

SZ: *I was thinking of Charlotte Zwerin's term "cinéma vérité police" (Zuber 238). She meant people who criticize any kind of manipulation whatsoever, or people who'll say any kind of manipulation means you don't have reality.*

AM: We get the best editors, Charlotte is the best in the world for documentary—but because editors rarely get the kind of credit they deserve in a film and because they're not generally interviewed as much as the producers, they get somewhat paranoid. And they come up with statements a little stronger than they might under other circumstances. So being thrown off balance to begin with, they tend to try extra hard to show the importance of the editing, which takes away from some of the importance of, say, the camera work. Whatever that may be or not be, she sure is the best. She is extremely good at getting the best out of my material, I know that.

You know, I talk about poetry. I have to give you an example of a poetic moment. I am sitting on the bus coming to the office, and I see an older man across from me talking to a woman, who he probably just met a couple of stops back. He's talking seriously about how he was in the war, the Second World War, and how so many of his buddies were just young kids, and these young kids always get killed in wars. But as he's talking to her, he keeps looking back at me, quite intensely, and of course I'm giving him the gaze, right? Finally, he says, "Here it is, it's 9 o'clock, I get up at 8:30 every morning" and looking back at me, he says, "I have a full day's activities and I'm totally blind." Poetry.

It gets to another thing I'd like to emphasize, too, and that is great literature, great art, great movies are without purpose. Now that little poem, what's the purpose? It's a poem. It has wonderful justification as a poem. It's a poem. It's something that engages you, it maybe enlightens you, but it has no specific point of view. It doesn't pass judgment. It enlightens.

On another occasion, I saw across from me a very overweight black woman with a hunk of a head on her shoulders. Nobody was looking at her, if only for the fact that they might embarrass her. But I was looking at her in a kindly way, and I kept looking at her. In fact, there was a woman next to me, and I nudged her and I made a motion like that and we were both looking at her. When suddenly, the little black girl next to her, maybe nine or ten years old—had to be her daughter—gets up, flips around in front of her mother, and nestles her head between her mother's breasts and falls asleep.

That's the kind of thing that I'm looking to film. And just as those are two entirely different scenes, they have the similarity of being poetic.

Before I forget about it, somebody came across a quotation from Orson

Welles of all people. . . . Anyway, I came across this quote that I thought was quite nice: "A cameraman should have behind the lens an eye of a poet." Unfortunately that's not usually the criteria for a good cameraman.

SZ: *Capote, in the film you made about him, mentions how he wanted to get the audience to feel what he was feeling. It seems to me that is another similarity, stylistically, that you have with Capote.*

AM: But at the same time, this is the hard part for people to understand. . . . He has that ability to notice what other people wouldn't notice. . . . There were dozens of other people, some of them right next to me, in both of those occasions on that bus. No one else noticed, but I did because there's something in me that drew my attention.

SZ: *It's more than looking, it's a seeing.*

AM: Yes. Seeing with the eye of a poet. I think in a way, you know better than I, I think poetry is kind of, in a way the purest kind of literature, in a way. It's not the new journalism, but it doesn't have a meaning. It has an existence that is undeniable. . . . As Edie in *Grey Gardens* says, "It's all time and place."

I so often make the comment that in a documentary film, because you are dealing with real live people, you have a special responsibility to be very accurate, and also that responsibility carries over because after the film you maintain a relationship with the people in the film.

So, it's been six months since Edie died, the daughter. She was eighty-four years old, just about the age that her mother died. So, I got a call from [Edith] Bouvier Beale, her cousin. They are having a special memorial service, in the Hamptons, and they want me to come. But it's only really the family, so no one else is going to be there. So I go; they assemble at a Catholic church. In front of the altar is a little basket holding Edie's ashes and a little bird on top. The priest gives the usual story about how everybody can, in following Jesus, inhabit another world and all that stuff. Then, [Edith] Bouvier Beale, the cousin, gets up and gives a talk. For a good twenty minutes, I would expect, it's all quotations from the film. So, the good word goes on.

Can you imagine what being in *Salesman* meant for Paul Brennan? The irony is that he's portrayed as a failure, but as a person he's such a success. And we became lifelong buddies, David and I and him.

SZ: *If a documentary is feature length, it gives more time to explore character. In ways that I associate with the novel, you give a chance for the character to really unfold.*

AM: Yeah. I have one argument with Tolstoy, not that I've read that much of him, but as you may remember in *Anna Karenina* the opening lines go like this: "All unhappy families are different in their own way; happy families are all the same." That's what he says, right? It's not true. Because journalists have this prejudice toward telling stories of unhappy families, they don't pay attention to the happy ones. And so, we have few role models of well-functioning people or families, and we need that.

In 1963, I connected with two very good filmmakers, Orson Welles and Jean-Luc Godard. Barbet Schroeder was about to produce a film where he drew on the talents of half a dozen French film directors, distinguished directors. One of them was Godard. And each one was to do a fifteen- to twenty-minute piece, a story that takes place in Paris. Because I knew Barbet, and he knew my work, Barbet said, "Look, wouldn't it be great if you did the camera stuff on Godard's sequence?" So he calls up Godard, tells him about me, and he says, "Yes, send him over." So the next day, he had everything all set up, the actors knew what they were going to do. And I walked in not even knowing what it was about, and I felt it. My filming was really one continuous shot almost. It's a kind of masterpiece of collaboration.

That same year, my brother and I were at Cannes. We met up with Orson Welles, who says, "Come on, let's go to Madrid and spend a good week together." So, we make this little film of him talking about a film we would make. He's describing how he could best work with us, and of course, it has to be on 16mm. Then he talks about how he has a script, that he knows what he wants to do, but he's throwing away the script. Then he talks about divine accidents.

What is a documentary but one divine accident after another? I mean, reality is a force outside of ourselves that we play a small part of.

Works Cited

Kael, Pauline. "Beyond Pirandello." In *Deeper into Movies*. Boston: Little, Brown, 1973. 206–11.

Plantinga, Carl. *Rhetoric and Representation in Nonfiction Film*. Cambridge, UK: Cambridge UP, 1997.

Robertson, R. B. *Of Whales and Men*. N.Y.: Alfred A. Knopf, 1954.

Vogels, Jonathan, B. "'Outrageous Acts of Faith': The Films of Albert and David Maysles: 1962–1986." Diss. Boston University, 2000.

Zwerin, Charlotte. Personal interview, August 6, 2002, in Sharon Zuber's "Reshaping Documentary Expectations: New Journalism and Direct Cinema." Diss. College of William and Mary, 2004.

Maysles on DIFF, Castro, Flies on Walls, and the Poetic Eye

MARTY MAPES/2004

AL MAYSLES has a fifty-year career of making documentary films. Among his more prominent credits are *Gimme Shelter*, *Salesman*, and five films about the artist Christo.

With his brother and filmmaking partner David, Al Maysles was among the first to use the style that came to be known as cinéma vérité. This style of documentary filmmaking shuns narrators and re-enactments, and simply lets the subjects speak for themselves.

Unlike most of the Denver International Film Festival's guests, Al Maysles was in town to honor, and not *be* honored. Beginning this year, the DIFF will give to outstanding documentary filmmakers a new award called the Maysles Brothers Award for Best Documentary Film.

I was fortunate to interview Mr. Maysles, a spry, white-haired man, softspoken, with a joyful sparkle somewhere behind his black-rimmed glasses.

Ornery Honorer

MARTY MAPES: *You've turned the tables. You are honoring a film festival and not the other way around.*
AL MAYSLES: It's an honor to be an honorer. Without being ornery.

MM: *And the DIFF will give it out in your name?*
AM: Yeah, that's right.

From *Movie Habit*, www.moviehabit.com. Reprinted by permission of the author.

MM: *And this year's winner?*
AM: Danny Shechter. Do you know his work? He's almost one step beyond Michael Moore in the forcefulness of his presentation.

Wise Man

MM: *I learned about Frederick Wiseman and came to love his style before I found out that he had learned from you.*
AM: And from two or three other guys.

MM: *Did you learn from somebody else or did you all arise at the same time?*
AM: We learned at the same time. Ricky Leacock, I would say, was in the forefront. And then [D. A.] Pennebaker and Bob Drew and myself. And *Primary* is the one that got it all started. It's funny, the title *Primary*, it's primary to the documentary movement.

Relations with Cuba, and Others

MM: *It's really hard to tell a story without a narrator to fill in the gaps—did you find any tricks along the way to help?*
AM: Just keeping a sharp eye, a poetic eye if you will. There's a knack for being at the right place at the right time. And also there's a knack that goes along with getting access to people. So many people say, "Well, it must take a long time before people accept the camera." (Shakes his head, points at himself) Right away. It's the way you look at them.

I formed that relationship with Fidel [Castro] for example. I came to Cuba in 1960 without any credentials or any contacts. Got off the plane, jumped into a cab, asked the cab driver, "Where's Fidel?" He said, "Oh, he's addressing a group of women." "—Take me there." So I get as close as I can, which in that public space was difficult, I could only get maybe within twenty feet, but I put a 200mm lens on the camera. And as he was talking I was picking [my camera] up (gestures slowly), got it onto my shoulder just as he turned to my direction, by chance, and we connected with our eyes. He was responding to my eyes, and I knew it was okay. So I put [the camera] all the way up on my shoulder and got this fantastic shot of him.

It wasn't long before I was spending two, full, twenty-four-hour days with him. There was a point where I was with him at a Chinese embassy reception, standing shoulder-to-shoulder with him. A messenger came rushing in, handed him a telegram. He tears it open, reads it, turns to me, and says, "Shall I translate it for you?" The state department had just broken off relations with Cuba.

So recently I sent him a letter recalling that moment with the implication that maybe, with the election, things will change, and there'll be another telegram. I want to be there, this time, with my little video camera.

Fly Swatter

MM: *Do you think the trick is to be invisible?*
AM: No, no. That's wrong. People have complimented me—or attempted to do so—by saying, "Oh, it's the fly on the wall, isn't that wonderful." The fly on the wall doesn't have any intelligence. And if you're totally invisible, you're not using your presence to be *more* present when something is happening. Maybe that's the best way to put it. You gotta be in the thick of it, but without imposing upon it by being accepted.

MM: *That is so hard to do.*
AM: I find it easy. And I think what makes it easy is if you're confident that you can do it. That's the first thing. Part of that confidence is that you feel that this is gonna be good for the person I'm filming, even if it's something a little bit embarrassing. It's telling the truth about that person.

Debra Dixon, who is here [at the DIFF], she edited a film that we worked together on, a film called *LaLee's Kin*, a film of a very poor family in the south. I remember we finished the film—which really told their life very, very clearly, without any punches being pulled, but very sympathetically. When we finished it, we showed it to the main character, grandma. She looked at it (makes a reluctant face), and she said (nods), "That's the truth." Then she followed up by saying, "But couldn't you have made it longer?" Then you really knew, that was the ultimate compliment.

Counterexamples

MM: *Can you think of a counterexample in your career? Where somebody says, "No, you can't film me," or "No, I don't like that, that's a very unflattering portrait"?*

AM: There's one instance of that. It's a long story, but you'll appreciate it. The first film that my brother and I made was a film called *Showman*, of a man by the name of Joseph E. Levine, who was a distributor, but in the process of our filming him he became a producer of Sophia Loren films. So we showed him the film. And he liked it. And his wife came over to us and she said: "I'm so glad he doesn't have a Jewish voice."

Now even in the film you see that he came from a very poor family in an anti-Semitic neighborhood. What frequently happens is that, when you're subject of anti-Semitism, you tend to believe some of it. If you're only a film distributor, the middle guy, without being creative, "Oh, it's a Jewish moneylender," all these stereotypes. So there was some of that, especially when friends of Levine said, "Oh, my God, that film is so anti-Semitic." So he was a little bit confused about whether to like the film. Sometimes he liked the film, sometimes he didn't, but that's an odd case.

On another occasion, as we were filming him, he had a guy working for him doing the public relations. And the two of them were so different from one another it wasn't going to work out. So they had a meeting one day. And we wanted to get into the meeting because we thought maybe the guy was being fired. But he didn't want us in there so we couldn't film. So instead we went to the guy's office to wait for him when he came back. So he comes back to the office, and as he's walking in, one of his assistants says, "Gee, I heard they dropped a bombshell on you." So we got that on film. We got a better story under the right circumstances. He sat down. We put the camera down. I looked at him, I said, "If it's okay with you, we'd like to keep filming." (Nods). He picks up the phone, he tells the whole story to his best friend. That was the right way to do it. The other way would have been too embarrassing to both of them.

Wiseman's Bias

MM: *I was in the room when somebody asked Frederick Wiseman whether the Heisenberg Uncertainty Principle applied to human behavior.*

AM: What did he say?

MM: *He said no it doesn't.*

AM: How did he explain it?

MM: *He said it* is *okay to be an observer. Just by observing you don't necessarily change the events.*

AM: That's right.

MM: *You would say the same thing.*
AM: Yeah, yeah. Depends on how you handle it. For some people it's a real problem. But especially his early films I disagreed with his way of doing things. It was always good guy bad guy. And that's not fair. Do you know [Frederick Wiseman's film] *Titicut Follies*?

MM: *Yeah.*
AM: I didn't like that one at all, and I'll tell you why. I've worked in mental hospitals so I know something about that. And I felt that, with the best of intentions on his part, he tried to show how bad the system was there, right? How bad the people running it [were], right?

MM: *So he already had a point of view.*
AM: So he had that, right. And then he showed very little of the patients. But the little that he showed of the patients were in one state of psychosis or another. So making a film in defense of the patients, he actually hurt them by dehumanizing them. And in fact I've learned recently that that hospital already had underway serious plans for reform. And he didn't pay any attention to that.

MM: *Do you catch yourself saying, "I need to be more objective"?*
AM: I don't have a problem with that. Part of it is that before making films, by the time I was twenty-eight, I was a psychologist, teaching psychology at Boston University. And in psychology, whatever you learn, you learn to be very careful about containing your prejudices.

Two to Tango

MM: *It seems like you had a great collaboration with your brother David. Did you work well together?*
AM: One thing I think that helped was that we chose non-competing roles. He did the sound; I did the camera. But it was more than sound, and more than camera. He supervised [the editing]. So that was more than sound. So we had really equally important roles.

Many a brother, they're in terrible competition with one another and they never get along. In our case, I think the relationship was facilitated by the fact that we had parents who were very much in love with each other, very good parents. My mother for example was a very, very active civil rights person, before that even became popular. And so we had more than just a tolerance of people of other ethnic or color . . . whatever background, rich or poor, whatever. We totally accepted whatever differences there might be. That helped.

MM: *Was it hard to adjust, after you lost him?*
AM: Well, I worked with Susan Froemke. And we, again, we had a very complementary relationship.

Film-to-Video Transfer

MM: *You have had a very long career so far.*
AM: Fiftieth year coming up next year.

MM: *You've seen a lot of changes. I'd like to ask you about some specific ones. First of all, film to video.*
AM: (Smiles) Oh yeah, great! Good.

MM: *Really? I don't like the look of it. I'm kind of a film snob.*
AM: I'm holding judgment on that until I see it side-by-side. Maybe I don't want to. But I like to put it this way. The Hollywood film, the fiction film—okay, you're looking for high production value. Documentary? Let's sacrifice a little bit of that if it means that we're gonna get closer to what's going on, less imposition, make it all possible because it's five dollars for an hour instead of a couple of thousand. And still, the beauty is another kind.

MM: *The subject . . .*
AM: Yeah. And you don't want to sacrifice that beauty. You've seen *Salesman*?

MM: *Yeah.*
AM: When Paul is sitting alone in the cafeteria and just looking off into the room. He's had a hard time already, he's taking a break. I was lucky. I had ten minutes of film. I must have had a new roll or something. But I tell you, it would have broke my heart if in the middle of that I ran out of film. But it would be all the less likely if I were shooting with a video camera, with an hour. That's very important.

Now, people say, "Yeah, but with video you're shooting all the time, so you end up with a thousand hours of tape." Well, that's *your* fault, that's not the camera. I'll put it this way. Henri Cartier Bresson, the great still photographer. Probably the greatest still photographer. He always used the Leica. Thirty-six exposures. Would he be better off with a 2¼" image and only twelve exposures?

MM: *But then is he better off with a cheap digital camera with five thousand exposures?*
AM: He wouldn't abuse it. He never did abuse the privilege of having

thirty-six pictures instead of twelve. Every time he took that shot, you just didn't fire away. They just photographed [me] just now (pointing to photographers). They must have taken fifty shots. See now, for example, they should have been photographing me here now (talking to you). Every two minutes I've got twenty beautiful different expressions. Not that one of just looking at the camera, under the blaze of the lights. The light is fine, right the way it is right now. It's okay. It's not professional lighting. . . . (smiles)

MM: *But there it is . . . it's a better smile right now . . . right . . . now.*

AM: Orson Welles put it beautifully. Someone gave me his quote recently. "The cameraperson should have an eye behind the camera that is the eye of a poet." He's not talking about lighting, he's not talking about the size of the negative.

Albert Maysles

SHANA LIEBMAN/2004

THE MAYSLES BROTHERS revolutionized documentary making with nonfiction features *Salesman* (1969), *Gimme Shelter* (1970), *Grey Gardens* (1975), in which "the drama of life unfolds as is without scripts, sets, interviews, or narration." After David Maysles died in 1987, his brother Albert persevered. Despite the lack of recent commercial success, Maysles Films' large loft is still buzzing with young filmmakers enthusiastically engaged in one of Albert's many projects (the Dalai Lama in Canada; a Wes Anderson documentary; the Gates project in Central Park; a Polish Holocaust survivor; a nun's missionary work with homosexuals . . .) Just west of the whirlwind is Albert, a tiny, white-haired man crouched over a corner desk. The seventy-seven-year-old—who has earned a Guggenheim Fellowship, a Peabody, an Emmy, and five Lifetime Achievement Awards—couldn't be more unassuming, or as it turns out, more accessible.

SHANE LIEBMAN: *You're working on so many projects. When do you see films?*

ALBERT MAYSLES: I don't see movies. I don't have time or rather I don't make time. I was invited to present an award to Barbra Kopple at Silverdocs. She said to me, "I don't think you've seen any of my films." I said, "You're right." But I love to talk about films I haven't seen. I'm the biggest anti-Michael Moore person in the world, but I've never seen any of his films.

SL: *Why are you so anti-Michael Moore?*

AM: I don't like his methods. He said it himself: "People do themselves

---

From *The Independent*, October 2004. Independent Media Publications, www.independent-magazine.org. Reprinted by permission of *The Independent* and the author.

in. You don't have to provoke them." What an attitude toward people! I don't go with that at all. If he wants to build his case for gun control, he can do it in a very fair fashion and probably end up with something that is more powerful—but powerful for people who are discerning, not people who are easy prey for propaganda. We had enough of that with Hitler.

SL: *How would you describe your filmmaking style?*

AM: When I was in Russia, someone asked me to describe the way I work in a word. I said, "Serendipity." It's so much easier when you're doing films about political or social issues to just interview someone and more difficult to follow them around and get interesting moments. That's what I do—I get interesting moments. I film people experiencing whatever it is without taking the shortcut of interviewing or depending on music to heighten the drama.

SL: *How did you come to make* Salesman*?*

AM: My brother had a luncheon with Joe Fox, who was Truman Capote's editor, and he asked Joe what would be an interesting subject. Joe said, "What about door to door salesmen?" We found a Chicago outfit with guys selling the bible, and there were four guys from Boston, our hometown—four Irish guys.

In the best films, there is something in the makeup of the filmmaker that is poignant to the film itself. When I was growing up, the Irish would pick on Jewish kids. I had to defend myself everyday with my fists. So it was time for reconciliation. [Making *Salesman*] was sort of like a resolution of the Palestinian-Israeli conflict . . . on a slightly smaller scale.

SL: *Does the term cinéma vérité apply to your work?*

AM: I think that is a little bit pretentious, although I believe a film like *Salesman* and *Grey Gardens* is quite truthful. The term came into being in France when Rouch was making films like *Chronicles of a Summer*. He'd sit people around a table and get conversation going. That's not kosher by my standards . . . it's not as real as what I'm after. A French critic called my early films Direct Cinema and I think that makes sense—behind the scenes, close up.

SL: *Why do you make documentaries?*

AM: Almost any social problem is a problem because there wasn't a documentary made about it. This war would have been totally impossible if there was a documentary that gave us the facts before we got the lies.

SL: *What's the most important social issue right now?*
AM: Tribalism is the biggest danger to world peace. People thinking they are better than other people.

SL: *Whom would you most like to shoot?*
AM: I met Elie Wiesel—who is very adverse to anyone making a film about him. He had a bad experience with it and he says he's a person of words not pictures. I showed him a drawing my son made of Holocaust victims and he was moved. He told me that every so often he gets together with a former fellow prisoner and they read the Talmud together. That is a scene I'd like to film.

SL: *Whom do you admire?*
AM: Richard Leacock—who was [Robert S.] Flaherty's cinematographer. He, along with [D. A.] Pennebaker in the 1960s, began a whole new way of making documentaries. His film *Primary* [1960] about the election campaign with Humphrey changed everything.

SL: *Who has influenced your work?*
AM: I don't think I've been influenced by anyone. I got into making movies from being a psychologist. This was in 1955. Because I knew something about psychology and I worked in a mental hospital, I borrowed a movie camera. It's the human element of my films that is most important.

"A Bible Salesman or the Rolling Stones: They're All Just People"

GEOFFREY MACNAB/2005

THE SEVENTY-EIGHT-YEAR-OLD documentary maker Albert Maysles recently embarked on a new work called *In Transit*. The film entails him making a series of long-distance railway journeys, befriending fellow passengers, and persuading them to talk about their lives on camera.

"Why am I doing it, besides that I love to travel?" he asks himself. "I have a faith in strangers. When I was seventeen, in 1944, I went off to war. When I was in the station, leaving for the army, I was with a number of other kids my same age. We were joking around. Then, as the train began to move, I looked out of the window, still laughing about some joke, I saw my family looking very serious and looking straight ahead. They couldn't see me but they could see this train move off. They were thinking of course that I might never come back. That image has been in the back of my mind all my life. I don't want to get away from it because it was the most intense feeling of their love for me."

Maysles has already shot one episode of *In Transit* which comes close to recapturing the intensity of his departure for the army. Late last year, he met a woman on a train heading out of Pittsburgh. The woman revealed that her parents had been through a bitter divorce when she was only three years old. Her father, who won custody, vowed that she would never see her mother again. The night before she ran into Maysles on the train, she had received a call from a lady in Philadelphia. That was where she was now headed. "Part of why she was so open was that she was a

---

From *The Guardian*, 19 August 2005. Reprinted by permission of the author.

little bit nervous," Maysles observes. "She didn't quite understand what was going to happen. I'm filming all of this. She gets off the train. As she gets off the train, there's a woman who comes rushing down the stairs and opens her arms. They embrace and they talk and the mother puts her head over her daughter's shoulder and turns to me and says: 'Isn't she gorgeous?' "

Maysles has an uncanny knack for capturing such climactic and intimate moments on camera. It's easy to understand why strangers open up in front of him. He is a gentle, silver-haired presence in black spectacles who has the air of a father confessor. As he repeats several times, he loves people. "I have no difficulty in getting access or establishing rapport," he says. "Usually, it's just from the first moment of meeting someone. I think it's the way I look at them and establish trust right away. There's nothing in my method that is subversive or hurtful and I think people get a sense of trust right away."

Whether he is filming the Rolling Stones (the subjects of his 1970 classic *Gimme Shelter*) or Irish-American door-to-door bible salesmen (featured in his 1968 documentary *Salesman*), or a mother and daughter living secluded in a decaying East Hampton mansion (1976's *Grey Gardens*), his approach doesn't change. "People are people. We're out to discover what is going on behind the scenes and get as close as we can to what is happening." Maysles never intrudes in his documentaries. He seldom even asks a question. If one of his subjects looks directly at camera, thereby threatening to expose his presence, he'll lay the camera down. He is the antithesis of documentary makers like Michael Moore or Nick Broomfield, who foreground themselves in their work.

Touchingly, he still talks about his younger brother and long-term collaborator David Maysles (who died in 1987) in the present tense. "The camera is totally silent," he explains. "My brother doesn't use a boom hanging over people's heads. Instead he uses a directional microphone down low in his hands. There's no connection by wire between camera and tape recorder. We can move separately from one another. I have the camera designed in such a way that I don't need to put it down to read the aperture or the focus. I offer very little imposition on people or on the scene."

The Edinburgh retrospective features three remarkable, rarely seen shorts by the Maysles brothers. *With Love from Truman*, shot in 1966, captures Truman Capote just after *In Cold Blood* has been published. In *Meet Marlon Brando*, the brothers' camera is trained on the loquacious and mischievous movie star during a press junket. Brando is grilled by journalists from all over America and responds to their inane questions with ever more provocative and baffling answers.

Muhammad and Larry, meanwhile, is the most idiosyncratic film about the run-up to a world heavyweight boxing bout ever made. The subjects, an ageing Muhammad Ali and the young pretender Larry Holmes, are in training camp. Although they will shortly be climbing into the ring to fight, what shines through is their mutual respect and curiosity about one another.

Where did the Maysles style come from? The brothers set out in the late sixties to match in documentary what Capote had achieved in the nonfiction novel. During their film about Capote, the author holds forth on his aesthetic theory "that you can produce a work of art out of factual material that has the same impact as the most imaginative literature does . . . and it has this extraordinary extra dimension that it's absolutely true." This was a sentiment that the brothers agreed with absolutely. Fittingly enough, it was Joe Fox, Capote's agent at Random House, who suggested the subject matter for *Salesman*, their breakthrough nonfiction feature film.

There is still debate today about the subterfuge that Capote used when researching and writing *In Cold Blood*. A recent article in the *New York Times* alleged that the author "told some lies to tell a truth" and "sold out" the two killers whose stories he chronicled in his book. No one has ever accused Albert Maysles of such deceptions. The key to his working method is his background. Albert began his career as a psychologist and still sees himself as a scientist. "I think my training taught me above all to be unprejudiced. Psychology was social science, and so in a way my work has always combined a kind of scientific approach with art," he muses.

In other words, Maysles observes without judging. Whereas other filmmakers concede that their own prejudices are implicit in everything they do, from where they set the camera to how they edit, Maysles insists that documentary can capture the objective truth. He is sharply critical of filmmakers who resort to advocacy or polemic. He calls them "point of view people," which in his lexicon is the ultimate put-down. Not that his work is bland. "When I started making films, I was given two or three rules. It's got to be 35mm, it's got to have a strong point of view, and you've got to use a tripod," he states. It goes without saying that he never abided by any of these rules.

At any given time, Maysles always has several different projects on the boil. He is currently making a film about Budd Schulberg, the writer of *On the Waterfront.* He recently shot footage of Marlon Brando's memorial service in New York. He continues to work with artists Christo and Jeanne-Claude, and has spent years filming the build-up to The Gates, their project that entailed draping Central Park with over seven thousand saffron-coloured fabric panels. Now, in a radical departure for a film-maker who has always resolutely kept himself out of the picture, he is making a documentary about his own life. *Hand-Held from the Heart,* as the project is called, chronicles his fifty years as a film-maker.

"At some point in everybody's life, they like to make some sort of statement as to who they are. That's why people give us access when we make films. They can look at that film and say, yes, that's me, that's who I am. I am doing that service for myself," Maysles explains, admitting to just a trace of vanity.

Putting himself on camera will be considered heretical by some of his more purist cinéma vérité colleagues. They might frown, too, at his plans for a film about Mendel Beilis, a Russian Jew living outside Kiev who was falsely accused of murdering a thirteen-year-old Christian boy and using his blood in a religious ritual. For this film, Maysles will break with the habits of a lifetime and use historical reconstructions with actors. (If he does, he adds, "every word will be taken from the transcripts of the trial.") He dates the so-called "blood libel" accusation dates back to Norfolk, England, in the twelfth century when Jews were accused of killing Christian children to take their blood to mix with mud to celebrate passover. Discussing anti-Semitism, Maysles, whose family were Jewish immigrants from east Europe, temporarily loses his composure.

The only other subject that provokes the same ire is the behaviour of George W Bush. "It's shocking what must have gone on in the minds of Americans to put so many votes in his pocket," Maysles frowns and then adds that if he ever made a film about Bush, he would struggle to hide his point of view. "Right now, if the opportunity arose and there was the money for it and the story, in the case of the Bush administration, I would be quite happy to part from my high ideals."

Uncontrolled Cinema: Albert Maysles

WILLIAMS COLE/2006

ALONG WITH HIS late brother David, Albert Maysles is one of the most important figures in American documentary credited with being one of the founders of what is variously called "Direct Cinema" or "Cinéma Vérité" and whose body of work includes *Salesman* (1969), *Gimme Shelter* (1970), and *Grey Gardens* (1975) among many others. In the documentary community he's known for his warmth and openness and his support of the craft. The *Rail*'s Williams Cole sat down with him in corner of his famous open office on West 54th Street.

WILLIAMS COLE (*BROOKLYN RAIL*): *What is your central philosophy of filmmaking?*

AL MAYSLES: Well, I think one of the most important things is to have reliable information and knowledge about other people and places—all kinds of knowledge that we, otherwise, would have incorrect or none at all. We could even say that the country is only a piece of geography until its citizens know one another to as much extent as possible. The documentary gives us a very basic familiarity with people that we, otherwise, would never know. At its best, a documentary directly shows other people's experience. That experience becomes the experience of the viewer. It can be so direct that the viewer feels actually present in those moments that are recorded. For example, the other day I was thinking of an experience I had as a child. In those days in the early thirties, every family had a strap and the father would use the strap on the child when the child got out of order. My father would never hit me, but one day he did. I must have really seriously provoked him. But it didn't hurt or anything. As I walked through the apartment, just after that, I passed

From *The Brooklyn Rail*, July–August 2006. Reprinted by permission of *The Brooklyn Rail*.

through his bedroom, and there he was, head against the wall crying. I just stared on and on and on. That kind of scene, that kind of experience, for me, if there were a camera on it, I could share that. My father could share it, and I could. Or in a larger and more contemporary sense, we know very little of what Iraqis are going through. How do we know what's really going on there unless we intimately see what an Iraqi family is going through?

BR: *How would you describe what people bring into the experience of viewing, say, a scene with your father, or an Iraqi family? Some media theorists would say that it's the context and the baggage that people bring into viewing that changes or doesn't change people.*
MAYSLES: You'd have to be, I think, deprived of humanity not to connect with the scene with my father. Of course, each person will connect somewhat differently, but it's all there for everyone. If it's a father, a son, an older person, a younger person, someone from an entirely different culture can have that scene and connect. It's interesting too, it takes the best part of—and I would call it entertainment—and applies it. If you look up the word "entertainment" in the dictionary, it's first defined as "diversion." But the second definition is "engagement." And the second one, I think, is the best one.

BR: *Yes, and that's a good segue to reality TV. Diversion vs. engagement. Now, over the past few years, people talk about reality in terms of entertainment a lot more. How do you think this came about and what is your opinion on it?*
MAYSLES: It started out with the press being somewhat skeptical of "realism." So it put quotation marks around "reality." Then they became sloppy, they dropped the quotation marks so that people think that it's more real than it is. I don't know if anybody can duplicate the beauty and the force of that scene with my father. It couldn't be quite as explosive. One problem with the "reality" thing is that, even if they want to film it in a truly documentary fashion, so that you get the real thing, the question is how many shows can you really put on with one family and still stick to something interesting? I could see two or three shows maybe.

BR: *Yes, as opposed to, say, your film* Grey Gardens, *these days reality TV producers almost have to manipulate the conflicts in these families to get a whole series out of it.*
MAYSLES: But the sadder part of it is that a family without the kind of dysfunctional conflicts ain't gonna make it. The very common journalistic

notion is that unhappy families are different and happy families are the same so why bother if it's a happy one? (*Chuckles.*) In fact, I don't think they've tried the other. It might work. The Dalai Lama is probably the most popular person in the world today. Where's his negativity? He gives lectures on happiness. It's a word that's just about disappeared from our language as we use it. And yet, that's our golden egg. But nothing related to that in the news mass media.

BR: *In terms of sit down interviews and narration, could you talk about how your style of Direct Cinema challenged the norm when you started?*
MAYSLES: Well, up until we started there wasn't any kind of equipment where a two-person crew can go out with a camera, not on a tripod, but on the shoulder and with a sound person that was in sync and disconnected. That was the technology. But then also, partly because the technology wasn't there, there wasn't a philosophy that went along with it. You had to as best you could try to get information, which is not as directly cinematic. Not as cinematic as it would be with a camera that's up close capturing the experience, of giving you the feeling of being present. So you had to substitute that with narration and a host to give it more credibility. These people weren't even there and they were talking about material that doesn't tell it fully either! So they had to add their own research or whatever to it. All of which doesn't direct us to what we can do now. Another way to spark it up would be to add music. In a way television hasn't caught up yet to the advances we made with so-called direct cinema. They're still using music, and the television commercial is a perfect example of what went wrong. People are substituting fancy cinematography, fast-cutting, over-dramatized music, because they don't have the real thing. And it works because people don't know the other. For example when we invented this kind of equipment that allowed us to be so close to people, it took over ten years before anyone was interested in promoting what we had. What did they care? They weren't showing our stuff. And they still don't. Just think about that. It's still seen as the work of "outsiders." Festivals often have hundreds of documentary entries and very few of them have a chance to make it onto commercial television.

BR: *Can you talk about the commercial situation? Why won't they show the stuff? Why won't they let filmmakers make their own films? What powers that idea?*
MAYSLES: They want control. The word control is very interesting; it crosses all kinds of lines in that discussion. A true documentary is shot with no control. You might even call it the uncontrolled cinema. Because

once you begin to control the audience it's not even the real thing. And so that's part of the problem with the reality shows. They want to control things, so we get the control but lose the reality.

BR: *Uncontrolled cinema, I like that. But then wouldn't someone come across and say cinema is controlled in editing? You still have to make a decision.*
MAYSLES: Right. But it's a whole range of decisions that you make. If you choose a range of decisions that get to the true character of the material itself, without violating what appears to be the case, then you control it so it won't be changed.

BR: *You're controlling something that was once uncontrollable.*
MAYSLES: So you can keep it uncontrollable. Our editors have always found that when they're editing it's the chronology that gets thrown out of position. Until we get really close to the end, and then without even thinking about it, it falls back into the original chronology. But with commercial entities it is usually about control, only about what they want to do. Let me give you an example. About ten years ago I got a call from the Rockefeller Foundations, saying, "We'd like to send you to North Korea to make a movie there." So I go. I get to Beijing, and I hear from them again, "There's a guy on your flight, Tom Johnson from CNN." They want me to meet him. So I'm in the waiting room the next day, waiting for the plane to take off, and I see the only other Caucasian, and I say, "You must be Tom Johnson," and he says, "Yeah." And I say "I'm Albert Maysles," and he says, "Oh, I know who you are." And the discussion stopped. I say, "Aren't you interested in what I'm doing?" He said, "Oh, no, we're doing our own stuff." So the film never got made. So here we are all these years later, and that much less with North Korea. The North Koreans gave me permission to make the film I wanted to make, too.

BR: *So the difference with places like CNN: they're coming from kind of a top-down business model. You're coming into it as someone who has access and experience and an idea of presenting the material to open up different parts of the world. They're just not interested; it's just a wall.*
MAYSLES: It's a commercial. Or what they think is going to be a commercial.

BR: *That's interesting because isn't it true that audiences have developed more of an appreciation of the vérité style and you would think that the commercial entities would flock to using that.*
MAYSLES: I'm an optimistic thinker. And just as reality in literature

has moved—everybody reads nonfiction now—the bestseller lists have nonfiction—so there's a significant movement in that direction in film as well. But already so many of the feature films are using documentary techniques.

BR: *For a while now—the hand-held look, very clearly documentary-style shooting.*

MAYSLES: In 1963 I made a little film with Jean-Luc Godard. We were talking about the documentary philosophy and technique. And in the middle of his talking about it he referred to, even in his own films, what he called a divine accident. And that just happened accidentally, and it was a great moment in the film. He says let's make a film full of divine accidents. But substitute the word divine for reality. Reality is almost a divine course, in that it controls everything, and you just abide by it. But the thing is he also said that the eye behind the camera should be the eye of the poet. Because if the poet wasn't there, if it was just a camera. People sometimes try to describe what I do by saying I have the eye of a poet.

BR: *Yes, you need that ability to pick out details, reactions, cut-aways. So I have a particular interest in social issue documentaries like the Enron film or* The Corporation, *or even* Fahrenheit 911, *which is an essay of sorts, an Op Ed. What's your opinion of films like that?*

MAYSLES: Well, it's not the same kind of information that a film without a point of view would have. I try to distance myself from the point of view. But there are times when you have a preference. And that's another kind of documentary, that's very important. A point of view film, had we had one, called, say, "Weapons of Mass Destruction," right at the start of the Iraq War, well, we couldn't have gone into it with a lie, or had we gone in we'd be out by this time. So it's very important that that kind of film exists.

BR: *I've heard you say that you'd like to make the world a better place through the kind of filmmaking you've had such a hand in creating. But what do you see as the major problem now?*

MAYSLES: The major, major things that have gone wrong with our culture is that people's respect of true knowledge has slacked off. For some time there's been a certain healthier skepticism about what has been given to us as being true. That's good but now it's become cynical criticism so we can't, in this country, believe anything. A society that feels it can't know anything truly can't know anything. Knowledge is worthless unless it's true. People have the same skepticism about any documentary as well. So even if I make a film that is fairly true the average person is deprived of that kind of confidence, and therefore doesn't get the full value of it. Also, the level of distrust of anything that you read is at its peak now. Or at least let's hope that it doesn't get worst; it can't go that much further.

BR: *So in a way, perhaps the poetry of the lens can sway things, because you actually see something happen . . .*

MAYSLES: Edmund Burke, the great English philosopher, said, "Evil will triumph as long as good people do nothing." So the converse of that is if you do something good, then evil has a less chance of getting out and making its way.

BR: *That's a good point.*

MAYSLES: (*laughter*)

Reel Life

LANCE AVERY MORGAN/2007

HE KNEW PRESIDENT Kennedy, was a great pal of Truman Capote, and captured the Rolling Stones and Beatles on film. He was the man behind the film, *Grey Gardens*, which is now the Tony-winning toast of Broadway. Considered by most to be the godfather of the modern documentary film, Albert Maysles, along with his brother, David, practically invented the art form. Here, in an exclusive to *Brilliant* magazine, Maysles gives insight into his career as a filmmaker that's inspired three generations of film auteurs.

"Albert Maysles and I had parallel filmmaking careers," remarked Norman Mailer about Albert Maysles. "He's a fascinating man and he's quite smart." Of course, Norman Mailer, eighty-four, arguably one of the most prolific writers of the twentieth century, was a contemporary of Maysles, eighty. Maysles' life has been so intertwined with notable political and entertainment figures that he would be intimidating if his demeanor and sensibility weren't so kind and his passion for documentary filmmaking so full of soul and purpose.

A trim, compact man given to wearing a black cashmere sweater and gray trousers, Maysles has a thick shock of silver hair and his signature black horn-rimmed glasses sit neatly on his face as he reflects on his career when I caught up with him at the New Milestones Film Festival benefitting the Travis County Mental Health and Mental Retardation. He was there surrounded by fans who revere him. Even French filmmaker Jean-Luc Godard once called Maysles "the best American cameraman."

Maysles' career was an integral part of a one-two punch. His brother, David Maysles, who died in 1987, was the soundman and supervising

---

From *Brilliant* magazine, October 2007. Reprinted courtesy of *Brilliant* magazine and Brilliance Media, 2008.

editor while Albert was the cinematographer, and both shared directorial duties. Their films were revolutionary in the 1950s and set the path for generations of filmmakers. In their documentaries, the drama of human life unfolds as is, without sets, scripts or narration. Before the Maysles brothers, documentary filmmaking usually contained a voiceover to guide the viewer's journey. Maysles broke that tradition by letting the story play out naturally . . . sometimes tragically so.

"In fiction, the director is God, and in nonfiction God is the director," Maysles likes to quote suspense filmmaker Alfred Hitchcock. When asked about comparing his work to the current reality television craze, he comments, "Reality TV is not real at all. It's controlled and there's very little value to be gained from that because they focus on the dysfunctional. It reflects the mistake that a story being told has to have a conflict with good versus bad. In my films, we just tell the story." When asked if he considers himself to be voyeuristic, he vehemently denies it and shares, "I'm a dedicated observer, just noticing what people are doing and recording their lives with respect and discretion. My guiding force is to see what's happening honestly. That's sometimes difficult for some people to comprehend—the difference between exploitation and an honest attempt to understand."

Born to Eastern European Jewish immigrants in Boston, he understood persecution from an early age. Knowing that his education could be a factor of self improvement, he graduated from Syracuse and Boston Universities. Maysles says, "I started out as a psychologist and always liked to listen instead of talk. It helped me become a keen observer and that has served me well." He made his first film in 1955 when he took a 16mm camera to Russia to film patients at several mental hospitals and the resulting film, *Psychiatry in Russia*, started him down the path to creating modern cinéma vérité.

In 1960, Maysles and a team of filmmakers went where only news crews were used to going—backstage of the Kennedy presidential campaign. In *Primary*, the film focused on Kennedy's road to the White House, while campaigning against Hubert Humphrey in the Wisconsin primary race, a pivotal primary because it was Humphrey's home state. "There's a part of that film where I captured Kennedy's point of view by holding the camera above the back of his head as he was passing through the crowds," says Maysles. "I enabled the viewer to feel what it was really like to be him in that situation with so many people." With its groundbreaking, no-frills technique, the film gives equal time to Humphrey, but it's readily apparent that Kennedy's magnetism and the calm campaign-trail grace of his wife Jacqueline would lead them to an eventual White House win. It aired as an ABC news special and is considered by many to have been a deciding factor in Kennedy's defeat over Nixon in the 1960 election.

And when the British invaded the United States . . . the British bands that is, the Maysles brothers were there to record it on film. Their forays into the world of music range from *The Beatles in the U.S.A.* (1964) to *Gimme Shelter* (1970) starring the Rolling Stones. *The Beatles in the U.S.A.* covers the breathless reception of the arrival of Beatlemania to the states, as well as the band's historical appearance on *The Ed Sullivan Show.*

Also in the turbulent 1960s, the silver screen's tough guy was the subject of *Meet Marlon Brando.* Then the Maysles set their sights on writer and social gadabout Truman Capote in the film, *With Love from Truman,* commissioned by National Educational Television. Capote, the literary set—and jet-set—phenomenon, was interesting fodder for any filmmaker. With the recent biopic films on Capote that tried to capture his true essence, the Maysles film is a genuine glimpse into the man behind the legend. "As Capote came out of the screening room, he had tears in his eyes," recalls Maysles. "He said it was the best thing ever done of its kind." They filmed Capote in the Oak Room at the Plaza Hotel, one of his favorite venues, as well as other New York sites reflective of his idiosyncratic life, such as his home in Sagaponek and the Random House offices where he was interviewed by *Newsweek.* That project sparked a friendship that begat a coveted invitation for the Mayles brothers to Capote's party of the century, his Black & White Ball in 1965, at Manhattan's Plaza Hotel.

The press that swirled around the party for a year leading up to it noted that only five hundred guests were invited. The Maysles brothers made the guest list. It would be an understatement to say that Capote was the boy of the moment with his widely touted novel, *In Cold Blood,* being the best selling book of the year and his flamboyant interviews on the late night talk show circuit. It's interesting to note that the Maysles approach to filmmaking, turning reality into art, mirrored Capote's literary point of view when he wrote *In Cold Blood.* "It was a great evening," says Maysles. "Everyone seemed to be there. Years later, after I met and married my wife, the subject of Truman's party came up, and, to both of our surprise, we were each there and we didn't know it at the time."

But how could the Maysles brothers top their Capote film? The answer came in the seminal film, *Salesman,* about Bible salesmen. The film captured the heartbreak of four unyielding door-to-door salesmen who deal with constant rejection from potential bible-buying customers, their homesickness and eventual burnout as they travel the country selling very pricey bibles to low-income Catholic families. Its Willy Loman-esque quality strikes a nerve with almost any viewer. "There are two extremes in filming," shares Maysles. "Exploitation on one end of the spectrum and overprotection on the other. We never had problems avoiding both extremes because of our respect for people."

After chronicling those subjects of modest means, the Maysles stepped back into the world of music with *Gimme Shelter*, which ranks, in many rock historian minds, as one of the best films reflecting the drop-out generation of the 1960s. It's a film that wrapped up a very turbulent 1960s when the Rolling Stones and Jefferson Airplane gave a free concert in Northern California, east of Oakland at Altamont Speedway. About 300,000 people attended, and the organizers placed Hell's Angels in charge of security around the stage. With pool cues and knives on hand, Hell's Angels did as much damage as the troublemakers in the crowd. They spent the concert beating up spectators, killing one. Maysles' film juxtaposes performances, violence, Grace Slick and Mick Jagger's attempts to simmer things down, with close-ups of young listeners dancing and doing drugs. Not only is the concert and audience footage peerless, the film also takes a look at the Rolling Stones band members as they watch concert footage and reflect on what happened.

The Maysles' foray into pop culture may have approached its zenith in 1975 with the film, *Grey Gardens*. It is shabby gentility at its best, and perhaps, also at its most uncomfortable. Expert statistics point toward most Americans being three paychecks away from homelessness. This film illustrates how fortune and beauty can evaporate and the effects it can have on those who had plenty of both. Former New York socialite Edith Bouvier Beale, aunt to Jacqueline Kennedy Onassis and a one-time belle epoch beauty, was close to eighty when the film was made. She and her daughter, Edie, then in her mid-fifties, comprise a pair of odd recluses. Complete with double-digit cats and raccoons, they live in Grey Gardens, a ghoulish, dilapidated twenty-eight-room mansion in East Hampton, New York. "We really hit it off with them, and they trusted us," says Maysles about the experience.

In the film, Edith is an eccentrically witty former singer. Her daughter, Edie, is verbose and dresses oddly with trademark ensembles that include scarf-like concoctions around her head. The women address the camera, talking over each other, moving from the present to events that happened decades before as if they'd just occurred. It's a tour de force look at the basics of mother-daughter relationships and the circumstance of having to make do. The documentary developed such a cult following that it was made into an off-Broadway play in 2005 and then became a Tony award–winning Broadway musical last season. That film project might best define Maysles' overall vision that, "documentary has to give us knowledge . . . and truth." The fictional film depiction of *Grey Gardens* is in the works. "We are talking to Jessica Lange and Drew Barrymore to star as the Edies," confides Maysles.

Truth in relationships is vital to Maysles. He had friendships with some of the most pivotal personalities of the past fifty years, including Muhammad Ali, Leonard Bernstein, Jimi Hendrix, Vladimir Horowitz, Wynton Marsalis, and several hundred more. Among many other projects, Maysles teamed with the artist Christo and Jeanne Claude several times to document their artistic triumphs, including *Running Fence, Islands, Umbrellas,* and several more, including most recently *The Gates* (of Central Park). Maysles' work has not gone unnoticed and over the years many accolades have been bestowed—The Emmys, The Academy Award nominations, the recognition from the Library of Congress. But to Maysles it has always been about the work . . . what shows up on the screen.

These days, Maysles is still working out of his Manhattan offices on a daily basis. Currently, he is sharing his inspiration on a multitude of projects. One of them, *In Transit,* is about trains as a metaphor for life. "I've had experiences on trains," says Maysles. "Even in childhood and back in 1944 when I went off to war. The film reminds me of my early days. This is a present-day project, depicting the stories that develop when people get off the train." When asked if making documentaries has changed, he offers, "Not that much, really. Raising money is still a problem. There are more documentaries and more ways to show them on DVD and the Internet."

As Socrates wrote, "An unexamined life is not worth living." Albert Maysles' career has been devoted to examining life, while his altruistic nature has led to the founding of the Maysles Institute, a nonprofit organization, in 2005. It's committed to providing training and apprenticeships in filmmaking to underprivileged youth who are missing a parent in jail. The result is an increase in self-respect and a parent-child reconnection. "You can do so much good while getting directly involved in what's going on in the world," Maysles shares. "There's a History Channel. But wouldn't it be great if there was a Peace Channel?"

INDEX